Common Sense about Uncommon Knowledge:
The Knowledge Bases for Diversity

G. Pritchy Smith

AACTE

The American Association of Colleges for Teacher Education is a national, voluntary association of colleges and universities with undergraduate or graduate programs to prepare professional educators. The Association supports programs in data gathering, equity, leadership development, networking policy analysis, professional issues, and scholarship.

Common Sense about Uncommon Knowledge: The Knowledge Bases for Diversity may be ordered from:

AACTE Publications
One Dupont Circle, Suite 610
Washington, DC 20036-1186
WWW: www.aacte.org

Printed in the United States of America
ISBN No: 0-89333-163-5

To Marcos, Rubin, T. J., Lucious, Jackie, Ed, George, Pete, Mary Lou, Paul, Billy Ray, Faye, Ruth, Terrance, Napoleon, and all the other students who made me think about what teachers need to know in order to teach culturally diverse students. I remember you.

Contents

Acknowledgments

Writing this book while working full time would have been impossible were it not for the moral and verbal support of many people. I owe a debt of gratitude to those who believed in me, encouraged me, and believed as I did that there was a need for a book that more clearly identified the knowledge bases for diversity in teacher education. Two such people are Carl Grant, Hoefs-Bascom professor at the University of Wisconsin-Madison, and Mary E. Dilworth, senior director for research and information at the American Association of Colleges for Teacher Education. Without their prodding and pushing, I might never have completed this book. Katherine Kasten, dean of the College of Education, and Dennis Holt, chairman of Curriculum and Instruction, provided appreciated words of encouragement during the low times. Kathe's comments on draft versions of the manuscript were especially helpful.

I also owe a debt of gratitude for long-term encouragement and other support received from the Rose Duhon-Sells, Distinguished Professor of Education at McNeese State University in Louisiana, and Asa Hilliard III, Fuller E. Callaway Professor of Education at Georgia State University. Neither of these individuals probably know the powerful impact they have had on my life and my way of thinking. In fact, I probably would never have even started this book had Rose not told me many years ago that I "had a gift for telling White folks some things they ought to know that Black folks just *can't* tell them." I began to listen to what Asa was saying and writing 25 years ago. His works have had an everlasting influence on my thinking as a teacher educator; and, although he denies he ever really did anything special on my behalf, I know he has watched my backside a time or two and helped me stay employed during some difficult times in my career.

I also owe much gratitude to students and colleagues at the Paul Quinn College and Jarvis Christian College, two historically Black institutions where I spent 10 years from 1975 to 1985 as a teacher educator. During these years I made strides forward in my personal growth as a multicultural educator. Many of the ideas in this book about how culture influences learning grew out of the dynamic cultural contexts provided by these two institutions.

Finally, my family—Janice Joy, Derek, and Parc, their loving wives, and the grandbabies Alexander, Hayden, and Wilding—provided emotional support and understanding during every weekend and holiday that I spent working on this book instead of being with them. Thanks to all.

PREFACE

I wish I could say that this book is a thoroughly original work, but it is not. There is almost nothing said in this book that has not been said before by other writers in the field of teacher education. In fact, many of the ideas, themes and concepts in this book have been written at sometime in someplace by scholars of color or multicultural theorists from many cultural backgrounds. I have for many years been reading the works of minority scholars because long ago I came to believe that the keys to unlocking the historical problem of the under education of minority youth in the United States would ultimately be found largely in the voices of minority scholars who had been marginalized from the mainstream literature. I realized as early as 1961, my first year of teaching a class of Mexican American, African American, and poor White students that "the knowledge bases" I had studied at the University of Texas had in no way prepared me to teach culturally and linguistically diverse students. Some of you who are reading this preface have either heard or read "the story" of this realization when I delivered the opening keynote address at the 1991 conference of the National Association for Multicultural Education in Orlando, an address that was later published as "Multicultural Education: The Foundation for Culturally Responsive Teaching of All Our Children" in *Multicultural Education for the Twenty-First Century*, edited by Carl Grant (1992). I have repeated the story as a fitting introduction to this book. It became even clearer to me when I was a doctoral student in the late 1960s at North Texas State University that the mainstream theorists and researchers, who were primarily European or European American, had not even the vaguest notions of the true cultural and school realities of minority children. Today, after all these years of reading and thinking, I may not always know precisely where I first came upon an insightful idea about teaching minority students, or even who first conceived the idea; but I do know that it was almost always found in the marginalized literature of journals and books that almost none of my White colleagues were reading.

If there is anything at all original about this book, it is the attempt to put between the covers of a single volume, perhaps for the first time, not only what many minority scholars and others have said at different times in different places about what should be "the knowledge bases for diversity" in teacher education, but also where uninformed teacher educators might locate the theory and research that undergirds each knowledge base. Thus, if this book enables teacher educators to conceptualize better the knowledge bases for diversity in teacher education and to find, synthesize, and teach the theory and research that undergird each knowledge base, then this book has accomplished its purpose.

— G. Pritchy Smith
September 1997

INTRODUCTION: *The Beginning*

...[T]hat which we are, we are—
One equal temper of heroic hearts,
Made weak by time and fate, but strong in will
To strive, to seek, to find, and not to yield.

—Tennyson, "Ulysses"

The beginning of this book is a story, the story of one class of students during my first year of teaching in 1961 at Central High School in San Angelo, Texas. This story about the lives of my first students marks the beginning of my 35-year odyssey "to strive, to seek, to find" without yielding better ways to teach culturally diverse students. I chose to begin this otherwise pedantic book with a story because I know of no better way to convince my colleagues in teacher education of the urgent need to restructure teacher education in the United States to include the knowledge bases on diversity. Besides, everyone loves a story. In fact, I know of no culture in the world that has not used story-telling to preserve and pass on to the next generation its heritage. Readers, particularly teacher educators and classroom teachers, will like this story because it will probably remind them of the first class they taught. One truth about teachers is that we never forget our first class of students. We are never quite as close to future classes as we were to that first group we taught. So it is with me. Although it has

been over 35 years since I taught them, the names and faces of the students in the following story are as fresh in my memory as if I had been in 8 am homeroom class with them this morning.

Let me set the scene and tell you about the school where I taught my first year in 1961. San Angelo Central High School at that time was one of the most innovative high schools in the nation. Shortly after the 1954 Brown decision, the district decided voluntarily to integrate its schools. To do so, it built one high school for the entire city. It was a magnificent campus, a campus of eight split-level buildings of glass, steel, and brick that looked like a college campus spread over ten acres of beautifully landscaped lawns and gardens. It was an architectural wonder. Teams of educators from abroad—Japan, Germany, even the Soviet Union—visited the campus. The colors inside each building were bright and inspiring. Every classroom wall that faced the hallway in each building was of glass and was draped. No classroom had a door. We were one of the first schools in the nation to have closed-circuit TV outlets in every room, one of the first to voluntarily integrate, and one of the first schools to adopt that new rage in education at that time—"ability grouping." It was not until later that I learned that ability grouping was just another way to segregate under the same roof.

I'll never forget my first day of teaching 11th-grade English in this "rail 3" class, the district's name for "slow learner" classes. On my first day of teaching, I walked into that class to face 23 boys and 3 girls. They were about a third White, a third

> **This story about the lives of my first students marks the beginning of my 35-year odyssey "to strive, to seek, to find" without yielding better ways to teach culturally diverse students.**

Hispanic, a third Black—none of them reading above the fifth grade level and some not reading at all. In this class was Marcos Espanoza who had just arrived from Mexico and who spoke not one word of English. Of course, I spoke no more than 10 words of Spanish, none of which were appropriate for the classroom. In this class, also, was *Rubin Bienvenido*, a tall, handsome boy with a movie-star smile, the only Mexican American who was a starter on the varsity basketball team. Oh, he was a hero of the school, and was chased by all the girls on campus regardless of their ethnicity. And he was to be one of the first of my students to be drafted to serve in the Vietnam War after graduation.

T.J. Brown, one of my African American students, was in that class too. T.J. moved as slow as any student I had ever known when he moseyed from his back seat to take the long walk to my desk at the front of the room to turn in his work. He wore the baggiest pants I had ever seen, bunched and tied at the waist with cotton rope. His shoes were scruffy and turned over on their sides, sometimes tied, sometimes not. Finally, after about a month of not getting "proper recognition," T.J. sauntered up to my desk in his slow-moving, easy walk and said, "Mister Smith, you don't know who I am, do you?" Brushing him off, I said, "Well, no, I guess I don't, T.J. Let's get back to our desk now; we need to start class." He looked up at me and said rather dramatically, "Mister Smith, I'm the fastest man alive. You remember that. I'm the fastest man alive!" After nearly two-thirds of the school year had passed, I was looking at the front page of the newspaper with a headline that read "Central High Student Sets Record for the 100-Yard Dash at State Track Meet." There was a front page photograph of T.J. as he crossed the finish line. I remember saying to myself, "Son of a gun, T.J., you very well may be the fastest man alive."

Lucious Washington, another Black student in that class, was quiet and worked diligently in English class. He was also in a physical education class I taught. He was an "extra-effort" kind of guy, the kind of student who would dive headlong into grassburrs and gravel just to catch a flyball. In fact, he played on the varsity baseball team, and his dream was to be another Jackie Robinson.

Jackie Hamilton was another African American student in my class. He was lovable, handsome,

arrogant, always bragging about the number of girlfriends he had, but functionally illiterate as a writer of standard English. He wrote this paragraph titled "The Things I Like About Myself":

> I am a wall rond man. I can tall to King and tall to Hud and not feel out of place. I am very good with the girl I have ten can get antying time. I love me clothes I have eight suites, twelve pair pant, and twenty-three shirt.

Through my ethnocentric eyes, it seemed as if Jackie's identity went no deeper than the fine clothing that hid his poverty. Jackie was a star, varsity football player, but what he wanted most of all was to be an aerospace engineer.

Ed Thackery, a White kid, was a compulsive liar. He would even tell a fib when the truth would have been better. After a few weeks, I just stopped believing anything he told me. We had an awful dispute in class over whether or not he had turned in his money for school insurance. He said he had. I said he hadn't. It was the typical spat between a teacher and student. I tried to out-yell him. Finally, he crumpled, put his head down on the desk, and sulked in silence the rest of the class period. Something happened that day. I don't think Ed ever again really engaged himself in classwork after that incident.

George Gray was what some people would call "White trash." In the South, we sometimes affectionately or not-so-affectionately call folks like George "Crackers." I found out that he had been in the accelerated classes until the 8th grade, when he had a motor scooter wreck that had left him with a permanent limp, a great exaggerated limp where his right leg bowed out with every step he took. If he was late, he wouldn't come to class because he was ashamed to walk in front of the other students. He liked to come early and be in his seat when the other students came into the room. I once gave him a copy of Hemingway's *For Whom the Bell Tolls*, thinking he might identify with what Hemingway saw as the "war wound." In fact, he did. When he brought the book back to me, he had tears in his eyes when he said, "Mr. Smith, this is the best book I ever read. Do you have anymore like it?" George was a mechanical genius. He made all kinds of miniature go-cart vehicles that he could drive, from what looked to me like old pieces of wood, lawn mower engines, and parts he found in his father's junk yard. When he made a turnaround in school work, his family invited me to a Sunday dinner of fried chicken, biscuits and gravy, and fresh garden-grown tomatoes. The house the city let the family live in for watching the town dump was a three-story house that was unpainted and seemed to tilt to one side. In fact, all the buildings where he lived seemed to lean and be on the verge of collapsing, even the shop where George built his go-carts. George's parents were plain and simple, grateful folks, so pleased that George was interested in school again. George took me to his special place, his room in a gable on the third floor. I remember seeing a tattered quilt on his bed and looking up at the ceiling where I could see light from the cracks between the shingles. Of course, I didn't say anything because he was so excited and so pleased to show me his private room, a special treat in a family with eight children and two adults. As I left George's house that day I remember asking myself if George would really make it.

Pete and *Mary Lou Salyer*, brother and sister, were in that class too. They were the children of an oil-well driller. Pete was "tough as a boot" and ran a gang of White kids who were always at odds with one of the Mexican American gangs. Mary Lou's big dream was to be a beautician, and every day she defiantly spent the first 10 minutes of class preening and putting on make-up and fingernail polish from a large makeup kit she placed on top of her school desk each day. It was as if she carried her entire identity in that makeup kit as she lugged it from class to class, day after day, month after month for the entire school year.

Cecil Roberts, another White student, was an effeminate, thin, delicately built young man who seemed to delight in swishing his femininity in the faces of his classmates. His male peers described him as "measly" and soon created the nickname of "Mecil" to convey their perceptions. Others who wanted to enact a crueler form of teasing called him "Cecilia" or "punk," an African American term for homosexual in those days. Cecil seemed to flit about the room like a butterfly, moving from desk to desk to be near and talk to the three girls in the class. If I asked Cecil to stop talking during class, he would often smile, and bat his eyelashes like

Clara Bow, and apologize by saying "No harm meant Mr. Smith, it was just girl talk." I really never felt like I knew how to respond to Cecil, not even on the occasion that I found him hiding behind my Volkswagen in the parking lot late one afternoon after school. He was crouched down on the curb in just his shirt and underwear. He was crying, and his right eye was red and swollen. When I asked what had happened, he told me some boys had beaten him up and driven off with his pants. I asked if he was crying because the boys had hurt him. He said, "No, I'm crying because the person I thought was my best friend told the other boys I was a 'queer' and helped hold me while the others beat me up." My heart went out to Cecil. I understand betrayal. Yet, I am ashamed to say that I could not talk openly to Cecil about his homo-sexuality as I drove him home from school that afternoon.

Billy Ray Moore, another White student, was the son of a well-known family with a successful funeral home business. Wealthier than the other students in the class, he drove an XKE and wore a large diamond ring. He knew he was expected to take over the family-run funeral home someday, and literacy just didn't seem very important to him.

Faye Green and *Ruth Jackson* were the two young African American women in that class. Faye was beautiful, had an attractive figure and big doelike, seductive eyes. She was quiet and read at about the 7th-grade level, did her work, and demurely flirted with the boys in class. Ruth, on the other hand, was one of those students we say "matured early." She didn't mess with boys. She was interested only in MEN! On my way to school each morning I would see Ruth hunkered down below the dash of some long, fancy automobile, called a "hog" in those days, in passionate embraces with some man who looked old enough to be her father. As I would walk by the car, she would look up and wave with a sheepish grin on her face as if I had caught her doing something she shouldn't have been doing.

Terrance Smith and *Napoleon Hayes*, both African American, were the class characters. Terrance Smith had a band, and he had changed his, and the band's name to "Terrance Trojan and the Trojanettes," a name that sounded to me like prophylactics and cough drops; but there was no doubt about it, he *could* sing and his dream was to become a recording star. It was Terrance who made my first day in this class so memorable. He marched into class late on the first day, walking briskly and efficiently, carrying a briefcase and wearing a long peach-colored scarf around his neck and a chartreuse glove on his right hand. With the same efficiency that he walked, he whipped the scarf from his neck and popped it in the air to let it float softly down on the top of his desk like a tablecloth. After he smoothed all the wrinkles from his scarf, he snapped open his briefcase and commenced to lay out his pencils, ballpoint pens, rulers, and erasers neatly placed and in a special order on top of the scarf. Then he placed his briefcase beneath his chair and sat at attention waiting for class to start as if he had made no grand entrance at all. This impressive performance, executed with such style, was to be the beginning of what was to become a daily ritual. He changed the color of his neck scarf almost everyday, but the glove on his right hand was always chartreuse. Here was a guy who wore a glove 20 years before Michael Jackson wore his! It was much later in the year that I was to learn that Terrance wore the glove on a hand badly scarred from a severe burn he had received when he was a child.

His buddy, *Napoleon Hayes*, was the class clown. He had a shaved head and talked and joked, shucked and jived, and played the dozens incessantly. He was always woofin', and it was "yo momma this" and "yo momma that" every day. He was the percussionist in Terrance's band and planned on riding Terrance's shirt-tail to recording fame when they graduated from high school.

There were other kids in this class just as colorful, but time will not permit me to tell you the stories of all of them. Let me simply say that the school year began to pass by. Day by day, it became clearer that I was not really helping these kids. To be certain, there were small triumphs; but, in reality, I wasn't prepared to teach these students. I had a degree in literature, primarily White American literature and British literature. I hadn't even had a course in teaching reading. In those days, one couldn't even find a course on minority literature in the curriculum of most universities. I hadn't studied Black English or nonstandard English, and I certainly hadn't had a course in teaching English as a Second Language. I wasn't a culturally responsive

teacher. The University of Texas hadn't prepared me to teach adolescents of different races, cultures, and languages how to read and write.

I taught similar classes for four more years, then went back to graduate school to see if I couldn't learn more about being a better teacher. After completing a doctorate, I went back to San Angelo, Texas, almost 7 years later to see if I could locate most of these students and learn what had happened to them. In fact, even before I returned to graduate school, I had known already what had happened to many of these students. Over one-third of them had not finished the following senior year.

Most of their stories are tragic. *Lucious Washington* was killed outright in the Vietnam War. He never became another Jackie Robinson. A few years ago, I stood before the Vietnam Memorial in Washington, DC, and wept uncontrollably as I ran my fingers across the letters of his name carved in the stone. *Jack Barton*, the compulsive liar, lost his thumb in the war. There were other casualties, but I will return to that later.

Billy Ray Moore got his girlfriend pregnant their senior year. On the way to the prom, they were fighting, he struck her and lost control of the car. She lost an eye and aborted. Seven years later I found Billy Ray at the Red Rooster, a bar, in the middle of the day, already an alcoholic at 25 years of age. The family-run funeral home had been sold. Most of the money was gone. Billy Ray no longer wore a diamond ring, I noticed. *T.J. Brown* and *Jackie Hamilton* went to a junior college in Oklahoma on athletic scholarships. They were back in San Angelo after one year. T.J. may have been "the fastest man alive," but he would set no records in the college record book.

I found *Jackie Hamilton* bagging groceries at a Piggly Wiggly in the Black section of San Angelo. He was the one who helped me find out where many of the students were now. *T.J.* was in prison for drugs. No one knew what had happened to *Faye Green*, but *Ruth Jackson* was a single mother with three children, and she worked for a professional cleaning company that cleaned office buildings. *Terrance Trojan* was "on the West Coast doin' real good, folks say." *Terrance's* buddy, *Napoleon Hayes*, was in prison. I also found out that *Pete Salyer*, the gang leader, was in prison for transporting a minor and drugs across the U.S. and Mexican borders.

His sister, *Mary Lou*, whom I had watched apply makeup to her face every day for a year, was reputed to be a prostitute in Fort Worth, Texas.

Marcos Espanoza had finished that year and returned to Mexico. My single greatest achievement with Marcos occurred when he spent the entire 50-minute class period writing a book report on an elementary storybook I had acquired for him. As he was writing his paper, I would look up from my desk periodically to see Marcos laboring with pen and paper in his new language of English, his tongue sticking out the corner of his mouth as if he were intent on writing a perfect report. Every so often, he would ball up another piece of paper and start over. That night when I was grading papers, I opened his paper and found three words scrawled in the center of the page: "I like it." In some ways, these three words of English were a triumph. In other ways, these three words were a sad commentary on my failure with Marcos that year.

George Gray, the boy who lived at the trash dump, wrote me letters for nearly 10 years. I followed his life from the Job Corps to a job at a water-sewage treatment plant and on to a marriage that failed. The last letter I received from him described his life of living alone in a room in the back of a service station where he worked, in a small town in Oklahoma.

Rubin Bienvenido's story was part of the reason I left to return to graduate school. During the spring of my final year of teaching at San Angelo Central High School, I was returning to my classroom between classes to do some work during my preparation period. The hallway was full of students and alive with noise, as schools are between classes. As I walked down the hall, I kept hearing someone call out, "Meester Smeeth, Meester Smeeth." I kept looking back but couldn't see the person calling me. "Stop, Meester Smeeth, stop." Then someone broke through the crowd of students. There was Rubin in a wheelchair. He had lost both legs from knees down in the Vietnam War. We went to my classroom. He said, "Meester Smeeth, I came to see

> **I felt that I had failed as "the catcher in the rye."**

you. I came to show you my Bronze Star." My face must have shown that I didn't know what to say. He said, "Ees OK, Meester Smeeth, I'll be getting new legs soon, and I'm going to electronics school." We talked awhile and, when I went home that night, I cried.

I think I cried not just because of Rubin but also because I felt so inadequate as a teacher. I told my wife that night that there had to be something incredibly wrong with an educational system that failed to reach so many kids and that there had to be something incredibly wrong with a university that had not prepared me any better than I had been prepared to teach these kids. As hard as I had tried, it seemed as if I hadn't known how to help these kids. I felt that I had failed as "the catcher in the rye." Deep down, I felt like I had not reached the hearts and minds of the kids who lived in Sandra Cisnero's "house on Mango Street," like I hadn't understood in my soul and bones "why the caged bird sings." I resigned that spring.

In June, the day after all the other teachers were gone, I went back to the school to clean out my desk. Even today I can remember the echo of walking in the empty hall. There is no sound like the sound of reverberating footsteps in the heavy silence of an empty school building. I cleaned out my desk, leaving the center drawer until last. After I dumped most of the contents in the wastebasket, I noticed something stuck in the crack of the drawer. I pulled it loose and opened it up. Lo and behold, it was *Ed Thackery's* insurance envelope, and inside it was a dollar for his school insurance. I still have that dollar to remind me that I was wrong about *Ed Thackery* the very time I needed to be right.

Today, at the moment we are poised to step over into the 21st century, when I think back to these students, I cannot help but think about the tremendous pool of talent we have lost in America. In truth, these students were not really different in potential from the students in my college-prep classes. It is true that they could not read and write on grade level, but any one and all of them could have, given the proper prior conditions and instruction. Yes, 35 years have passed. Yet, hardly a day, at most not a week, passes that I do not think about them. Sometimes now, even so many years afterwards, when I am sitting alone in my study during the early morning hours before the sun rises, trying to write or just think in solitude, my eyes sometimes well-up with tears as the memories haunt me. Sometimes, in my mind I hear Rubin calling out, "Meester Smeeth, Meester Smeeth." Sometimes the memory of Rubin seeps into my consciousness as he is sitting legless in his wheelchair, showing me his Bronze Star. Other times I see the image of Mary Lou's pouting face just as it was on those days I asked her to put away her cosmetics or the expression of humiliation and defeat on Cecil's face the day his best friend betrayed his trust and called him "a queer" in front of his classmates.

At other times during these early hours of the morning, I cannot help but wonder, also, why so many of my colleagues in teacher education have stubbornly resisted for so many years to make the preparation of teachers for culturally diverse classrooms a priority. Some of them have told me that they do not know "what they would teach that is any different from what they are already teaching" and, if such information exists, that they "don't know where to find it."

In truth, much more is known today about effectively teaching culturally diverse students than was known in 1961 when I first started teaching. There are at least 13 knowledge bases of theory and research that provide a better understanding of educating students like Marcos, Lucious, and countless other students whose stories have been told, again and again, under different names by different writers. This book, in fact, is about those knowledge bases and where to find the theory and research that undergirds each one of them.

More is known today than was known by my teacher education professors at the University of Texas in 1961 about the foundations of *multicultural education* and *the sociocultural contexts of human growth and psychological development in marginalized ethnic and racial cultures.* Had I studied these knowledge bases at the University of Texas, perhaps I would have understood how my own ethnocentrism had led me to see my students as hopelessly culturally deficient rather than as capable young men and women who were grappling with their own complex cultural, racial, social, gender, and sexual identities. Perhaps I would have understood that Jackie's African American cultural context was programming him for a much more complex identity than mere "clothing and athletics."

We know more today about *cultural and cognitive learning styles and about the language, communication, and interactional styles* of students from many different cultures. Had I known more in 1961 about how culture influences learning, I might have conceptualized teaching as more than "telling and testing." Had I known something about the principles of teaching English to non-native speakers, perhaps I could have been more successful with Marcos. Perhaps if I had studied Black English or Ebonics, as it is called today, and understood signifying, playing the dozens, and woofin', I would not have over reacted and sent Napoleon so often to the office for disciplinary action. Perhaps I could have used the rich characteristics of Napoleon Hayes' and Jackie Hamilton's language to build bridges to the language I found so beautiful in the poetry and fiction I was trying to teach them.

Today we also know much more about the *essential elements of culture, the principles of culturally responsive teaching and curriculum development,* and *effective strategies for teaching minority students.* We know now that it is important to create a school culture and curriculum that includes the cultures of all our students, not just the culture of our White middle-class students. We know now that teaching about the cultural heritages, both ancient and modern, of our students lifts their aspirations, develops stronger self-esteem and confidence, and affirms their worth and place in the universe. Had I known these things in 1961, I could have taught that most of the great Egyptian pharaohs were of Black African descent and that the great African Egyptian contributions to architecture, art, science, mathematics, philosophy, and writing were the foundations for the Golden Age of Greece later. I could have talked to my students about the great universities established in Africa, where some of the Greeks learned part of their foundation of knowledge centuries before Christ's birth. I could have had Jackie Hamilton, who wanted to be an aerospace engineer, read the biographies of the great 20th-century African American scientists and inventors. I could have excited him with stories of Garrett Morgan, the African American who invented the modern traffic light and sold his patent to General Electric in 1923, and Garrett Morgan, the inventor of the gas mask. Maybe Jackie would have been touched by the stories of Dr. Charles Drew, who pioneered the development of the blood bank, or Dr. Daniel Hale Williams, who was the first person to perform open-heart surgery.

Maybe I could have instilled pride in Rubin Bienvenido by tales of how some of his ancestors, the natives of the Americas, the great Maya, Aztec, and North American Native American civilizations, transformed Europe with the medical and agricultural technologies and products, such as potatoes and corn, that prevented famine and provided a diet that enabled Europe's population to grow and rule the world for the next five centuries. I could have explained how the Iroquois League and other Native American social and political organizations provided the democratic models for Ben Franklin and Thomas Jefferson when they framed our Constitution.

Perhaps if I had been educated through a more inclusive curriculum at the University of Texas, I could have introduced Terrance Trojan to the musical achievements of James Weldon Johnson or the literary achievements of Paul Dunbar, the African American poet who was a major influence on Gwendolyn Brooks. Perhaps I could have even developed a burning need to read and to make artistic achievements in Faye Green and Ruth Jackson with the novels of Zora Neale Hurston or the sculpture of Edmonia Lewis, the first African American sculptress.

We also know a great deal more about the *foundations of racism* and the *effects of policy and practice* on maintaining a status quo that replicates the societal inequities faced by many minority and poor White students. In addition, more is known about *culturally responsive assessment.* Had I studied these knowledge bases in my teacher preparation program at the University of Texas, I could have better understood that ability grouping and culturally biased testing were aspects of institutionalized racism and classism that relegate too many minority and poor White students to second-class education. I might have had the knowledge and confidence to question policies and practices that were harmful to my students. I might have had the courage to become a social activist.

Finally, we know much more today about *gender and sexual orientation* and about the types of *experiential knowledge* that help prepare teachers to better understand and educate diverse students. Had I

studied these knowledge bases perhaps I could have helped Mary Lou Salyer, Faye Green, Ruth Jackson, and the young men see that there were social roles available to women other than pleasing men, that life can be more than fingernail polish and flirtation. Had I known then, as I do now, about the lives of great women who were missing from the pages of history, I might have inspired the young women in my class with stories and biographies of heroines such as Margaret Sanger, Jane Addams, and Ida B. Wells. I might have helped Cecil believe in himself and learn that literary history is replete with gay and lesbian fore-bears such as Walt Whitman, James Baldwin, and Gertrude Stein who created a place in the stream of humanity where others had dared not to tread. In truth, had the University of Texas placed me for my student teaching internship in a school of culturally and racially mixed students rather than in a White suburban high school in Austin, I might have been better prepared to teach this first group of students in San Angelo. I might have understood that as a professional teacher, I had a personal responsibility to expand my social and professional life to include people different from myself. Instead, I had been programmed in the teacher education program to accept the social taboos of the day and to relish the privileges society had bestowed upon me.

The story of my first students and my own struggles as a novice teacher has important implications for teacher education reform. In the final analysis, the most important reasons for reforming teacher education to include knowledge bases about diversity are the students—students like Rubin Bienvenido, Lucious Washington, Mary Lou Salyer, and George Gray—real flesh-and-blood students with whom we laugh and cry each day we teach, not just as nameless numbers lost in demographic data that tell us America is changing. Most of my first students who are still living are now 50 years old. Some, no doubt, have grandchildren. Yet most novice teachers are no better prepared today to teach the grandchildren of my first students than I was prepared to teach them in 1961. The cycle of monocultural teachers teaching multicultural students must be broken and will require teacher educators who have "heroic hearts...strong in will to strive, to seek, to find and not to yield" until the cycle is broken. We must not lose another generation.

CHAPTER 1
Toward Defining Culturally Responsible and Responsive Teacher Education

We must be the change we wish to see in the world.

— Mahatma Gandhi

In the schools, colleges, and departments of education in the United States, two camps of teacher educators who do not talk much to each other have emerged—the genericists and the multiculturalists. On the one hand, an examination of course titles and course content at the majority of U.S. teacher education institutions leads to the conclusion that most teacher educators are genericists. That is, they generally believe that no special knowledge and skills other than the mainstream, traditional knowledge bases of teacher education are needed to train teachers for classrooms of students from culturally and linguistically diverse backgrounds. In short, genericists believe that if the teachers they train would only work as vigorously and intensely with non-White minority, culturally diverse, and poor White students through the regular curricula of the elementary and secondary schools as they do with White middle-class students, these teachers would deliver high-quality education and the perplexing, historical problems of "underachieving" students from culturally diverse minority and poor White groups would be solved.

Genericists usually believe that "good teaching is good teaching." What the genericists really mean when they say "good teaching is good teaching" is that good teaching for White middle-class students is also good teaching for all students without any consideration given to factors of race, culture, social class, gender, and other significant aspects of diversity. Therefore, genericists usually intentionally or unconsciously construct a teacher education

curriculum that is either *race-blind* and *culture-blind* or that perpetuates a negative knowledge base regarding minority children. A race-blind and culture-blind teacher education program gives almost no consideration to the social and cultural realities of minority children of color. In fact, there is such an extreme absence of information on race and culture that one would erroneously assume that student populations are monocultural and that no children of color and diverse cultures even attend public and private schools in the United States. Upon viewing the textbooks and course syllabi of a race-blind and culture-blind program, a person from another country would be more likely to conclude that the United States is a homogeneous monoracial, monocultural society than to conclude that this country is a multiracial, multicultural society. Furthermore, genericists plan and teach not just a race/culture-blind curriculum but also a "diversity-blind" curriculum. In truth, most genericists are able to discuss in their teacher education classrooms a few conservative social class or socioeconomic concepts and even about the needs of special children; but most are "not comfortable" talking about such classroom contextual factors as race, culture, gender, or sexual orientation.

In contrast to the diversity-blind teacher education program, genericists sometimes construct a second type of curriculum that gives undue attention to the "literature of failure" rather than to the "literature of success" regarding minority children. This type of curriculum perpetuates the negative assumptions about minority children that far too many White, middle-class, preservice teachers bring with them to the university classroom. The "literature of failure" regarding minority children in this type of teacher education program consists of research findings that present repeated comparative test-score profiles of low-achieving minority students and high-achieving White students. This kind of teacher education program seems not to emphasize that such test profiles are not evidence of inferior levels of *potential* among minority students but are, in fact, evidence of poor schooling and lack of societal commitment to equal outcomes for minority students. In addition, the negative "literature of failure" presents minority-group social and cultural factors as pathological conditions that even the best teaching cannot overcome. Thus, the literature of failure and perhaps what could also be called a literature of pathology in most generic teacher education programs constitutes a "knowledge base" that does more harm than good.

On the other hand, there are teacher educators, multiculturalists, and reconstructionists who constitute a much smaller group of scholars and practitioners who hold that generic teacher training is not sufficient. That is, they assert there really is a body of special knowledge, skills, processes, and experiences that is different from the knowledge bases of most traditional teacher education programs and that is essential for preparing teachers to be successful with culturally and linguistically diverse student populations. They also assert that learning how cultural variables interact with other variables of diversity such as race, gender, social class, special needs, and sexual orientation is of primary importance in the education of teachers. These culturally responsive teacher educators believe that culture

...The scholarly works of the multiculturalists have not been integrated well into the mainstream teacher education literature.

deeply influences the way children perceive and go about school learning and that the more a teacher understands the cultures and other aspects of diversity of the students in a classroom, the more likely the teacher can provide a classroom context that will result in successful, high-quality education for culturally and linguistically diverse students. Whereas culturally responsive teacher educators believe that there are alternative knowledge bases that have greater value for training teachers for cultural diversity than do some of the traditional knowledge bases, they do not advocate the wholesale elimination of most traditional knowledge bases that constitute the teacher education curriculum at most colleges and universities. That is, they do not believe that most of the traditional knowledge bases for teacher education have no *value* at all for preparing teachers of minority children, but they do believe that the value of some traditional knowledge bases is dependent upon the applicability of these knowledge bases to a variety of cultural and social contexts.

For example, the traditional knowledge base on classroom management and discipline studied by preservice teachers in generic teacher education programs has value only if its applicability is examined in the cultural context of, say, African American children in inner-city schools, Mexican American children of working immigrant parents in a rural school, or Native American students in a reservation school. That is, if a particular model of classroom management is inconsistent with the child's cultural belief system and community context, the model is likely to have limited value. Thus, culturally responsive teacher educators believe one of the major elements missing from traditional generic teacher education programs is the examination of the traditional knowledge bases in a variety of cultural contexts.

The distance between the genericists and the multiculturalists that has evolved historically is illustrated by the fact that the scholarly works of the multiculturalists have not been integrated well into the mainstream teacher education literature. That is, neither the textbooks typically used in undergraduate elementary and secondary teacher education programs nor the professional literature on the knowledge base for teacher education programs contain many references to the works of multiculturalists. For example, during the last 30 years, an enormous amount of theory and research has been generated about the psychological, social, and intellectual development of African American children, as well as some other ethnic minority groups; yet the textbooks used for courses in human growth and development and adolescent psychology make almost no mention of this literature. Similarly, the Center for the Study of Applied Linguistics and other independent research organizations and individual researchers have generated volumes of literature regarding the linguistic minority child's acquisition of standard English; yet the typical textbooks used in such courses as "The Teaching of Language Arts" and "The Teaching of Reading" either ignore almost entirely or make only token and superficially passing references to this enormous body of theory and research. Indeed, throughout the textbooks used in undergraduate courses such as "Introduction to Education" or "Foundations of Education," one might expect to find cited the works of John Ogbu, Asa Hilliard III, Barbara Shade, James Banks, Donna Gollnick, Phillip Chinn, Christine Sleeter, Carl Grant, Prentice Baptiste, Geneva Gay, Carlos Cortes, Manuel Ramirez, A. Castenada, Henry Trueba, Eugene Garcia, and many other nationally recognized scholars in the fields of multicultural and bilingual education. If the views of these scholars are studied at all by undergraduates in teacher education, they are studied almost exclusively through a textbook used in a separate course titled "Multicultural Education" or "Introduction to Bilingual Education" or textbooks used for a single course such as "Sociology of Education." In addition to these three typically omitted "knowledge bases," there exist other well-defined areas of theory and research regarding the education of culturally diverse students that are missing not only from the pages of textbooks but also from the curricula of most teacher education programs.

The Professional Literature

The absence of the theory and research regarding how culture influences learning is also characteristic of the professional literature about the knowledge bases for teacher education. To date, most all of the attempts to define the knowledge bases for teacher education have skirted the bodies of theory and research that hold the most promise for better educating culturally diverse students. Culture-specific research findings remain largely unmentioned. For example, *Knowledge Base for the Beginning Teacher* (Reynolds, 1989) is an important, seminal effort to collect and define the body of theory and research undergirding the knowledge base for teacher education; yet this work falls woefully short of treating the knowledge bases necessary for preparing teachers to teach successfully culturally diverse student populations. To be fair, *Knowledge Base for the Beginning Teacher* contains two chapters that peripherally treat effective schooling for minorities. Cazden and Mehan (1989) in their chapter, "Principles from Sociology and Anthropology: Context, Code, Classroom and Culture," present what might be considered an excellent introduction to several significant pieces of the knowledge base for effectively teaching minorities. Florio-Ruane (1989) in her chapter, "Social Organization of Classes and Schools" devotes a small sub-section to "The Special Problems of Minority Children" but centers primarily upon the knowledge-base related to the analysis of school culture rather than the students' cultures.

These two chapters present significant aspects of the knowledge base for beginning teachers and point out to teacher educators where some of the bodies of research relevant to preparing teachers for effectively educating minorities may be found. The other 22 chapters of *Knowledge Base for the Beginning Teacher*, however, contribute little toward identifying knowledge bases with special relevance to minority education.

A similar criticism can be made about the *Handbook of Research in Teacher Education* (Houston et al., 1990), the *Handbook of Research on Teaching* (Wittrock, 1986), and the classic *Encyclopedia of Educational Research* (Mitzel, 1982), a basic knowledge-base resource sorely in need of revision to include research generated since the fifth edition was published over a decade ago. While none of these works exclude entirely references to the theory and research about minority achievement and cultural dimensions of the teaching-learning process, they represent the predominate view that teacher preparation is generic. Again, to be fair, The *Handbook of Research in Teacher Education* does contain three chapters out of 48 that directly address knowledge bases relevant to preparing teachers for culturally diverse classrooms. Grant and Secada (1990) in their chapter, "Preparing Teachers for Diversity," examined empirical studies in multicultural education, gender equality, and second-language issues, and noted that the paucity of research "...suggests the marginal status and low importance that has been given to research on the preparation of teachers to work with diverse student populations" (p. 404). Garcia (1990) in his chapter, "Educating Teachers for Language Minority Students," addresses significant knowledge bases for preparing teachers for culturally and linguistically diverse students. Reynolds (1990) in his chapter, "Educating Teachers for Special Education Students," identifies the knowledge base necessary for the preparation of teachers of handicapped students.

More recent publications have similar shortcomings. The second edition of the *Handbook of Research on Teacher Education* (Sikula, 1996) commendably devotes an entire subsection to diversity and equity issues but fails to point teachers toward clearly defined knowledge bases for effectively teaching diverse student populations.

The Teacher Educator's Handbook: Building a Knowledge Base for Preservice Teachers (Murray, 1996) is another valuable, seminal effort to identify a knowledge base for teacher preparation programs;

> *...schools, colleges, and departments of education have a moral and ethical responsibility... to enable teachers to respond to the educational needs of their diverse student populations...*

but, in truth, this publication presents the preparation of teachers as largely a diversity-blind endeavor. For the most part, the basic reference works for teacher education reflect a subtle color and culture-blindness that implies that race and culture are not factors that have special relevance for the preparation of teachers.

Definition of a Culturally Responsible Pedagogy for Teacher Education

What is a *culturally responsible pedagogy* for teacher education? In this treatise, "pedagogy" refers to the art and science of teaching, to both the intuitive and research-based knowledge and practices that guide the classroom teacher's management of student learning, and to both content and methodology. As used here, *pedagogy* implies a multitude of ideas and includes not only all that is implied in the frequently used term *culturally responsive teaching* (Bowers & Flinders, 1990; Ladson-Billings, 1994b; Villegas, 1991) but also a moral and ethical imperative for schools, colleges, and departments of education. In brief, a culturally responsible pedagogy for teacher education is a teacher preparation program that prepares teachers to be respectfully sensitive to the cultures of their students, to learn about and know the cultures of their students, and to use understandings about how culture influences learning in their day to day planning for teaching students.

A *culturally responsible pedagogy* means that schools, colleges, and departments of education have a moral and ethical *responsibility* to prepare teachers to be culturally responsive, that is, to enable teachers to respond to the educational needs of their diverse student populations by planning and developing culturally rich curricula and by using instructional methodologies that are based upon knowledge about how culture influences cognitive learning styles. Ideally, to have a culturally responsible teacher education program, a school, college, or department of education would have a mission statement that recognizes that multicultural teacher education *is* teacher education and would provide a series of multiculturally rich experiences consisting of formal course work and interactive classroom and field experiences that accomplish its mission.

A culturally responsible teacher education program is one (a) that directly teaches about several cultural groups, most of which have special relevance for the local rural and metropolitan communities to which candidates will return; (b) that presents the knowledge bases of theory and research studies about these selected cultural groups; and (c) that enables preservice and inservice teachers to learn processes and methodologies for the study of other cultural groups. This view is in partial contradiction to the recommendations of Cazden and Mehan (1989):

> Sometimes an attempt is made to transmit to teachers specific information from research studies about the culture of different groups. . . .But there are limitations and even dangers in this solution.
>
> The limitations come from the practical impossibility for beginning teachers to learn about the many cultures that may be represented in their class. The dangers come from the likelihood that such knowledge will contribute only stereotyped categories and labels that then become barriers to understanding the behavior of a particular child working on a particular school task, and contribute to lowered expectations about that child's possible achievement. Moreover, such information is likely to be considered controversial, even racist, by adult members of the groups described, and any action that undermines trust between home and school is, by that fact alone, detrimental to children's learning.
>
> Instead of trying to transmit information about specific cultures, teacher education can help beginning teachers learn how to learn experientially about students and their families and encourage them to reflect on their own cultural background rather than unthinkingly live it as an unexamined norm.

> In conclusion, it is important to note that we are not recommending a general solution for all educational situations. Instead, we are recommending a general procedure, one that can be used to find solutions in local circumstances. The basic idea is that beginning teachers should learn how to gain information from the local community and transform it for pedagogical use. (pp.54-55)

In terms of program outcomes, a culturally responsible teacher education program graduates teachers who think and act multiculturally rather than monoculturally, who develop curricula that are multicultural rather than monocultural in content, who utilize methodologies that are congruent with cultural learning styles, who can reflect about relevance of knowledge bases in a variety of cultural contexts, and who understand that becoming a multicultural educator is a developmental process without a known point of completion. They understand that becoming a multicultural educator involves the individual's quest to understand and respect his/her own cultural heritage and to develop the knowledge, skills, and attitudes to become functional within other ethnic cultures as well as the mainstream culture. They understand that multicultural education enables the individual to believe in one's intrinsic worth, to transcend monoculturalism and, ultimately, to become multicultural. As a personal, educational, and professional venture, this developmental process is at the center of individual's noble quest to define one's relationship and responsibility to the common good in an interdependent, global society. Hence, it is a goal of a culturally responsible teacher education program that teachers will ultimately perceive "commitment to the common good" to mean the reconstruction of society to be fair, just, and free of oppression.

Realistically, teachers who have completed a *culturally responsible* teacher education program recognize that they are not prepared to teach children from *all* cultures, but they do know they have studied four or five major cultures and the theory and research about how elements of these cultures influence the school learning environment and the teaching-learning process. Even more importantly, through the in-depth study of four or five cultures and the body of literature about these cultures, they have internalized a methodology for adapting to and learning about the many other cultures from which their future pupils may come. Thus, they know that for as long as they teach they must continue to add to their knowledge base the customs, belief systems, communication and linguistic styles, mores, and behavior patterns of new additional cultures. They know also to reflect intelligently about how to develop curriculum that includes elements of these new cultures. They know how to identify dominant culturally-influenced cognitive styles and how to recognize the individual student's variances from the dominant cognitive style of that student's culture.

Additional program outcomes of a *culturally responsible* teacher education program center upon dramatic paradigm shifts in the way teachers think about minority children. That is, if preservice and inservice teachers were to study the appropriate knowledge bases of theory and research, they would view minority students as described by Williams (1994) not as "deprived, underachieving, unmotivated, and at risk [but instead as] culturally diverse, capable, motivated, and resilient (p. 1)."

Finally, a culturally *responsible* and *responsive* teacher education program centers its expressed program outcomes in mission and goal statements that boldly express the intent to graduate teachers who are not merely educated to adapt to a society of social inequality and inequities but, instead, are

educated to correct injustices. As the statement by Gandhi used to open this chapter implies, the next generations of teachers "must be the change we wish to see in the world." Teacher preparation programs must empower new teachers who will, in turn, empower their pupils to create a more fair and just democratic society. This social reconstructionist perspective is an inextricable part of the definition of a culturally responsible and responsive teacher preparation program.

In Search of the Knowledge Bases for Culturally Responsible and Responsive Teacher Education

If teacher education faculty members at an institution of higher education wished to revise their teacher education programs to include knowledge bases that are especially relevant to preparing teachers for culturally and linguistically diverse classrooms, where would they look for guidance? Unfortunately, no single source exists that presents a comprehensive blueprint regarding all of the knowledge bases for diversity in teacher education. More often than not scholars, theoreticians, and researchers have focused their scholarship on the importance of one or two key knowledge bases rather than a comprehensive listing of knowledge bases that ought to be included in a modern teacher education program. Thus, no sophisticated, comprehensive taxonomy of knowledge bases for diversity in teacher education has emerged in the literature at this time. Even more difficult to find is a treatise that not only identifies a comprehensive listing of knowledge bases, but also provides information on where uninformed teacher educators can readily find the synthesized bodies of theory and research that undergird each knowledge base and, therefore, constitute the "content" to be studied by preservice and inservice teachers.

Key Pieces of Literature. However, there are several key pieces of literature that collectively provide a suggested framework of recommended knowledge bases and identify either directly or indirectly some of each knowledge base's supportive theory and research. The best of these references

> *...No sophisticated, comprehensive taxonomy of knowledge bases for diversity in teacher education has emerged in the literature at this time.*

include Gay's "Multicultural Teacher Education," a chapter in Banks and Lynch's *Multicultural Education in Western Societies* (1986); Gollnick's "Multicultural Education: Policies and Practices in Teacher Education," a chapter in Grant's *Research in Multicultural Education: From the Margins to the Mainstream* (1992), Zeichner's *Educating Teachers for Cultural Diversity* (1993); Gay's "Building Cultural Bridges: A Bold Proposal for Teacher Education" (1993); Hollins, King and Hayman's *Teaching Diverse Populations: Formulating a Knowledge Base* (1994); Baptiste and Archer's "A Comprehensive Multicultural Teacher Education Program: An Idea Whose Time Has Come," a chapter in Atwater, Radzik-March, and Strutchen's *Multicultural Education: Inclusion of All,* (1994); and Boyer's *Teacher Education and Schools of the Future: Issues of Race, Class and Gender* (1994), an unpublished manuscript for a publication forthcoming from the Association of Teacher Educators' Commission on Preparing Teachers for Diverse Populations.

Other valuable resources recommended for study by teacher education faculty members who wish to educate themselves about knowledge bases relevant to preparing teachers for culturally and linguistically diverse classrooms include Dilworth's *Diversity in Teacher Education: New Expectations* (1992), O'Hair and Odell's *Diversity and Teaching: Teacher Education Yearbook I* (1993), and Sleeter's *Keepers of the Dream: A Study of Staff Development and Multicultural Education* (1992). Teacher educators will also find *Developing Multicultural Teacher Education Curricula* (Larkin & Sleeter, 1995) and a subsection, "Preparing Teachers for Cultural Diversity," in *Currents of Reform in Preservice Teacher Education* (Zeichner, Melnick, & Gomez, 1996) are valuable resources for infusing the knowledge bases for diversity into teacher education programs. *Critical Knowledge for Diverse Teachers & Learners* (Irvine, 1997) is another important volume of essays about what teachers should know to teach students of diverse backgrounds. A review of these publications and their reference sections indicates that over the past 25 years there has been *no shortage* of recommendations regarding what preservice and inservice teachers should study and experience to become more effective teachers in culturally diverse class-

rooms, but that it has only been recently the term "knowledge base" has been used to describe the content of culturally responsible and responsive teacher education programs. A review of these publications also clearly indicates that there is considerable consensus among authorities regarding what knowledge bases of theory and research ought to be included in a culturally responsible and responsive teacher education program.

Thirteen Essential Knowledge Bases to Prepare Teachers for Culturally and Linguistically Diverse Classrooms

What follows is a description of 13 knowledge bases that should be infused into the curriculum of preservice and inservice teachers who are being prepared to become effective teachers in culturally diverse classrooms (see Appendix 1).

First, each knowledge base is broadly defined. Second, some of the essential elements of each knowledge base are presented. In most instances, a brief rationale for including each of the knowledge bases in teacher education programs is provided. Third, the literature of theory and research for each knowledge base is identified. Although the literature of theory and research for each knowledge base is not claimed to be comprehensive, key resources are presented that will enable teacher educators not only to have starter resources for educating themselves but also to locate and construct their own collections of supportive and instructional materials for including the knowledge bases in their courses.

> *...over the past 25 years there has been no shortage of recommendations regarding what preservice and inservice teachers should study and experience to become more effective teachers in culturally diverse classrooms...*

Chapter 2
Knowledge Base 1: *Foundations of Multicultural Education*

To me, if you'd been telling the truth, I wouldn't have to be arguing for a multicultural or a culturally plural curriculum. I think about the reality in my classroom. I've got people there from all kinds of ethnic groups and they all have prior experiences that are related to the general culture in some way. I think it's disrespectful to ignore that and say, "Well, I'm only going to listen to the cultural and ethnic experiences of a single group." That's academically incorrect and intellectually dishonest.

I don't even like to use the word, "included," because it seems like you're begging. The problem is a problem of truth. The curriculum as it is presently taught is invalid. So you don't have to include me. You just have to make your curriculum valid. Then I will be included.

— Asa Hilliard III

The theoretical, ideological, philosophical, and historical foundations of multicultural education constitute one of the most important knowledge bases characteristic of a culturally responsive and responsible teacher education program. Broadly defined this knowledge base consists of an introductory level of knowledge *about multicultural education.* It includes more specifically "the language" of multicultural education as a stand-alone discipline and as a field of study and practice. It is that knowledge base that introduces the preservice and inservice teacher to (a) definitions of multicultural education; (b) key terms that constitute the concepts and language of multicultural education such as *diversity, cultural pluralism, assimilation, culture, acculturation, xenophobia, ethnocentrism, Eurocentrism, racism, classism, sexism, homophobia, prejudice, discrimination, antiracism, antibias, inclusion, exclusion,* etc; (c) principles and philosophical tenets of multicultural education such as *differences are not deficits or culture influences the way students go about learning,* (d) commonly known models of multicultural curriculum infusion such as those described by Banks (1988a), Sleeter and Grant (1988a, 1994), and other well-known scholars and theoreticians in the field of multicultural education; (e) well-known models of the personal stages of development from ethnocentrism to multiculturalism and globalism such as those described by Banks (1992) and Bennett (1986); and (f) the literature of theory and research that undergirds multicultural education as an academic discipline. In short, this knowledge base consists of that content commonly found in more than 20 textbooks published for use in teacher education courses titled "Multicultural Education."

> *The absence of the foundations of multicultural education as a content knowledge base in teacher education programs is appalling...*

The absence of the *foundations of multicultural education* as a content knowledge base in teacher education programs is appalling, particularly in light of the fact that the parameters of this knowledge base, including the supportive literature of theory and research, have been collected and organized already into so many existing textbooks appropriate for delivering this knowledge base as a separate course in core teacher education programs. Some teacher education programs do cover this knowledge base in a required course in multicultural education, but most do not (Gollnick, 1992). In fact, only 19 of 51 State Departments of Education reported coursework in multicultural education as a requirement for teacher credentialing (Evans, Torrey, & Newton, 1997). What is even more appalling, however, is that a majority of instructors and professors in teacher education programs have not, themselves, read even one of the basic textbooks in multicultural education. Whereas most professors of education have read or studied at least one basic textbook in human growth and development, curriculum design, methods of teaching, educational psychology, and research design and statistics, it cannot be assumed, similarly, that most teacher educators have read a basic text or reference book about multicultural education. That so few teacher educators have read a basic textbook in multicultural education is partially explained by the fact that most of the current cadre of teacher educators earned their doctorates prior to the existence of courses in multicultural education. In fact, even most of the current instructors and scholars in multicultural teacher education have developed their expertise informally through reading and research, rather than through formal coursework.

Locating and Synthesizing Theory and Research for Knowledge Base 1.

The theory and research for the foundations of multicultural education as defined above have, of course, already been synthesized to a large degree and are presented in any number of textbooks written specifically for use in a multicultural education course found as a requirement in many teacher education programs. The problem for new

faculty members centers less upon their locating, synthesizing, and organizing the literature than selecting a basic textbook and collection of supplementary readings that constitute a synthesis appropriate to the overall mission, sequence, and content of the teacher education curriculum at their particular institutions. Because of the proliferation in number of teacher education textbooks in multicultural education and because of the variety of types of books, it is difficult to recommend any single book to teacher educators that is the most appropriate for faculty self-education about the foundations of multicultural education. It is equally difficult to recommend a single book as the most appropriate to use as a basic text in a required course in multicultural education for preservice undergraduates, graduate students, or inservice teachers. For preservice and inservice teachers with beginning level or no prior background, James Banks' *An Introduction to Multicultural Education* (1994) is an excellent primer. More comprehensive textbooks tailored to teachers at all grade levels and all subject areas include Nieto's *Affirming Diversity: The Sociopolitical Context of Multicultural Education* (1996), Gollnick and Chinn's *Multicultural Education in a Pluralistic Society* (1998), Sleeter and Grant's *Making Choices for Multicultural Education: Five Approaches to Race, Class, and Gender* (1994), Banks' *Multiethnic Education: Theory and Practice* (1988c), and Bennett's *Comprehensive Multicultural Education: Theory and Practice* (1995). Although Sleeter's *Keepers of the Dream: A Study of Staff Development and Multicultural Education* (1992) is not intended to be a basic text in multicultural education, it does provide an excellent review of the literature that constitutes much of the theory and research related to Knowledge Base 1. More importantly, Sleeter's book helps define the parameters of what is known through research about inservice teachers' experiencing staff development in multicultural education and, therefore, is extremely useful to teacher educators as they construct their own organizations of theory and research for Knowledge Base 1.

A second category of books that include part of the theory and research relevant to the foundations of multicultural education as a knowledge base consists of texts tailored to specific grade and program levels such as early childhood and elementary or certification areas such as special education and deaf education. Texts that are illustrative of those written explicitly for preservice and inservice early childhood teachers include Ramsey's *Teaching and Learning in a Diverse World: Multicultural Education for Young Children* (1987), King, Chipman, and Cruz-Janzen's *Educating Young Children in a Diverse Society* (1994), and Vold's *Multicultural Education in Early Childhood Classrooms* (1992). Examples of texts targeted primarily to the elementary teacher that are activity-based but also cover basic theory, concepts, and principles of multicultural education are Tiedt and Tiedt's *Multicultural Teaching: A Handbook of Activities, Information, and Resources* (1995), and Hernandez's *Multicultural Education: A Teacher's Guide to Content and Process* (1989). Resources that do not necessarily cover the basic theory, concepts, and principles of multicultural education described as essential elements of Knowledge Base 1 but are recommended as texts to extend the study of cultural diversity issues in teacher training programs for special education and deaf education are Harry's *Cultural Diversity, Families, and the Special Education System: Communication and Empowerment* (1992) and Christensen and Delgado's *Multicultural Issues in Deafness* (1993).

A third category of books extend the beginning level content of Knowledge Base 1 to more complex levels and to a variety of issues and themes. Books illustrative of this category include edited collections such as Banks and Banks's *Multicultural Education: Issues and Perspectives* (1997) and *Multicultural Education in Western Societies* (1986) and Sleeter's *Empowerment through Multicultural Education* (1991). In delivering Knowledge Base 1 in teacher education programs teacher educators often use several of these books as supplementary readers to a basic textbook in multicultural education. Similarly, a number of teacher educators find Shultz's *Annual Editions: Multicultural Education 97/98* (1997) a useful collection of supplementary readings that represent the editor's selection of the best contemporary journal articles on the topic of multicultural education. With regard to facilitating the development of a credible research base for Knowledge Base 1, teacher educators will find valuable resources in Grant's *Research & Multicultural Education: From the Margins to the Mainstream* (1992) and James A. Banks' and Cherry A. Banks' *Handbook of Research on Multicultural Education* (1995).

CHAPTER 3
Knowledge Base 2: *Sociocultural Contexts of Human Growth and Psychological Development in Marginalized Ethnic and Racial Cultures*

Grandmother, next to mother, was the most important person in the home...Her place, in fact, could be filled by no one else...old people were revered for their knowledge...the old were objects of care and devotion to the last...they were never given cause to feel useless and unwanted, for there were duties performed only by the old and because it was a rigidly kept custom for the young to treat their elders with respect.

— Luther Standing Bear, Lakota

The sociocultural contexts of human growth and development in marginalized ethnic and racial cultures constitute an essential knowledge base for teacher education programs that profess to prepare teachers for culturally diverse classrooms. Most existing textbooks used to provide a solid grounding in the social and psychological development of children to preservice and inservice teachers include almost no information about minority cultures. For the most part, teacher educators and the textbooks they use continue to pretend that the dynamics of child, adolescent, and adult development are not affected by culture. Thus, if teachers are expected to understand their culturally diverse students, content of the human growth and development component of teacher education programs (typically courses in child and adolescent development) must be drastically revised.

The essential elements of the knowledge base on sociocultural contexts of human growth and development from infancy through adulthood for members of nonmainstream cultural and ethnic groups ought to consist, minimally, of (a) ethnic patterns of social, physical, and cognitive development and (b) patterns and stages of ethnic identity including self concept and self-image development. In addition, this knowledge base ought to include the influences of culturally determined and unique patterns of family organization, childrearing practices, and other processes of socialization and development. Other elements of this knowledge base center upon culturally shaped dimensions of motivation, the literature on resilience and the critical theory perspectives that challenge conventional norms for human growth and development and conventional definitions of "developmentally appropriate practice." If preservice and inservice teachers study the appropriate bodies of literature, they will understand that norms for human growth and development vary from culture to culture and that much of the traditional knowledge base studied in the psychological foundations courses is Anglocentric or Eurocentric and not necessarily appropriate for interpreting and understanding the behavior of culturally diverse pupils of color.

Locating and Synthesizing the Theory and Research for Knowledge Base 2

The theory and research for Knowledge Base 2 has been synthesized far better for behavioral scientists and for instructors of psychological foundations courses than for student consumption. Even so, to infuse Knowledge Base 2 into child development, adolescent development and human growth and development courses, instructors will have to synthesize a number of bodies of literature that have emerged from distinctly separate strands of investigation and from a variety of disciplines including psychology, counseling, anthropology, sociology, and teacher education. Those instructors who attempt a comprehensive synthesis of theory and research for Knowledge Base 2 also need to be mindful of some general characteristics of the various bodies of theory and research.

Much of the theory and research on Knowledge Base 2 has been synthesized in two seminal publications. Phinney and Rotheram's *Children's Ethnic Socialization and Development* (1987) focuses upon that aspect of Knowledge Base 2 that is referred to as "ethnic socialization and ethnic identity development" and provides an excellent introduction to definitions of such terms as *ethnicity, ethnic identity, ethnic self-identification, ethnic awareness,* and *ethnic attitudes* that are characteristically used throughout the literature. Also, through chapters contributed by scholars and researchers from the United States, Canada, Australia, New Zealand, and Mexico, this publication provides a synthesis of vastly divergent bodies of theory and research literature that can be organized, as noted by Phinney and Rotheram (1987), into four unifying themes:

① Important differences in attitudes, values, and behaviors distinguish ethnic groups; these differences affect the socialization of children within their own group and the attitudes and responses to other groups.

② The impact of ethnicity on children and the way children understand and deal with it vary significantly with age and developmental level.

③ The process of ethnic socialization differs in important ways depending on the particular group children belong to, and on whether that group is the majority group or a minority group in the society.

④ Children's ethnic socialization is a function of both the immediate environment and the sociocultural context; social and historical change is continually altering the relationships among the groups and the meaning of ethnicity for children. (pp. 274-276)

Children's Ethnic Socialization and Development also identifies some of the most significant topics and subtopics that are related to understanding ethnic identity development.

Similarly, Bernal and Knight's *Ethnic Identity: Formation and Transmission Among Hispanics and Other Minorities* (1993) identifies some of the most important topics that constitute the parameters of ethnic identity development as a knowledge base. In this collection for example, Ocampo, Bernal, and Knight (1993) synthesize the theory and research that connect ethnic identity to gender and race identity. Bernal, Knight, Ocampo, Garza, and Cota (1993) explore Mexican American identity. From a cognitive development perspective, Aboud and Doyle (1993) present their proposition that stages of development in ethnic identity and prejudice are correlated to similar development in social cognition. Using research on Asian American, African American, Mexican American, and White adolescents, Phinney (1993) discusses ethnic identity development from the perspective of ego identity theory. Additional chapters highlight other equally significant topics related to the knowledge base on ethnic identity development. Both the range of topics and the chapters are greater in number, in fact, than can be reviewed substantively in this chapter. The important point to make here, however, is that the chapters in Bernal and Knight's book constitute the kind of readings that preservice and inservice teachers should be experiencing in their teacher education programs.

Literature with an Afrocentric Framework. Another body of literature that should be integrated into Knowledge Base 2 but has been ignored historically is that which presents an Afrocentric framework for theorizing about, researching, and interpreting the diversity of African American family life, African American socialization patterns, and African American identity development. Until the decade of the 1980s and to some degree presently, this literature had not been synthesized sufficiently for use in teacher education programs. Instructors in psychology departments and schools, colleges, and departments of education were forced to construct their own collections of literature from a handful of books similar to Billingsley's *Black Families in White America* (1968) and Staples' *The Black Family: Essays and Studies* (1971), and a few journals marginalized from mainstream literature such as *Journal of Black Psychology, Black Scholar,* and *The Western Journal of Black Studies.* Even in the 1990s, almost none of psychological foundations textbooks used in teacher education programs cite the works of the scholars of this body of literature, and only a few teacher educators include this literature in their own professional reading. It is not likely, however, that preservice and inservice teachers can be considered educated nor well-prepared to teach African American children if they are not exposed to this vast and growing body of theory and research. At least four contemporary books provide good syntheses of theory and research as a starting place for teacher educators to educate themselves regarding the parameters of this literature and to begin infusing this information into the curriculum. These four recommendations include McAdoo's *Black Families* (1983), Berry and Asamen's *Black Students: Psychosocial Issues and Academic Achievement* (1989), Rodgers-Rose's *The Black Woman* (1980), and Gary's *Black Men* (1981).

Teacher educators who teach principles of human growth and development must also integrate into Knowledge Base 2 what is known about motivation in African Americans. Perhaps the best starter resource for the uninformed teacher educator to identify relevant research is the seminal review of 103 race-comparative and 30 race-homogeneous empirical studies on African American motivation conducted by Graham (1994). Graham's extensive review of research literature organized studies into the topical categories of need for achievement, locus of control, attribution expectancy, and ability self-

concept to test three often-made assumptions: (a) that African Americans lack specific personality traits associated with achievement, (b) that African Americans do not believe in internal or personal control of outcomes, and (c) that African Americans have negative self-perceptions about their abilities. Finding no support for any of these assumptions that are too often held by some teachers, Graham concluded:

① As measured by research on need for achievement, there is no strong evidence that African Americans lack personality traits associated with motivation.

② It cannot be concluded that African Americans are more likely than their White counterparts to endorse external and/or uncontrollable causes for achievement, nor is there evidence that perceived uncontrollability has maladaptive motivational consequences.

③ Both expectancy for future success and self-concept of ability among African Americans remain relatively high even when achievement out-comes indicate otherwise. (p. 103)

Literature of Resilence. The literature on resilience constitutes another body of theory and research relevant to Knowledge Base 2. The "resilient child" literature has found its way into mainstream scholarship. Because much of the scholarship has been targeted to educational audiences such as teachers and teacher educators, this literature's synthesis is already largely packaged for infusion as a content area in teacher education programs. The theory and research on resiliency has been based largely, though not solely, on urban children, particularly African American urban youth. An exception is Werner's *Overcoming the Odds: High Risk Children from Birth to Adulthood* (1992), the classic longitudinal study that followed 505 high-risk children on the island of Kauai from 1955 into their thirties. The general findings of this body of literature show that many urban youth (a) do, indeed, overcome adverse conditions and are self-supportive, responsible, and productive, (b) have such characteristics and skills as stress resistance, hardiness, resilience, social competence, autonomy, problem-solving abilities, and (c) have a keen sense of the future. Much of the resiliency literature has been synthesized by Bernard (1991), Garmezy (1991), McIntyre, Wait, & Yoast (1990), Rutter (1990) and Winfield (1991). Because much of the research is based on the premise that studying resilient youth who overcome adverse conditions provides some solutions to improving education for minority and urban youth, the resiliency literature seems to merit a place in the teacher education curriculum to counteract and change the negative attitudes of many preservice and inservice teachers who express that "nothing can overcome the backgrounds of these students."

Literature in Counseling. Scholarship in the field of counseling is a rich but often untapped source for much of the theory and research literature on sociocultural contexts of human growth and development for marginalized cultural, ethnic, and racial groups of students. In fact, several basic texts written for training counselors to work with multicultural youth populations have synthesized the psychological literature relevant to Knowledge Base 2 far better than have most texts written to prepare teachers to work with culturally diverse students. Counseling texts illustrative of those from which teacher educators can extract the theory and research that undergird Knowledge Base 2 are Pederson and Carey's *Multicultural Counseling in Schools: A Practical Handbook* (1994); Sue's *Counseling the Culturally Different: Theory and Practice* (1981); Gibbs and Huang's *Children of Color: Psychological Interventions with Minority Youth* (1989), Stiffman and Davis' *Ethnic Issues in Adolescent Mental Health* (1990); and Atkinson, Morten, and Sue's *Counseling American Minorities: A Cross-Cultural Perspective* (1979). These publications include scholarly treatments of cultural and ethnic identity development and reviews of literature relevant to understanding the psychological, social, emotional, and cognitive development of African Americans, Asian Americans, Native Americans, Hispanics, and other groups.

Literature on the Critical Theory Perspective. Another body of theory and research that should be integrated into Knowledge Base 2 is the critical

theory perspective regarding the conventional norms for human growth and development and definitions of "developmentally appropriate practice" in a multicultural society. Although many of the same bodies of theory and research mentioned above are used by critical theorists to support their positions, critical theorists provide a sociopolitical perspective on human development that preservice and inservice teachers do not typically but should experience in the psychological foundations component of teacher education programs. In addition, some reviews of other bodies of theory and research not mentioned heretofore will help curriculum planners of teacher education programs identify more comprehensively the key references for Knowledge Base 2.

A good starting point for teacher educators who do not feel well grounded in critical theory perspectives about human development is Mallory and New's *Diversity & Developmentally Appropriate Practices* (1994). This publication through chapters written by distinguished scholars in the field of early childhood education presents one of the best syntheses of literature available to challenge traditional Eurocentric/Western assumptions about development that historically have excluded culturally and developmentally different children.

Finally, the construction of a comprehensive body of literature to support Knowledge Base 2 would not be complete without specific topics from the works of some scholars not mentioned above. Clearly, preservice teachers and inservice teachers should study Banks' (1988c, 1992) six-stage model of ethnic identity development; Helms' (1990, 1994) racial identity model, Hale-Benson's (1986) discussion of childrearing and socialization into womanhood and manhood in African American culture; Comer's (1980, 1986, 1987, 1988, 1989) perspectives on school power, self-concept development, and social skills development; and Ogbu's (1978, 1982, 1987, 1988a, 1988b) analysis of castelike and voluntary and involuntary minority groups' socialization in an unjust opportunity structure that mitigates against members of oppressed groups. Additional key resources for understanding African American identity development include *Expressively Black: The Cultural Basis of Ethnic Identity* by Gay and Baber (1987) and *Shades of Black: Diversity in African American*

Identity by Cross (1991). Resources for understanding the classroom implications of the stages of ethnic identity among White students include the works of Helmes (1990) and Tatum (1992).

In addition, teacher educators who are compiling their own organization of the bodies of literature relevant to Knowledge Base 2 are advised to read "Chapter 3: Principles of Human Growth and Development" in *At the Essence of Learning: Multicultural Education* by Geneva Gay (1994). In this chapter, Gay discusses traditional, general principles of human growth and development in "the contexts of ethnic diversity and multicultural education" (p. 64).

The paramount importance of understanding the relationships between *principles of human growth an development* and *cultural context* has been described by Gay in the following manner:

> The human development concepts most frequently invoked in educational theory are continuity, sequence, and progression; critical tasks and periods in development, motivation; individual diversity and human universality; cumulative effects of experience; and maximizing personal potential Multicultural education adds the dimension of cultural context to these. It contends that these principles cannot be fully understood or translated into practice for culturally different students unless they are interpreted through the screens of their diverse ethnic identities, cultural orientations, and background experiences. (p.64)

Gay has articulated as well as anyone else in the field the relationships between mainstream, universal principles of human growth and development and *cultural contexts*. She has conceptualized the general principles of human development into four categories: *holistic growth, universal psychological needs and developmental tasks, identity development and individuality*, and *universality*. Based on these four categories, she has also constructed a conceptual framework that correlates many general principles of human growth and development to a "multicultural translation" of each principle (see Table 1 on the next page).

In addition to providing a visual representation of how general principles of human growth and development can be viewed in cultural contexts, Gay's framework suggests one way Knowledge Base 2 could be organized thematically. Although education faculty and instructors of the content in Knowledge Base 2 could design a variety of conceptual frameworks by which the content of Knowledge Base 2 will best be organized for integration into the overall teacher education curriculum, using Gay's already established framework has a time-saving advantage. This advantage may be especially useful to those teacher educators who are just beginning to educate themselves about Knowledge Base 2 and feel somewhat overwhelmed about how to commence.

Several points can be made about the status of the sociocultural contexts of human growth and psychological development of marginalized ethnic and racial groups as a knowledge base suitable for including in the teacher education curriculum. First, there exists a relatively large body of theory and research on the social and psychological development of children from minority ethnic and racial groups; but, even so, the research base, particularly replicated findings, is not yet sufficiently developed to meet the standards of mainstream psychology for including psychological "truths" or "principles" in psychology textbooks. Second, despite the fact that the study of the psychological development of ethnic and racial minority groups is a relatively new field, it is sufficiently developed to advance preservice and inservice teachers' understanding of culturally diverse children. For example, as Matsumoto (1994) points out, the research base is sufficiently developed to prove the existence of psychological findings that are *etics* (findings that appear to be consistent across cultures) and *emics* (findings that appear to be culture-specific and thus different across cultures). This small fact alone is evidence that the research base is sufficiently developed to enable preservice teachers to learn how to deconstruct mainstream knowledge in psychology, one of the important purposes for including this knowledge base in teacher education programs. Third, the body of theory and research on African Americans and Mexican Americans is more extensive than for other ethnic and racial minority groups although the knowledge base on other groups appears to be expanding rapidly.

TABLE 1
General Principles of Human Development and Their Multicultural Translations

GENERAL PRINCIPLES	MULTICULTURAL TRANSLATIONS
Holistic Growth	
Human growth is multidimensional and holistic.	Ethnic and cultural factors are key aspects of human development.
Human growth is sequential.	Sequence of growth is influenced by cultural environments.
Human growth varies in rate.	Rate of growth is affected by cultural conditions.
Universal Psychological Needs & Developmental Tasks	
Behavior is internally and externally motivated.	Motivation varies by ethnic and cultural group, situation, and context.
Psychological needs are hierarchical.	Psychological needs are satisfied in culturally specific ways.
Identity Development	
Self-acceptance leads to greater academic achievement.	Ethnic identity development, self-concept, and academic achievement are interrelated.
Improvement of individual abilities enhances personal competence of students.	Ethnic identity is a major part of personal competence for diverse students.
Individuality & Universality	
Individual differences in human growth and development are normal.	Ethnicity and culture are key determinants of individuality.
Human dignity must be respected.	Cultural socialization determines behavioral expressions of humanity.
There are both similarities and differences among individuals and groups.	Strengths and abilities are culturally contextual.
Individual learning styles and preferences should be accommodated.	Cultural filters diversify human potential.

Adapted from Gay (1994), pp. 63-90

CHAPTER 4
Knowledge Base 3: *Cultural and Cognitive Learning Style Theory and Research*

You White teachers think White. You don't know nothing. My Arlene, she is one smart girl... Teach her good and she learn good. That's your job.

— Mrs. Yellow Eyes, mother
Rethinking Schools (October/November 1991, p. 10).

The theory and research on culturally distinct learning styles of ethnic/cultural minority students is an essential knowledge base for culturally responsible and responsive teacher education programs. Noting that "culture and ethnicity have a strong impact on shaping learning styles," Gay (1994) provides a rationale for including the knowledge base on cultural learning styles in teacher education programs:

> [T]eachers must understand cultural characteristics of different ethnic, racial, and social groups so they can develop instructional practices that are more responsive to cultural pluralism. Cultural characteristics of particular significance in this undertaking are communication styles, thinking styles, value systems, socialization processes, relational patterns and performance styles. (p. 2)

This knowledge base includes an extensive body of literature on how cultural patterns influence the educative process. The knowledge base that preservice and inservice teachers should study consists of (a) descriptive profiles of cultural learning styles for African Americans, Mexican Americans, Native Americans, and other cultural groups for which sufficiently developed theory and research exist, (b) the theory and research that undergird the cultural learning-style profiles for each group, and

(c) the skills to use the profiles wisely. Using cultural learning-style profiles wisely means that teachers need the skills and intuitive abilities to assess the degree to which an individual student departs from the learning-style patterns generally characteristic of that student's cultural group.

Cultural learning-style profiles consist of predominant patterns of favored sensory and learning modalities, cognitive processes, mind sets, attitudes, interests, points of focus and orientation, social attributes, and approaches to learning that have been distinctly and uniquely shaped by culture. Typically, the patterns occur with sufficient frequency within a cultural group that they have been documented by observation and research, but the whole of a learning-style profile consisting of multiple patterns is not meant to be descriptive of all members of the cultural group. Cultural learning-style profiles also consist of generalizations that describe (a) how a culture conditions members of that culture to collect and process data, draw conclusions, and construct knowledge; (b) how culture predisposes members of the group to value or not value learning by doing, abstract thinking, analysis, synthesis, holistic and relational thinking, and analytical and reductionistic thinking; and (c) how culture influences perception and preferences for individual and group learning structures.

In addition, part of the preservice and inservice teacher's mastery of this knowledge base is learning appropriate and inappropriate uses of cultural learning styles. Thus, a significant aspect of this knowledge base includes comprehending that cultural learning-style profiles have broad applicability to a teacher's understanding of how culture intersects important junctures of human behavior that affect perception, interaction, cognition, and other processes significant to the educational environment bu*t* that cultural learning-style profiles are not schemata within which to force individual learners. For example, teachers must understand that what theory and research define as the African American learning style is not likely to match the learning style of any single African American student or all African American students. Cultural learning styles are to be distinguished from individual learning styles. Individual learning styles are subject to the influence of a large number of variables other than culture. Individual learning styles are influenced by individual personality traits and characteristics, family socialization experiences, degree of assimilation into the dominant culture's values, worldviews, learning processes, and, no doubt, the complex interactions with many other variables not yet fully understood. Whereas individual students should not be labeled and made to fit group cultural learning style profiles, cultural learning style profiles do have great value in helping teachers culturally contextualize their teaching and augment their repertoire of teaching strategies beyond the conventional didactic, individual and whole-class methodologies believed by some educators to be effective for middle-class European American students. Despite the danger that teachers with shallow knowledge about cultural learning styles may stereotype individual learners, teachers who do not study the existing scholarship on cultural learning styles are likely to continue to contribute to the undereducation of students from racial and cultural minority groups.

> *The cultural learning styles of African Americans and Mexican Americans seem to have commanded the earliest and perhaps the most attention during the 1970s.*

Current Status of the Cultural Learning Style Knowledge Base

Cultural learning style has been an established, recognized construct since the mid-1970s, yet theory and research on cultural learning styles has been largely absent in the educational psychology textbooks, learning theory courses, and the mainstream literature of teacher education. For example, the October 1990 issue of *Educational Leadership* was devoted to the theme of learning styles, yet less than a half-page was devoted to "cultural" learning styles with the remainder centering entirely on culture-free discussions of a variety of learning style models.

Faculty members who plan to infuse the cultural learning style knowledge base into their teacher education programs should be aware of the historical trends and current status of theory and research in this area of scholarship. First, the literature is more extensive on African American and selected Hispanic groups than for other groups although considerably more literature exists on Native American and Asian American cultural learning styles than is generally known by teachers and teacher educators. The cultural learning styles of African Americans and Mexican Americans seem to have commanded the earliest and perhaps the most attention during the 1970s. Some of the research base often cited in the literature about African American learning styles, most often in relation to language and communication, dates back to the early works of Lorenzo Dow Turner (1941, 1949) and Melville Herskovitz (1935, 1958), but most of the research that has been conducted since the late 1960s centers more on cognitive style than on communication style. Kagan and Madsen (1971, 1972) conducted seminal cross-cultural research on cooperation and competition among Anglo and Mexican American students; and Ramirez and Castenada (1974) established the field-sensitive learning styles of Chicano (Mexican American) students. Early research that began to sketch the parameters of what was called an "Hispanic" learning style, more often than not, was either based upon data collected on Mexican American students or was based upon the common "elements of Hispanic culture that originate from Ibero-Catholic tradition" (Diaz, 1989, p. 2). Educators were not always clear about the generalizability of this research to the many other specific Hispanic groups in America.

Second, the literature on cultural cognitive styles is general for some cultural groups but shows a growing trend in some cases toward addressing the more finite cultures within the broad cultural categories. More recently, the literature on Hispanic learning styles reflects a trend toward finer distinctions based upon sub-group cultural and social experiences of Puerto Ricans (Diaz, 1989; Torres-Guzman, Mercado, Quintero, and Viera, 1994; Walsh, 1991), Mexican American, Cuban American, and other Latino groups (Diaz, 1989). A similar trend is noticeable in the literature related to Pacific Rim and Asian American cultures including the Filipino (Santos, 1983), the Chinese (Tong, 1978; Huang & Hatch, 1978; Sue, Sue & Sue, 1983; Aaronson and Ferrer, 1987), the Japanese (Yamamoto & Iga, 1983), the Korean (Yu & Kim, 1983), and the Vietnamese (Chinn & Plata, 1986). On the other hand, the literature on Native American learning styles tends to be more general rather than specific to the many and various tribal cultures. More literature on a generic Native American learning style such as that described by Burgess (1978), Pewewardy (1994), and Swisher and Pavel (1994) exists than tribal-specific, learning-style profiles such as that described in an Odawa school setting by Mohatt and Erickson (1981). Scholarly discussions regarding the learning styles of poor Whites range from arguments that poor Whites do not have a cultural learning style (Selakovich, 1978) to arguments that Appalachian students represent a distinct ethnic minority culture that influences the Appalachian student's approach to school learning (Eller-Powell, 1994).

Third, theory regarding cultural learning styles has generally been regarded as having a "soft" research base. This criticism is much less justified in the 1990s than it was in the mid-1970s. In general, empirical evidence to support theoretical constructs has been slow in coming. However, the empirical evidence that has been accumulating during the last two decades has provided a respectable beginning research base. Clearly, the research base undergirding learning styles profiles is not as empirical as quantitative researchers would prefer. Much of the research is ethnographic and observa-

tion based. On the other hand, the research base is much more solid than is the research base for many common teaching practices.

Synthesizing the Knowledge Base on Cultural Learning Styles for Infusion into the Teacher Education Curriculum

Unfortunately, no single volume of scholarly work has pulled together and integrated the knowledge base of theory and research that does exist on several culture-specific learning styles. This literature remains largely scattered throughout the journals of several disciplines although some single works in recent years have organized the learning style information on several cultural groups better than others. Although no single existing book would serve as a comprehensive learning style textbook for use in teacher education programs, the use of two or three different books along with selected journal articles would provide sufficient coverage of the current state of cultural learning styles theory and research to improve considerably the cultural responsiveness of most teacher education programs.

At the present time, teacher educators must synthesize the theory and research on cultural learning styles from several sources. Perhaps the best primer to introduce the concept of "cultural learning style" to preservice and inservice teachers with beginning-level knowledge is Morris' *Extracting Learning Styles from Social/Cultural Diversity* (1978), an edited publication that contains separate chapters on the learning styles of African American, Chicano, Native American, poor White, and Chinese American students. However, teacher educators who are compiling a comprehensive synthesis of the literature on cultural learning styles will need to augment the theory and research presented in Morris' publication with more recent sources. Shade's *Culture, Style, and the Educative Process* (1989a), for example, is the most extensive presently existing single book about cultural learning styles. Shade's edited collection of chapters by numerous authors places major emphasis on African American, Mexican American, and Native American students, although literature reviewed throughout the book makes reference to other cultural groups.

Shade's second edition, *Culture, Style and the Educative Process: Making Schools Work for Racially Diverse Students* (1997), has been revised suitably for use as textbook appropriate for undergraduate- and graduate-level courses in teacher education. One of the best reviews of literature on cultural learning styles is the annotated bibliography by Huber and Pewewardy (1990). Another excellent review of the literature and research on cultural learning styles from the perspective of persistence of ethnicity across social class has been conducted by Banks (1988b).

A significant aspect of the theory and research literature on cultural learning styles that preservice and inservice teachers should study is the "literature of caution." Centering upon the debate and contradictions in the educational literature on cultural learning styles and the wise and unwise use of such information, this genre of literature has been synthesized well by Grant (1991). In addition to studying the "literature of caution" reviewed by Grant, preservice and inservice students should be introduced to the four points made by Gay (1994) as sensible guidelines for wisely matching teaching styles to cultural learning styles:

① Learning styles are multidimensional, fluid, individually and culturally determined, and, to some degree, situational.

② Gender may have a significant influence on learning styles. Research suggests that males and females, within and across ethnic and cultural groups, have some unique learning style characteristics (Gilligan 1982; Halpern 1986).

③ In addition to the perceptual orientation described by Barbe and Swassing (1979), other key components of learning styles are environmental setting, substantive content, motivation, procedural preferences, and interpersonal qualities.

④ Some of the learning style components are stable across time and context, while others vary greatly. Once basic learning patterns are established they tend to prevail thereafter as the *primary points of reference and central tendencies* for processing information, thinking, and problem solving. Students enter into the learning process through their preferred styles, but they do not always operate exclusively in a single learning style (Kochman 1981; Shade 1989). It is also possible for students to learn how to operate effectively in different learning styles—that is, how to "style shift." (p. 139)

With regard to constructing a comprehensive synthesis of theory and research on African American learning style, teacher educators need to review and include several classic references. Certainly, analytical vs. relational cognitive style profiles as described by Cohen (1969) and Hilliard (1976) should be included as should Hale-Benson's classic *Black Children: Their Roots, Culture, and Learning Styles* (1982, 1986). For almost two decades, Shade (1978, 1982, 1983, 1986, 1989a, 1994) has been the most prolific scholar on African American learning style. At least five chapters by Shade in *Culture, Style and the Educative Process* (1989a) synthesize and extend much of her previous scholarship on African American learning style. Certainly "Chapter 8: Afro-American Cognitive Patterns: A Review of the Research," which appears also in the second edition (Shade, 1997), provides an exceptional review of literature regarding such dimensions of African American learning style as the perception factors of sensory modality preference and cue selection (person-vs-object, interpersonal and affective, and extraversion-introversion); information retrieval and recognition patterns; and information analysis and evaluation patterns. The scholarship of Boykin (1979, 1982, 1983, 1986, 1994) and Boykin and associates (Boykin & Toms, 1985; Boykin & Allen, 1988) also constitutes an important part of the theory and research on African American learning style, particularly Boykin's concept of psychological/behavioral verve and his nine-point comparison of African and European cultures. Finally, the review of literature provided by Irvine (1990) constitutes a significant collection of references essential to constructing a comprehensive synthesis of theory and research on African American learning style.

Similarly, constructing a comprehensive synthesis of theory and research on Native American learning style for infusion into teacher education programs will require teacher educators to rely upon a variety of sources. Some of these sources (Burgess, 1978; Mohatt & Erickson, 1981; Pewewardy, 1994; and Swisher & Pavel, 1994) have already been mentioned. To these sources, Pepper and Henry (1989), Kaulback (1989) and More (1989)—all of which are in Shade's *Culture, Style, and the Educative Process* (1989a)—should be included. In addition, Reyner's *Teaching American Indian Students* (1992), an edited collection of scholarly essays, contains syntheses of theory and research literature indirectly and directly related to Native American learning style. For example, in Reyner's publication, Swisher and Doyle (1992) provide thorough reviews of Native American learning style concepts such as learning to learn, visual modality, field dependence/ independence, public/private talk, and cooperation/competition.

Teacher educators will need to synthesize the theory and research on Mexican American learning style variables from a variety of sources since no single publication exists that is appropriate to use as a textbook in teacher education courses. In addition to references already mentioned (Kagan & Madsen 1971, 1972; Ramirez & Castenada, 1974; and Diaz, 1989), other recommended references include Cortes (1978) and Shade (1989b) and Saracho (1989), two chapters in Shade's *Culture, Style, and the Educative Process* that synthesize much of the relevant theory and research. A resource to identify studies on learning style elements that are related to personality traits is *Chicano Psychology* by Martinez (1977). Studies on learning style attributes related to stages of Mexican American identity development have been reviewed in the chapter on Knowledge Base 2 (see Bernal and Knight, 1993). Given that bilingualism constitutes a significant element of the learning styles of many Hispanic American students, other relevant literature is reviewed in the section of this book on Knowledge Base 4.

In that preservice and inservice teachers must know and understand cultural belief systems, values, and worldviews of various cultural groups to understand and apply cultural learning styles to their instructional practices, these are also key components of the Knowledge Base for Cultural Learning Styles. Cultural belief systems, values, and worldviews of diverse cultural groups are also

important subcomponents of "teacher knowledge" in several other knowledge bases, particularly Knowledge Bases 2, 4, 5, 6, and 11. Recommended sources for compiling comprehensive profiles of belief systems, values, and worldviews of African American, Asian American, Hispanic American, and Native American cultures are emphasized in Knowledge Base 5 and found throughout various bodies of literature recommended elsewhere in this book.

There are actually two distinctly separate bodies of theory and research on learning styles. One body of literature consists of those previously mentioned works that center on *cultural* learning styles. The second body of literature can be described as *culture-free* or *culture-blind* and *race-blind*. This second body of theory and research centers on learning styles, thinking styles, and cognitive styles outside the context of culture. Although slight and general references to *culture* sometimes are made, this literature almost never uses the such terminology as *African American learning style, Mexican American learning style*, and *Native American learning style*. Much of the theory and research on culture-free models of learning styles has been synthesized by Reiff (1992). Perhaps one of the most important resources in this category is *Learning and Thinking Styles: Classroom Interaction* by Presseisen, Sternberg, Fischer & Knight, and Feuerstein (1990). Of these authors only Feuerstein, the Israeli psychologist who discusses his theory of structural cognitive modifiability, places significant emphasis on ethnicity and culture. In addition, the environmental, emotional, sociological, physical, and psychological elements of cognitive, affective, and physiological styles identified by R. Dunn & K. Dunn (1978) and R. Dunn (1983) and the literature synthesis on learning styles by Dunn, Beaudry & Klavas (1989) constitute part of this category of literature. The energic model developed by Gregorc (1979, 1982) and described by Gregorc and Butler (1984) also belongs in this second body of literature. Based on the theory of multiple intelligences developed by Gardener (1983), Lazear (1991a, 1991b) has developed models designed to teach for and with multiple intelligences. Although Lazear does not use the term "learning style," his "seven-ways-of-knowing" and "seven-ways-of-teaching" models bear a relationship to the culture-free literature.

CHAPTER 5

Knowledge Base 4: *Language, Communication, and Interactional Styles of Marginalized Cultures*

In the difference of language to-day lies two-thirds of our trouble... schools should be established, which [Indian] children should be required to attend; their barbarous dialects should be blotted out and the English language substituted...

— The "Peace Commission," 1868

On the one hand, from the standpoint of what language minority students need to have the best possible education, it could be argued ideally that the knowledge bases recommended by authorities in bilingual and ESL education are the same knowledge bases regular elementary, middle, and secondary school teachers should study. According to Garcia (1990), the content for linguistic minority teachers' training programs has been identified in three well-known descriptions—the list of 34 intercultural competencies developed by Chu and Levy (1988), the bilingual/multicultural standards published by the National Association of State Directors of Teacher Education and Certification (1984), and the content domains implied in the list of sample courses developed by Collier (1985). Only the latter two explicitly require proficiency in English and a second language. Although described as sample courses characteristic of a contemporary training program for linguistic minority teachers, Collier (1985) provides the following list of recommended knowledge bases:

- First and second language acquisition and bilingualism

- Teaching native language arts

- Methods of teaching a second language (e.g., ESL, SSL, VSL)

- Methods of teaching content areas, both bilingually and through the second language

- Multicultural education including teaching the culturally and linguistically different exceptional child

- Program models, policy, school-community relations, and administrative issues in bilingual education and ESL

- The phonology, morphology, and syntax of English

- The phonology, morphology, and syntax of another language, in addition to English (for bilingual teachers)

- Assessment in bilingual/ESL settings

- Curriculum development in bilingual settings/ESL settings

- Reading and research in foundations of education (anthropology, sociology, history, philosophy, and social psychology related to the education of minority language students)

- Use of instructional technology for teaching first and second languages and content areas

From *University Models for ESL and Bilingual Teacher Training* (p. 86) by J.P. Collier, 1985, Rosslyn, VA: National Clearinghouse for Bilingual Education. Copyright © 1985 by National Clearinghouse for Bilingual Education. (Adapted from Garcia, 1990, p. 727)

On the other hand, given the reality that few colleges of education have satisfactorily mounted excellent Bilingual/ESL teacher-training programs (Garcia, 1990) and the highly charged conservative political climate spurred by xenophobic and mean-spirited initiatives such as the English Only movement, it is unlikely that regular teachers can be required to study the full range of content and skill knowledge bases recommended for Bilingual and ESL certification. Thus, what is recommended here for regular teachers as Knowledge Base 4 on Language and Communication and Interactional Styles of Marginalized Cultures is a compact knowledge base that will surely fall short of the expectations of experts in Bilingual and ESL education but constitutes far more training than regular teachers have received in the past.

This necessary knowledge base in a culturally responsible and responsive teacher education program consists minimally of (a) the theory and research on language acquisition, particularly of native speakers of languages and dialects other than English, (b) cultural communication and interaction styles (verbal and nonverbal), and (c) principles and strategies of teaching English as a second language to speakers of culturally unique English dialects and speakers of first languages other than English. As envisioned here, Knowledge Base 4 could be delivered with a measure of integrity in two, three-credit hour courses or minimally in one three-credit hour course. After all, it is long past the time when schools, colleges, and departments of education and state departments of education should have required all regular and special education teachers to take at

least an introductory course in teaching linguistically diverse students.

The rationale for including Knowledge Base 4 in regular teacher education programs is obvious. It seems ridiculous that colleges of education should send neophyte, monolingual teachers, who are also too frequently monocultural, into inner-city classrooms of African American students and Hispanic students without a serious study of Black English as a sociolinguistic system and some serious preparation similar to but less extensive than that received by recipients of bilingual certification. The specific purposes of including this knowledge base on language acquisition, communication, and interaction styles should be (a) to make preservice and inservice teachers aware of the vast language and linguistic diversity in the United States and to rid them of their biases toward language minority students and dialect speakers, (b) to provide them with practice in applying principles and strategies for teaching content and English language arts skills to students of limited English proficiency, and (c) when possible, to provide them with the instructional expertise to enable students to be bilingual.

Identifying a precise knowledge base for all schools, colleges, and departments of education is not easy due to the unique and diverse language populations served by institutions in various geographical regions of the United States. In addition to a diverse range of English dialects, Development Associates (1984) estimates that among speakers of languages other than English in grades K-6, about 76 percent are from Spanish language backgrounds, 8 percent from Southeast Asian language backgrounds, 5 percent Far East Asian language backgrounds, 5 percent from European language backgrounds, and 5 percent from other language backgrounds that include Native American languages. As Reyner (1988) has recommended, institutions that are preparing teachers for tribal schools and other schools, both urban and reservation, with Native American student populations should emphasize developing teacher expertise in native languages and communication styles. In schools, colleges, and departments of education preparing teachers most likely to teach African American students, heavy emphasis must be placed upon a formal study of Black English as a sociolinguistic system, African American communication style and interaction patterns, and expertise in teaching students who speak Black English. Schools, colleges, and departmemts of education preparing teachers most likely to teach Spanish-speaking children must emphasize a linguistic knowledge base that includes Spanish, Chicano English or perhaps other varieties of mixed language systems. Faculty members in schools, colleges, and departments of education serving geographical regions with much greater language diversity will have to make other value decisions regarding the inclusion of a language-specific knowledge base.

Locating and Synthesizing the Knowledge Base on Language, Communication and Interactional Styles of Marginalized Cultures

With regard to the knowledge base for training language minority education teachers, Garcia (1990) notes that a "serious body of literature addressing instructional practices, organization, and their effects is emerging" (p. 728). Teacher educators who are just beginning to assemble bodies of theory and research literature for Knowledge Base 4 will find treatises by Fillmore and Valadez (1986) and Garcia (1990) excellent general references that are useful in identifying the parameters of this enormous area of scholarship. Another category of literature that is a significant part of Knowledge Base 4 consists of the numerous edited publications that synthesize research studies in the area of bilingual education and second language acquisition. Publications illustrative of this extensive genre of literature include Trueba, Guthrie, and Au (1981), Homel, Palij, and Aaronson (1987), and the series of research handbooks edited by Ambert (1988, 1991). Another important category of

> *Few publications include in-depth theory and research on multiple minority language groups.*

literature that constitutes part of the content of Knowledge Base 4 focuses upon single language-minority groups and aspects of their unique linguistic cultures. Finding a single source suitable as a textbook that provides comprehensive coverage of the undergirding theory and research for most language-minority student groups is difficult. Scholarship in the field has been largely group-specific rather than inclusive until recently. That is, published works have tended to center on African American English speakers; Hispanic speakers who are bilingual, speakers of Spanish only, or speakers of Hispanic English or Chicano English; or Appalachian/Mountain speakers of nonstandard English dialects, etc. Few publications include in-depth theory and research on multiple minority language groups.

However, one publication suitable for teacher education programs that is illustrative of multiple-group coverage is *Multicultural Communication Skills in the Classroom* by Adler (1993). This publication provides coverage of significant aspects of Knowledge Base 4 such as bidialectism, bilingualism, socioliguistic characteristics of several nonstandard English systems, and the assessment of nonstandard language. More depth is provided on phonological, syntactical, and lexical characteristics of Black English and Appalachian Mountain English than for Asian and Hispanic speakers of English as a second language. To provide a comprehensive knowledge base of theory and research for multiple groups, teacher educators typically must use multiple texts or develop supplementary collections of readings.

Black English. What should preservice and inservice teachers know about Black English (also referred to as African American English, Black dialect, and Ebonics in the literature)? Minimally, teachers should know (a) some historical information on lexical, phonological, morphological, and syntactical retentions from African languages, (b) the major phonological, morphological and syntactic retention characteristics of Black English as a sociolinguistic system, particularly the 15 to 20 major points of interference with standard English, (c) the stylistic verbal ruses such as *playing the dozens, woofin', coppin' a plea, signifying, sounding,* etc., and (d) stylistic nonverbal dimensions of communication, particularly body language.

An excellent synthesis of the literature on Black English as a sociolinguistic system with its own unique lexicology and its own rules regarding phonology, morphology, and syntax has been provided by Evelyn Baker Dandy in *Black Communications: Breaking Down the Barriers* (1991), a book that is frequently used as a text in teacher education programs. Dandy also provides a good coverage of stylistic aspects of verbal and non-verbal communication such as *rappin', woofin',* and *playin' the dozens.* Teacher educators who wish to build their own in-depth synthesis of theory and research that exceeds that provided in *Black Communications* will find an enormous body of literature on African American verbal and nonverbal communication styles that reaches back to the classic works of Lorenzo Dow Turner (1949) and proceeds to the more recent scholarship of Baratz and Shuy (1969), Stewart (1969), Labov (1970, 1972), Dillard (1972, 1977), Baratz and Baratz (1972), Burling (1973), Baron (1975), Williamson (1975), Smitherman (1977, 1985), Foster (1979), Kochman (1981), Schofield (1982), and Hanna (1988).

Teacher educators who are seeking special resources to use in teacher education courses should examine *Super Literacy* by Hoover (1996), a multi-faceted curriculum and recommended set of methodologies for teaching reading, writing, and speaking to African American and other students whose first language or dialect is not standard English. An excellent primer for teacher educators to use to introduce the study of Black English to preservice and inservice teachers is a special issue of *Rethinking Schools* edited by Perry and Delpit (1997), *The Real Ebonics Debate: Power, Language, and the Education of African American Children.*

An important aspect of the knowledge base on African American English is, of course, the early research on linguistic retentions from African beginnings in contemporary African American English. It is this knowledge that preservice and inservice teachers do not have that seems necessary to change their perceptions from believing that African American English is simply an "ignorant perversion of standard English" to the more respectful belief that African American English is "a full rich sociolinguistic communication system with consistent rules of phonology, morphology and syntax." A brief but good synthesis of this historical literature on lexical, phonological, morphological, and syntactical retentions from African languages has been published by Asante (1990). Other relevant categories of literature include such classic ethnographies as *Them Children* by Ward (1971), *Ways with Words* by Heath (1983), and *He-Said-She-Said* by Goodwin (1990) and the emerging literature on how teachers can use African American language forms pedagogically. *Signifying as a Scaffold for Literary Interpretation: The Pedagogical Implications of an African American Discourse Genre* by Lee (1993), for example, presents a pedagogical approach that brings forms of signifying into the classroom as "prior knowledge" to enhance students' interpretation of African American literature.

Hispanic American Bilingualism. The knowledge base of theory and research on linguistic diversity among Hispanic Americans far exceeds the brief description that can be provided in this chapter. Adler (1993) describes the complexity of this part of Knowledge Base 4:

> There has been a fair amount of research on the varieties of English and Spanish spoken by Hispanic Americans in the United States (Duran, Emight, and Rock 1985). For example, two nonstandard forms of English are spoken by Southwest Hispanic Americans: Pachuco or Calo and Chicano English. In addition to these latter forms of English some Hispanic Americans speak African-American English, as well as a fourth variety of English, namely standard American English. Outside the Southwest, there are spoken varieties of Spanish, such as Puerto Rican Spanish, Cuban Spanish, Isleno, and Ladino (Judeo-Spanish). Specific regional Hispanic dialects also exist, such as Nuyorican English, spoken by some Puerto Ricans in New York. (p. 39).

Despite the complexity of this knowledge base, teacher educators who are preparing regular preservice and inservice teachers rather than bilingual specialists to teach in classrooms with Spanish-speaking students will find previously mentioned edited volumes and research handbooks in bilingual education to be useful sources. In addition, most textbooks written for such courses as "Methods of Teaching English as a Second Language", "Introduction to Bilingual Education," or "Teaching the Linguistically Diverse Student" devote considerable emphasis to theory and research on teaching Spanish-language speaking students.

Native American and Low-Incidence Minority Languages. Much of the literature regarding Native American bilingualism and the recent revival of teaching Native American languages to school children has been synthesized in Reyner's *Teaching American Indian Students* (1992), an edited volume that is suitable for use as a textbook in teacher education programs. The chapter by Leap (1992) identifies significant starter references on American Indian English including collections edited by Leap (1977), Bartlett, Jasper, and Hoffer (1982), and St. Clair and Leap (1982). In addition, Reyner's book includes excellent bibliographies and resource lists almost never found in traditional teacher education textbooks that will enable teacher educators to begin constructing their own organizations of theory and research on Native American linguistic factors. Teacher educators seeking ready-made syntheses of theory and research regarding low incidence language groups will most likely have to conduct their own searches or depend upon such publications by the California Department of Education as *Handbook for Teaching Pilipino-Speaking Students* (1986), *Handbook for Teaching Japanese-Speaking Students* (1987), *A Handbook for Teaching Cantonese-Speaking Students* (1989), *A Handbook for Teaching Portuguese-Speaking Students* (1989), *Handbook for Teaching Korean-American Students* (1992), and others. Teacher educators who have a special need for information on Haitian and Jamaican Creoles will find the work of Bobo and Thompson (1990) invaluable.

CHAPTER 6
Knowledge Base 5: *Essential Elements of Cultures*

The question is not necessarily how to create the perfect "culturally matched" learning situation for each ethnic group, but rather how to recognize when there is a problem for a particular child and how to seek its cause in the most broadly conceived fashion. Knowledge about culture is but one tool that educators may make use of when devising solutions for a school=s difficulty in educating diverse children.

— Lisa Delpit, *Other People's Children.*

The purpose for educators' learning the cultures of their students is to understand the *individual child*. After all, a child of any cultural group is an individual with his or her own unique talents, skills, and abilities. Delpit (1995) is correct to say that culture is only one tool for understanding a child; but is an important one, too important to omit from a teacher's education. If preservice and inservice teachers are to provide high-quality and effective education, they must know the cultures of their students. It has been argued by some authorities that it is impossible, if not absurd, for teachers to know well all the cultures of their students, particularly in a multicultural society that has welcomed to its shores people from approximately 150 nation states in the world, each of which, like the United States, frequently is a nation state consisting of many subcultures. It is difficult to argue against the impossibility of preservice teachers learning much about many cultures in two-year or four-year teacher education programs by the time they enter the classroom or even in a lifetime, for that matter; but it must be argued that teachers ought to know what the essential elements of *any* culture are and, therefore, have a schema for learning about the cultures represented by students in their classrooms.

It is also true that preservice teachers can know far more about several major cultural groups in their local area than universities and teacher education

curricula have heretofore emphasized. If it seems absurd to expect teachers to know something about all cultures, it seems equally absurd that most teachers who graduate from traditional teacher education programs know almost nothing about African American, Asian American, Hispanic American, Native American, and other cultures that have historically made major contributions to the national culture. The truth is that most teacher education graduates receive their training and teach in communities and schools that are often predominantly bicultural, tricultural, or are restricted to an identifiable number of major cultural groups. After all, segregated schooling remains the norm for most children of color, particularly those of low socioeconomic backgrounds. Individual school populations that truly reflect the national diversity are rare, and schools in which the students are first speakers of 30 or more languages and reflect multiple national, ethnic, and cultural origins are found frequently in perhaps only four states. In most instances, teacher education programs can tailor programs to emphasize two to five specific cultural, national, and ethnic groups with high regional or local visibility. In this modern era, schools, colleges, and departments of education must simply move beyond the stage of producing monocultural teachers who have little academic and experiential knowledge about other cultures.

Essential Elements of Cultures as a knowledge base consists of at least two subcomponents. The first is a schema for learning about any culture. That is, preservice and inservice teachers ought to know the following as characteristics of any culture:

- Patterns of knowledge and ways of knowing

- Patterns and relevance of values, belief systems, worldviews, customs, traditions, mores, and spirituality

- An ancient through modern history including a culture's people (heroines and heroes), artifacts, and contributions (art, literature, music, dance, science, technology, mathematics, philosophy, architecture, government, etc.)

- Unique ways different voices of a culture express relationships to other cultures and particularly the dominant culture

- Patterns of culturally unique skills and behaviors

- Patterns of perception and cognition (cognitive styles)

- Language and communication styles including verbal and nonverbal nuances.

The second component of this knowledge base centers upon a study of each of the above essential elements of culture in the context of specific local or regional cultures, i.e., African American, Mexican American, Navajo, Korean American, Iranian American, and other groups depending upon the geographical location of the school, college, or department of education. Teacher education students rightly ought to be able to take a variety of courses in the arts and sciences and various departments outside the college of education that center upon the first four essential elements of culture listed above. In universities that have rich offerings of multicultural courses across the university curriculum, it is the responsibility of the college of education to require such coursework in the general education, elective, and major and minor content areas of study in the teacher education students' degree programs. Realistically, however, as Hood and Parker (1994) found in their study of diversity at a comprehensive Northeastern university and a Midwestern research institution, most teacher education students continue to be exposed to a European and Anglo-centered university curriculum rather than one that explores minority and ethnic perspectives. Teacher education programs located at institutions where ethnic studies courses are limited or near to non-existent must provide exposure to the first four essential elements in the teacher education curriculum. To be specific, if the English department does not provide a course in African American literature or multicultural children's literature, the instructors of the English/language arts methods courses will have to introduce secondary English education students and elementary education students to such valuable teaching resources as Magill's *Masterpieces of African American Literature* (1992) and Ramirez and Ramirez's *Multicultural Children's Literature* (1994).

The remaining three essential elements of culture—patterns of unique skills and behavior, patterns of perception and cognition, and language and communication styles—seem to be content areas best suited to coverage by infusion into teacher education courses, particularly the psychological and cultural foundations courses, rather than courses in other departments of the university. In fact, *patterns of perception and cognition* and *language and communication styles* are two areas of study of such expansive theory and research that they merit treatment as two separate knowledge bases discussed elsewhere in this book.

> *...most teacher education students continue to be exposed to a European and Anglo-centered university curriculum rather than one that explores minority and ethnic perspectives.*

Identifying and Synthesizing the Content for the Knowledge Base on Essential Elements of Cultures

One purpose of teacher candidates' studying each of the above seven elements of culture in the context of specific local and regional cultures is, of course, to enable them to strive for accuracy and authenticity when teaching *about* cultural groups. Without accurate and authentic information and perspective, teachers can neither teach respectfully about other cultures nor use cultural knowledge pedagogically. Thus, it is important that a teacher education knowledge base on any culture be accurate, fair, respectful, and sensitive to describing the rightful place of a cultural group in historical and contemporary times. To develop a teacher education knowledge base with these characteristics about, say African American culture, Mexican American culture, Native American culture, or any other culture is neither an uncomplicated nor straight forward task. Such a task is, in fact, fraught with potential pitfalls. Although space limitations do not permit full examination of the issues involved in trying to identify, synthesize, and teach the respective content for the seven elements of culture, some questions must be addressed: How does a teacher educator, or a teacher for that matter, certify what is "accurate" and "authentic" knowledge about a culture? How does a non-member of a culture identify the fine line of difference between a generalization and a stereotype when teaching about another culture's values, belief systems, worldviews, etc.? These are legitimate questions with difficult, complex answers.

On the one hand, it would be easy to argue that teacher educators cannot step outside their own cultural ethnocentrism sufficiently to address respectfully the worldviews and beliefs of other cultures. It can be argued that European American teacher educators are on shaky ground expounding on predominant values of Chinese Americans or that Mexican American teacher educators may not feel in their "souls and bones" the predominant values of Japanese American culture well enough to convey their meaning accurately and authentically—that, in fact, shallow knowledge will perpetuate stereotyping. Furthermore, these arguments may be partially responsible for the existence of so

many generic, culture-free teacher education programs in the United States. Perhaps teacher educators have doubted their own cross-cultural competencies so much that they have believed it best to leave the values of other cultures alone.

On the other hand, this treatise argues that if the cycle of provincial monocultural teachers' teaching multicultural student populations is ever to be broken, teacher educators must take bold steps forward to bring conversations about cultural values and belief systems to the teacher education classroom. To argue that a teacher educator of one culture cannot teach respectfully about the belief systems of another culture is similar to arguing that an instructor of one religious faith cannot teach a comparative religion course. Of course, there is always the danger of misrepresentation, but this danger pales in the light of the magnitude of the disaster of continuing to send teachers into classrooms who are unprepared to understand individual students from cultures different from their own.

Patterns and Relevance of Values, Belief Systems, Worldviews, Customs, Traditions, Mores, and Spirituality

How then, can teacher educators synthesize a knowledge base on diverse cultural belief systems that is risk-free? They cannot—at least not at this point in time. They can, however, do far better than is presently being done in teacher education programs by validating the accuracy and authenticity of the content about belief systems through research studies and the narrative voices of members of diverse cultural groups. What is meant by the latter is that teacher educators must have teacher candidates read and study profiles of belief systems as described by minority scholars about their own cultures. This is not to suggest that there is necessarily in-group agreement about what constitutes a particular culture's belief system. On the contrary, there is often a wide range of differing points of view within a cultural group regarding its values and beliefs. The point is that the body of literature that represents the within-group diversity, as well as commonly agreed upon generalizations about belief systems, is glaringly absent from most teacher education programs and must be brought into the mainstream literature. A well-constructed knowledge base of any sort and particularly one about cultural belief systems should be deliberately constructed with planned inclusion of works by minority scholars who are representative of the cultures that constitute U.S. society.

Where can teacher educators find information about cultural belief systems and values? Unfortunately, no single-volume source exists that contains cultural belief system/value system profiles for all or a majority of ethnic groups. Teacher educators must construct this knowledge base from a variety of sources until such a comprehensive reference work is published. What is clear is that the sources are numerous. Generally speaking, since cultural belief systems/values influence identity development, cultural learning styles, and communication styles, many of the works cited in chapters of this book on Knowledge Bases 2, 3, and 4 are also sources from which information about cultural belief systems can be extracted to construct profiles.

The field of multicultural counseling is an additional excellent source for finding theory and research on cultural worldviews. Much of the research to support specific dimensions of worldviews has already been synthesized by a number of scholars for textbooks in the field of multicultural counseling. A case in point is *Counseling the Culturally Different: Theory and Practice* by Sue, et al. (1981). Sue (1981) defines the worldviews of minorities in relationship to that of the dominant culture:

> It has become increasingly clear that many minority persons hold worldviews different from members of the dominant culture. A worldview may be broadly defined as how a person perceives his/her relationship to the world (nature, institutions, other people, things, etc.). Worldviews are highly correlated to a person's cultural upbringing and life experiences (D.W. Sue, 1975; Jackson, 1975). Not only are worldviews composed of our attitudes, values, opinions, and concepts, but also they may affect how we think, make decisions, behave, and define events. For minorities in America, a strong determinant of

worldviews is very much related to racism and the subordinate position assigned to them in society. ...[I]t must be kept in mind that economic and social class, religion, and sex are also interactional components of a worldview. (p. 73)

Included in Sue's book are a chapter on dimensions of world-views and separate chapters that present research-based world view profiles for Asian Americans, African Americans, Hispanic Americans, and Native Americans. Another work that presents discussion of worldviews is *Multicultural Counseling in Schools: A Practical Handbook* edited by Pederson and Carey (1994). For example, a chapter, "Worldviews: Culturally Learned Assumptions and Values," by Sodowsky and Johnson (1994) in Pederson and Carey's edited volume provides an insightful discussion and literature review regarding the systematic study of worldviews as described in the classic model developed by Kluckhohn (1968) and the revision of Kluckhohn's model by Kohls (1984a).

Although many multicultural counseling textbooks exist, other illustrative works in this genre of literature include *Children of Color: Psychological Interventions with Minority Youth* edited by Gibbs, Huang, and associates (1989) and *Minority Children and Adolescents in Therapy* edited by Man Keung Ho (1992). These works do not present world views and value systems in charts, but both present cultural vignettes that highlight dimensions of worldviews for Asian American cultures, Native American cultures, Hispanic American cultures, and African American culture.

One source of tables of distinct cultural values for several U.S. minority groups, often presented in comparison to values of European Americans, is *Critical Issues in Gifted Education* edited by Maker and Schiever (1989). The contributors to this book take on the daunting task of identifying the manifestations of giftedness in Hispanic cultures (primarily Mexican American), Native American cultures, Asian American cultures, and Black cultures. This volume presents a table for each cultural group that displays absolute aspects of giftedness, cultural values, and behavioral differences. In addition, for several of the cultural groups tables have been constructed which contrast ethnic group values/

perceptions to European American or Anglo values/perceptions. Narratives in each chapter examine within-group diversity and gender and socioeconomic variables in the context of within-group diversity. Although cultural values presented in the tables are not clearly shown as research-based, chapter narratives, more often than not, present empirical evidence to support some of the culture-specific values.

Finally, some often cited and important profiles of worldviews and values found in the literature merit mention. A well-known paradigm for analyzing cultural value orientations is the one developed by Kluckhohn and Strodtbeck (1961). A well-known chart that lists U.S. values compared to the values of some other countries has been developed by Kohls (1984b). Two of the most frequently cited syntheses of theory and research literature that have been capsulized in chart form to compare African American and European American belief systems are those by Boykin (1986) and Hilliard (1976). Hillard's chart is reproduced in *Black Children: Their Roots, Culture and Learning Styles* by Hale-Benson (1986). Two of the most comprehensive listings of elements of Native American worldview have been developed by Burgess (1978) and Richardson (1981).

Ancient through Modern History Including a Culture's People, Artifacts, and Contributions.
The discussion of this element of Knowledge Base 5 merits several cautionary points. First, it is not possible within the space limitations of this chapter to define fully the parameters of this element and its undergirding literature of theory and research. Second, if space permitted, full treatment of this element would carefully outline the content knowledge needed by *all* preservice teachers and for each teacher certification degree program, i.e., art education, English education, math education, music education, science education, social studies and history education, elementary education, etc. However, such an extensive treatment is the subject of a separate book. Instead, what follows is a clarified definition of cultural content as it is conceptualized here, its purposes, and some illustrative clarifying examples in the context of selected types of teacher education programs (art education, English education. etc.).

What is meant by "an ancient through modern history including a culture's people, artifacts, and contributions" requires some clarification as it is referred to here. This element of Knowledge Base 5 refers to survey-level knowledge about the history and contributions of cultural, ethnic and other groups who have historically been omitted from the formal education of teachers. This element of the knowledge base also refers more to the academic knowledge about cultural groups' histories and contributions than to knowledge about contemporary community, "home," or street culture. It is somewhat equivalent to the Eurocentric content found in such courses as "Western Civilization I and II," "History of Art," "Music Appreciation," "British Literature I and II," and "World Literature" except that its focus is upon African American, Hispanic American, Asian American, Native American, and other cultural groups typically excluded by the Eurocentric canon of Western traditions. Although the line of demarcation between "home" knowledge about culture and "school" or "academic" knowledge about a culture is not always necessarily clear nor absolute, the distinction between these two types of cultural knowledge is understood generally well enough throughout the U.S. society to be useful in crafting a definition of this element of the knowledge base. Thus, the cultural content being discussed in this section consists not of "home" culture but of formal academic knowledge somewhat canonized by primarily but not exclusively minority scholars in the humanities, fine arts, social sciences, and other academic disciplines and often taught in such courses as "Survey of African American Literature," "Introduction to Native American Art," "Introduction to Multicultural Art in U.S. Society," "The History of Africans in the United States," "Ethnic Music in the United States," or "Women, Power, and Politics." The focus of this academic knowledge base is on understanding the contributions and artifacts of a culture with the term *artifacts* simply referring to the products of the creative spirit (literature, art, music, spiritual systems, architecture, technology, etc.).

Finally, the definition of this element of Knowledge Base 5 is not complete without a clarification of the phrase "ancient and modern history of a culture." It is unrealistic to expect preservice teachers to acquire scholarly depth in, for example, the ancient historical roots of African Americans but it is realistic that preservice teachers should have surface knowledge about ancient African cultures and civilizations equivalent to their surface level of knowledge about ancient Western cultures and civilizations. That is, preservice teachers ought to know that the roots of African American heritage trace back to African presence in "the earliest centers of civilization [that] included Kush (modern Ethiopia) in East Africa; the Zimbabwe, Bantu, and Kongo Kingdoms in South and Southeast Africa; smaller independent kingdoms in the coastal rainforest area, such as Old Yoruba, Ife, Benin, Nok, Dahomey, and Asanti; and the great kingdoms of Ghana, Mali, and Songhay in West Africa" (Gay, 1995, p. 37). It goes without saying that similar survey-level knowledge about the ancient history of other historically excluded cultural groups in the United States should be a routine part of the education of preservice teachers. The term *modern history* as used here, of course, actually refers to the contributions of previously excluded peoples and their viewpoints during the chronological period that is found in most U.S. history textbooks, typically that period of time that the traditional Western view describes as beginning with the European age of exploration and early colonization in the Americas to the present. Again, the point being made here is that whereas in-depth expertise in U.S. history may be unrealistic, preservice teachers ought to have as much knowl-

> *...the typical graduates of today's teacher education programs know little about the history or contributions of African Americans, Native Americans, Hispanic Americans, Asian Americans, other historically disenfranchised minority groups, and women...*

edge about the influence and stories of non-Europeans and women as they do about persons of male European heritage.

The purpose for including this specific element of Knowledge Base 5 ought to be self-evident, but apparently is not since it has been and still is excluded too often from the education received by most preservice teachers. Regrettably, the typical graduates of today's teacher education programs know little about the history or contributions of African Americans, Native Americans, Hispanic Americans, Asian Americans, other historically disenfranchised minority groups, and women, particularly to the fields of art, dance, drama, literature, music, mathematics, science, medicine, technology, philosophy, government, and other spheres of endeavor that are reflective of humankind's creative spirit. Although teacher educators do not need empirical evidence to document the cultural illiteracy of most preservice teachers, such evidence exists. For example, using four instruments including the Ethnic History and Culture Awareness Survey on a sample of student teachers at Ohio State University, Wayson (1988) found that "at least 60 percent...did not feel sure of their knowledge about how various cultures contribute to American society and 75 percent weren't confident about their knowledge of the history of minority groups in America" (p. 11). Similarly, Boyer (1994) has noted that teachers and teacher educators alike have difficulty with a simple five-question test that asks them to name two black playwrights, two Mexican American historians, two Native American writers or poets, two Puerto Rican actors or actresses, and two female inventors or scientists. Thus, to break the cycle of one generation of monoculturally trained teachers from simply repeating and transmitting to the next generation an Eurocentric curriculum, teacher education programs must first remediate the present generation of preservice teachers' lack of cultural literacy in the academic subjects. After all, teachers cannot develop and teach multicultural curricula if they themselves are culturally illiterate in the academic subjects by virtue of having experienced only Eurocentric curriculum content in their own public school and university courses.

How can schools, colleges, and departments of education provide exposure to and, in some cases, in-depth knowledge about the history and contributions of African American, Native American, Hispanic American, other historically excluded groups, and women? Because of the unique and varying programmatic structures of teacher education programs in the United States, the college or university unit responsible for the education of teachers appears to have the following two options or some combination of these options.

First, they can partially remediate cultural illiteracy among this generation of teachers by requiring undergraduates to take courses in the general education program, elective offerings, or the major and minor subject-area concentrations. Some institutions have already developed courses which provide multicultural content through infusion in selected regular university and college courses. Other institutions have well developed African American Studies, Hispanic American Studies, Native American Studies, and Women's Studies programs that provide lower- and upper-level undergraduate courses in such traditional knowledge domains as literature, music, art, and history. However, many institutions, particularly small regional state and liberal arts institutions, do not have well-developed ethnic studies departments. At these institutions, teacher education faculty members must request from and negotiate with their faculty colleagues in the other academic disciplines to develop curriculum content more reflective of inclusive knowledge bases than found typically in the traditional classical Eurocentric courses.

At institutions where elementary and secondary teachers are required to complete an academic major, minor, or both, careful consideration must be given to the selection of existing or the creation of new courses that adequately educate teachers about the histories and contributions of historically excluded groups to U.S. society. For example, the following questions about the multicultural content of an art education program are illustrative of the type of questions interdisciplinary faculty curriculum committees must address regarding other teacher education programs such as English education, history education, and so on:

- In what courses and at what level will preservice elementary and secondary and special education teachers encounter broad survey exposure to and in-depth study of the traditions of African American art and the present African American canon's selection of great artists?

- In what courses will undergraduate students majoring in art education be introduced to in-depth content on African American art? In what course or courses will art education majors be introduced to classic reference works such as *A History of African-American Artists from 1792 to Present* by Beardon and Henderson (1993), *The Art of Black American Women: Works of Twenty-four Artists of the Twentieth Century* by Henkes (1993), and *African American Art and Artists* by Lewis (1990)?

- In what courses will art educators be introduced to curriculum guides and to teaching materials and books written or prepared for the elementary and secondary levels to enable school pupils to learn about African American artists and African American art traditions?

- In what courses will art education majors be introduced to major resources for remaining contemporary in knowledge about African American art after graduation such as *The International Review of African American Art* and *American Visions: The Magazine of African American Culture*.[1]

Similar questions must be asked regarding Latino, Native American, Asian American and other cultures' art traditions.

The second option for remediating the present generation's absence of content knowledge about the history and contributions to U.S. society of diverse cultures is to provide more of the content knowledge bases in the general and special methods courses. Ideally, the multicultural content knowledge bases ought to be provided through art appreciation and art history courses, literature, dance, history, and other general education and academic major courses taught in the academic departments across the university; whereas the multicultural knowledge bases regarding teaching materials, curriculum guides, and elementary and secondary level school materials and resources should be introduced through such special methods courses as "Teaching Language Arts," "Methods of Teaching Secondary English," "Methods of Teaching Art," "Methods of Teaching Science," "Methods of Teaching Mathematics," etc. When this ideal arrangement is not possible, instructors of special methods courses must bear a greater responsibility than normal for introducing preservice teachers to multicultural content in the subject areas. Realistically, however, most institutions that are doing an adequate job of providing preservice teachers with the cultural content knowledge bases are doing so through some combination of courses from both the academic disciplines and the schools, colleges, and departments of education.

In institutional settings where the Eurocentric educations of teacher candidates must be remediated with little assistance from other academic departments, teacher education courses must provide the content knowledge about the histories and contributions of various ethnic groups. To do so is difficult, given the limited number of credit hours in many teacher education programs. Even more problematic is the limited depth of content knowledge about the histories and contribution of ethnic groups that can be provided. Despite these difficulties, however, teacher education programs must do the best they can. Such efforts are likely to fall short of the depth needed but be far better than no coverage at all. Thus, the recommendation being made here is that teacher candidates should be required somewhere in the teacher education program to read and study ethnic group vignettes which emphasize histories and contributions. To follow through on this recommendation, teacher educators will find a number of resources that provide already compiled vignettes that will at least provide surface literacy regarding many ethnic and cultural groups in the United States. Among the best publications suitable to use as textbooks are *Educating for Diversity: An Anthology of Multicultural Voices* edited by Grant (1995) and *Teaching Strategies for Ethnic Studies* by Banks (1997). The former provides historical vignettes for African Americans, Central Americans, Mexican Americans, Chinese Americans, Cuban Americans,

Hawaiian Islanders, Japanese Americans, Jewish Americans, Korean Americans, Middle Eastern Americans, Iranian Americans, Arab Americans, and American Indians. Banks' publication also provides vignettes for similar ethnic groups. Teacher educators who wish to compile their own ethnic vignettes on the above and other ethnic groups will find the *Harvard Encyclopedia of American Ethnic Groups* edited by Thernstrom (1980) a somewhat dated but valuable resource.

Specific knowledge about the contributions of ethnic groups and significant ethnic individuals to specific fields seems to be presented most appropriately in special methods courses. To be specific, instructors of "Methods of Teaching Music" must present and emphasize significant contributions from African American, Asian American, Native American, Hispanic American, and other distinct cultural heritages. Teacher candidates' background research for curriculum plans, unit plans, and lesson plans must emphasize diverse ethnic groups' and individuals' contributions to the subject field of music. Such assignments should lead teacher candidates to use such resources as *Teaching Music with a Multicultural Approach*, a set of four videos and a book published by the Music Educators National Conference (1991) that explains the history and philosophy of the music of African Americans, Hispanic Americans, Asian Americans, and Native Americans. Likewise, the instructors of methods courses for teaching science, mathematics, social studies, language arts, and literature, etc., must craft inquiry assignments to extend teacher candidates' knowledge of minority/ethnic groups' and individuals' contributions to these fields. Thus, through coursework teacher education students in science and mathematics methods courses will be introduced to such resources as *Blacks in Science: Ancient and Modern* by Van Sertima (1989), *A Salute to Black Scientists and Inventors* (1985), and *Multicultural Mathematics: Teaching Mathematics from a Global Perspective* by Nelson, Joseph, and Williams (1993). In fact, the textbooks for special methods courses are improving with regard to providing the historical contributions of various ethnic groups to specific academic disciplines. An example of such a textbook is *Science in the Multicultural Classroom: A Guide to Teaching and Learning*, a relatively new elementary science methods text-book by Barbra (1995). Equally as important as learning *historical contributions*, teacher candidates must learn *how* to teach appropriately about specific ethnic/cultural groups. Therefore, they must read and study, for example, in "Methods of Teaching Social Studies" such publications as *Teaching About Native Americans* by Harvey, Harjo, and Jackson (1990) or in language arts and reading methods courses *Through Indian Eyes: The Native Experience in Books for Children* by Slapin and Seale (1992). Both of these references are attempts to clarify to non-Indian teachers how and what to teach about Native Americans that is respectful and accurate.

Teacher candidates' content knowledge of histories and contributions of specific cultural groups can also be extended through methods courses by having them read and review material written for younger students. Teacher candidates in music methods courses should read and review school students' materials such as *Traditional Black Music* by Jerry Silverman (1994), a curriculum series of 15 books written for students ages 10 and up; *Shake it to the One You Love Best: Playsongs and Lullabies from Black Musical Traditions* by Mattox (1989), a songbook and tape set of playsongs, clap games, ring games, and lullabies from African American tradition; and *We All Go Together: Creative Activities for Children to Use with Multicultural Folksongs* by Lipman (1994), an activity-based songbook that presents songs from African American, Anglo American, European American, and other heritages.

Math and Science. Illustrative teaching materials and school curriculum kits for teacher candidates to review in mathematics and science methods courses include *Multiculturalism in Mathematics, Science, and Technology: Readings and Activities* (1993); *Multicultural Mathematics Poster and Activities* (1984); *Multicultural Mathematics: Interdisciplinary Cooperative Learning Activities* by Zaslavsky (1993), *Africa Counts: Number and Pattern in African Culture* by Zaslavsky (1979), *African Americans in Science, Mathematics, Medicine, and Invention: A Multicultural Curriculum* (1993), and *Mathematics from Many Cultures* (1993) by Irons, et al.

Secondary English. Similarly, in methods courses for teaching secondary English, teacher candidates' knowledge of ethnic voices can be expanded by reading and reviewing literature anthologies for young and adolescent students. Examples of anthologies of Hispanic literature are *Iguana Dreams* edited by Poey and Suarez (1992), *Growing up Latino: Memoirs and Stories* edited by Augenbraum and Stavans (1993), and *Growing up Chicana/Chicano* edited by Lopez (1993). Similar anthologies of literature by writers from other cultural and ethnic groups include *The Big Aiiieeeee! An Anthology of Chinese American and Japanese American Literature* edited by Chan, et al. (1991), *Growing up Asian American: An Anthology,* by Hong (1993), *Growing up Native American* edited by Riley (1993), *American Indian Literature* edited by Velie (1991), *African American Literature: An Anthology of Nonfiction, Fiction, Poetry, and Drama* edited by Woreley and Perry (1993), and *Coming of Age in America: A Multicultural Anthology* edited by Frosch (1994). Teacher educators who teach courses in methods of teaching English and language arts will also find *Reading Across Cultures: Teaching Literature in a Diverse Society,* edited by Rogers and Soter (1997), a valuable resource of insights and suggestions.

In conclusion, other authorities have conceptualized cultural knowledge as a component in teacher education somewhat differently and have made other recommendations regarding how cultural knowledge should be acquired by preservice teachers. Two exceptional treatises that present specific recommendations regarding how cultural knowledge should be infused into restructured teacher education programs are Understanding the Dynamics of Race, Class, and Gender by Gollnick (1992) and *Building Cultural Bridges: A Bold Proposal for Teacher Education* by Gay (1993). Gay, for example, goes so far as to recommend that preservice teachers declare a concentration in a cultural group (e.g. African Americans, Mexican Americans) just as they declare a subject area major.

CHAPTER 7

Knowledge Base 6: *Principles of Culturally Responsive Teaching and Culturally Responsive Curriculum Development*

The notion of "cultural relevance" moves beyond language to include other aspects of student and school culture. ...[C]ulturally relevant teaching uses student culture in order to maintain it and to transcend the negative effects of the dominant culture.

— Gloria Ladson-Billings, *The Dreamkeepers*

Principles of culturally responsive pedagogy and culturally responsive curriculum development constitute an emerging but essential knowledge base for teacher education programs that profess to prepare teachers for culturally diverse classrooms. Despite the absence of any mention of the terms *culturally responsive teaching* or *culturally responsive pedagogy* in most mainstream textbooks traditionally used in teacher education courses, several teacher education scholars have advocated including the theory and research on culturally responsive teaching as a valid knowledge base in teacher education programs (Au & Kawakami, 1994; Bowers & Flinders, 1990; Delpit, 1991; Huber, 1991; Irvine, 1991; Ladson-Billings, 1990; Smith, 1991; Zeichner, 1993).

Culturally Responsive Pedagogy

In brief, culturally responsive pedagogy, often used as a synonym for culturally responsive teaching in the literature, uses the students' cultures and strengths (sometimes referred to as the "students' cultural capital") to build a bridge to success in school achievement. In doing so, culturally responsive pedagogy places other cultures (i.e., African American, Hispanic American, Native American, and Asian American, etc.) alongside middle class mainstream culture at the center of the instructional paradigm. Ideally, culturally responsive teachers have in-depth knowledge of both "home culture" as represented in the students' life experiences and "high culture" as represented by the more formal academic knowledge about a cultural group's identity, language, history, and contributions. More importantly, culturally responsive teachers translate cultural knowledge into instructional practices, thereby affirming the student's culture as an integral, valued part of the school environment. In the literature, this process is referred to as achieving *cultural synchronization* or *congruency* as contrasted to *cultural dissonance, cultural incongruity,* or *cultural incompatibility.* Thus, a central postulate in the theory of culturally responsive pedagogy is that much of the difficulty ethnic and language minority students encounter in schooling is due to a mismatch between their culture and the school's culture. Culturally responsive pedagogy seeks to remedy this situation by culturally contextualizing the teaching-learning processes.

As noted above in the introductory definition, the theory and practice of culturally responsive pedagogy consists of a number of interrelated premises. The first premise is that culture influences the way students learn. The second premise is that teachers must understand the culture of their students and translate this understanding into instructional practice. The definition of culturally responsive pedagogy provided by Villegas (1991) stresses these two premises:

A culturally responsive pedagogy builds on the premise that how people are expected to go about learning may differ across cultures. Cultural differences present both opportunities and challenges for teachers. To maximize learning opportunities, teachers must gain knowledge of the cultures represented in their classrooms, then translate this knowledge into instructional practice. (p.24)

A third premise centers on the notion that much of the difficulty ethnic/racial minority and language minority students experience is due to *cultural incongruity* between the school's White middle class culture and the student's culture. This cultural mismatch (Villegas, 1988) often exists in the general school environment of policies and practices but is also frequently found between the teacher's culture and the student's culture. Two theoretical constructs that are at the center of culturally responsive teaching and that emanate from the contrasting concepts of *cultural incongruity* and *cultural congruity* are (a) the greater the gap between the child's culture and the school's culture (degree of cultural incongruity), the greater the likelihood of failure or low student achievement and, conversely, (b) the greater the overlap (degree of cultural congruity) between the student's culture and the school's culture, the greater the likelihood of success or high student achievement. Much of the research base for culturally responsive pedagogy has been driven by these two constructs; in fact, most of the research findings provide empirical evidence supporting the validity of these two constructs.

That ethnic minority and language minority students often experience difficulty in school learning due to cultural conflict is stressed by Irvine (1990) in her discussion of cultural synchronization. Although Irvine centers her definition of cultural synchronization within the educational experience of African American learners, one can infer at the macrocosmic level that *cultural synchronization* refers to the degree of harmony between a culture and all elements of the larger world that are external to that culture. Thus, there is a lack of cultural

synchronization when ethnocentric individuals of one culture attempt to communicate with individuals of another culture; there is a lack of cultural synchronization between minority cultures and societal institutions that are based upon the world view of a majority culture. Irvine refers to cultural synchronization synonymously and interchangeably with *cultural correspondence* and *cultural continuity* and as an antonym to *cultural discontinuity* and *cultural contradiction*:

Because the culture of Black children is different and often misunderstood, ignored, or discounted, Black students are likely to experience cultural discontinuity in schools, particularly schools in which the majority, or Eurocentric persons, control, administer, and teach. The combination of Afrocentric children and Eurocentric schools results in conflict because of lack of cultural correspondence or sync. This lack of cultural sync becomes evident in instructional situations in which teachers misinterpret, denigrate, and dismiss Black students' language, nonverbal cues, physical movements, learning styles, cognitive approaches, and worldview. When teachers and students are out of sync, they clash and confront each other, both consciously and unconsciously, in matters concerning proxemics (use of interpersonal distance), paralanguage (behaviors accompanying speech, such as voice tone and pitch and speech rate and length), and nonverbal behavior (gesture, facial expression, eye gaze). When Black students are in sync with their teachers and school, and no cultural contradictions appear to exist, these children can be expected to be more Eurocentric than Afrocentric in their behavior, attitudes, language, style, and use of standard English and language. (p. xix)

As illustrated above, Irvine also uses cultural synchronization as the theoretical framework for macro- and microcosmic analyses of cultural incompatibilities between African American students and school personnel, policies, and practice.

A fourth premise of culturally responsive pedagogy is that classroom teachers can create the desired environment of cultural synchronization or congruence by culturally contextualizing the teaching-learning processes. Bowers and Flinders (1990) contend that the knowledge base for culturally contextualized teaching "...includes the content areas of the curriculum; an understanding of the physiological, psychological, and cultural influences on the learning process; and an understanding of the cultural and language processes that constitute the dynamic environment of the classroom" (p. 22). These knowledge bases constitute much of what teachers must know to be culturally *responsive* teachers. According to Bowers and Flinders, culturally responsive teaching is a process of highly complex interactions that is sensitive to the ecology of cultural patterns of thought and behavior, particularly those that may result in miscommunication and alienation. Central to the concept of culturally responsive teaching is the teacher's ability to recognize and let go of the Cartesian (Western) traditions of viewing the student as a culture-free individual, the classroom as a management problem, teaching as a primarily didactic act consisting of objectives and behavioral outcomes, and intelligence and achievement as phenomena that lend themselves to reductionistic assessment and measurement. For the most part, the knowledge bases of theory and research for culturally responsive teaching, according to Bowers and Flinders, are those that enable teachers to understand the cultural dimensions of the classroom ecology. Thus, the literature that enlightens the teacher about *pattern*, *schema*, and *template* with regard to culture and language is essential to the education of preservice and inservice teachers. This literature of course, has been treated extensively elsewhere in this book in chapters about Knowledge Base 4 and 5 and to some extent in the chapters about Knowledge Bases 2, 3, and 7.

More finite tenets and descriptors of culturally responsive pedagogy that extend the theory of culturally responsive pedagogy beyond the four broad premises discussed above have resulted from research conducted by Gloria Ladson-Billings and described in her book, *The Dreamkeepers: Successful Teachers of African American Children* (1994a).

Ladson-Billings' two-year study of eight exemplary teachers of African American students is seminal because its focus was on successful teachers' beliefs and classroom practices. Through interviews and observations, she documented what exemplary successful teachers of African American students believe and do that differs from less successful teachers. She concluded that successful teachers have a set of beliefs and practices that can be described as "culturally relevant" and that stand in vivid contrast to the beliefs and practices characteristic of "assimilationist" teaching.

Ladson-Billings organized her findings into six points regarding how culturally relevant teachers perceive themselves and others, four points regarding the social relations of culturally relevant teachers, and five points regarding culturally relevant teachers' conceptions of knowledge. These points are collectively presented in the left-hand column of Table 2.

In addition, Ladson-Billings extrapolated from her findings the following six overarching tenets of culturally relevant teaching practices:

① Students whose educational, economic, social, political, and cultural futures are most tenuous are helped to become intellectual leaders in the classroom.

② Students are apprenticed in a learning community rather than taught in an isolated and unrelated way.

③ Students' real-life experiences are legitimized as they become part of the "official" curriculum.

④ Teachers and students participate in a broad conception of literacy that incorporates both literature and oratory.

⑤ Teachers and students engage in a collective struggle against the status quo.

⑥ Teachers are cognizant of themselves as political beings. (pp. 117-118)

TABLE 2
Culturally Relevant vs. Assimilationist Teaching

CONCEPTIONS OF SELF & OTHERS	
Culturally Relevant	**Assimilationist**
Teacher sees him/herself as an artist, teaching as an art.	Teacher sees him/herself as technician, teaching as a technical task.
Teacher sees him/herself as part of the community and teaching as giving something back to the community, encourages students to do the same.	Teacher sees him/herself as an individual who may or may not be a part of the community; He/she encourages achievement as a means to excape community.
Teacher believes all students can succeed.	Teacher believes failure is inevitable for some.
Teacher helps students make connections between their community, national, and global identities.	Teacher homogenizes students into one "American" identity.
Teacher sees teaching as "pulling knowledge out" —like "mining."	Teacher sees teaching as "putting knowledge into"—like "banking."

SOCIAL RELATIONS	
Culturally Relevant	**Assimilationist**
Teacher-student relationship is fluid, humanely equitable, extends to interactions beyond the classroom and into the community.	Teacher-student relationship is fixed, tends to be hierarchical and limited to formal classroom roles.
Teacher demonstrates a connectedness with all students.	Teacher demonstrates connections with individual students.
Teacher encourages a "community of learners."	Teacher encourages competitive achievement.
Teacher encourages students to learn collaboratively. Students are expected to teach each other and be responsible for each other.	Teacher encourages students to learn individually, in isolation.

continued on next page

TABLE 2 (con't)

CONCEPTIONS OF KNOWLEDGE	
Culturally Relevant	**Assimilationist**
Knowledge is continuously re-created, recycled, and shared by teachers and students, It is not static or unchanging.	Knowledge is static and is passed in one direction, from teacher to student.
Knowledge is viewed critically.	Knowledge is viewed as infallible.
Teacher is passionate about content.	Teacher is detached, neutral about content.
Teacher helps students develop necessary skills.	Teacher expects students to demonstrate prerequisite skills.
Teacher sees excellence as a complex standard that may involve some postulates but takes student diversity and individual differences into account	Teacher sees excellence as a postulate that exists independently from student diversity or individual differences.

Adapted from Ladson-Billings (1994a), p. 34, 55, 81.

Finally, Ladson-Billings found the following five premises that describe culturally relevant teaching:

① When students are treated as competent they are likely to demonstrate competence.

② When teachers provide instructional "scaffolding," students can move from what they know to what they need to know.

③ The focus of the classroom must be instructional.

④ Real education is about extending students' thinking and abilities.

⑤ Effective teaching involves in-depth knowledge of both the students and the subject matter. (pp. 123-124)

Several observations about Ladson-Billings' findings raise important issues concerning restructuring teacher education programs to prepare teachers for culturally diverse classrooms. First, many of the beliefs and teaching practices that are characteristic of culturally relevant teachers leap out as being diametrically opposite to many of the beliefs and teaching practices of preservice and inservice teachers, particularly the majority of monocultural, politically apathetic White females from suburban, middle class backgrounds described by Zimpher (1989) and Feistritzer (1983). Second, many of the beliefs and teaching practices of culturally relevant teachers seem more akin to things learned from "life," intuition and craft wisdom (described in Chapter 8) than concepts and behaviors learned in a formal teacher education program. Third, at the present time there is almost no research to shed light on whether or not formal teacher education programs can be restructured in ways that will result in teachers who replicate the characteristics of successful teachers of African American students. Thus, these known and unknown factors are important considerations as teacher educators make decisions regarding how the elements of Knowledge Base 6, defined as principles of culturally responsive pedagogy, should be integrated into a teacher education curriculum.

Locating the Theory and Research on Culturally Responsive Pedagogy

Although it intersects with other knowledge bases, particularly Knowledge Bases 3, 4, and 7, *culturally responsive pedagogy* has its own separate body of literature. The inclusion of this knowledge base in the teacher education curriculum means that preservice and inservice teachers would (a) make a formal study of the language, definitions, concepts, principles, practices, and theory and research on *culturally responsive pedagogy* and (b) practice principles of culturally responsive teaching in supervised clinical settings. Content-level mastery of this knowledge base includes learning through studying the literature the relationships among such terms as *cultural synchronicity* (Irvine, 1990), *cultural salience* (Hilliard, 1988a), *cultural congruity* and *congruence* (Au & Jordan, 1981; King, 1994, Au & Kawakami, 1994), *culturally appropriate* (Cazden & Leggett, 1981), *culturally responsive* (Mohatt & Erikson, 1981; Villegas, 1991), *culturally compatible* (Vogt, Jordan, Tharp, 1987; Villegas, 1988), *culturally responsible* (Pewewardy, 1994) versus such terms as *cultural mismatch* (Villegas, 1988), *cultural contradiction* (Irvine, 1990), *culturally assaultive* (Clark, DeWolf & Clark, 1992) and *cultural dissonance* and *discontinuity* (Irvine, 1990).

Presently, the parameters of the knowledge base on culturally responsive pedagogy are not contained in a single book that might be used as a text in teacher education courses. However, several chapters in *Teaching Diverse Populations: Formulating a Knowledge Base* by Hollins et al. (1994) capture much of the theory and research on culturally responsive pedagogy. For example, the chapter on cultural congruence in teaching by Au and Kawakami (1994) provides an excellent review of the research literature across racial and ethnic cultures with regard to dialect speakers, participation structures, narrative and questioning styles, speakers of English as a second language, and peer groups. In this same volume, Boykin (1994) discusses cultural conformity and cultural capital and other concepts related to culturally responsive education for African American students. Like Boykin, Ladson-Billings (1994b), King (1994), and Foster (1994) center their discussions of culturally

relevant teaching primarily in the context of African American students and teachers; whereas Pewewardy (1994) writes about culturally responsible pedagogy for Native American students. In addition, a second book, Irvine's *Black Students and School Failure: Policies, Practices, and Prescriptions* (1990), provides extensive reviews of the theory and research that undergird culturally responsive pedagogy, particularly for African American students. Bowers and Flinders' *Responsive Teaching: An Ecological Approach to Classroom Patterns of Language, Culture, and Thought* (1990) also merits mention as a third resource.

Finally, as mentioned previously, *The Dreamkeepers* by Gloria Ladson-Billings (1994a) is a fourth valuable research-based resource that extends the tenets of culturally responsive teaching beyond the four main premises discussed in the previous section of this chapter. For the time being, teacher educators will have to use these four books and compile their own collections of readings from journal articles as cited previously to infuse the knowledge base on culturally responsive pedagogy into the academic content of teacher education programs.

Principles of Culturally Responsive Curriculum Development

Knowledge Base 6 also includes principles of culturally responsive curriculum development, an area of knowledge and competence related to culturally responsive pedagogy but discussed more frequently in the literature on multicultural education. Teacher education programs must provide direct learning experiences for preservice and inservice teachers to *learn how* to develop culturally inclusive curricula for their classrooms and how to participate on curriculum writing teams for developing schoolwide and districtwide curricula that are multicultural. The two primary knowledge bases minimally necessary to develop sound multicultural curriculum are principles of multicultural curriculum development and ethnic and cultural literacy. The difficulty of a teacher education program's providing these knowledge and skills is highlighted by the current state of affairs in most traditional teacher education programs. The truth is that most teacher education programs are not presently producing teachers who can write culture-free curricula much less write well-designed multicultural curricula. The reality for the new teacher is that survival the first year of teaching means they must fall back on a set of "curriculum guidelines" and school textbooks. More often than not, the school curriculum is little more than what the textbooks contain. At best, most graduates from traditional teacher education programs have had some learning experiences that required them to develop a few sample lessons or sometimes "a thematic unit" that may or may not have been multicultural. It is also true that the majority of teacher education students have not themselves experienced a curriculum that was sufficiently multicultural to provide them with the ethnic and cultural literacy necessary to develop multicultural curricula. Whereas it could be argued that no two-year education program can realistically remediate the typical preservice teacher's cultural literacy deficiencies, a culturally responsive teacher education program must try.

Since the content knowledge about cultures necessary to develop multicultural curricula has been addressed in this book under Knowledge Base 5: Essential Elements of Cultures, this subsection of Knowledge Base 6 centers only on a discussion of the six broad principles of multicultural curriculum development that should be transmitted to preservice teachers in a culturally responsive and responsible teacher education program:

① *A well-designed multicultural curriculum contains learning experiences and lessons that move the student from the "culturally familiar" or "culturally relevant" to the unfamiliar.* Some multicultural lessons, particularly in the beginning but at all age and grade levels, should begin with the culturally familiar and build a bridge to (a) the school culture, (b) achievement in the traditional academic skills and subjects of the school (reading skills, math skills, etc,), and (c) broadened horizons that expand students' experiences to include knowledge and skills typically beyond or outside their own culture.

② *A well-designed multicultural curriculum contains learning experiences and lessons that develop the student's ethnic identity from negative to positive, from "ethnic psychological captivity" to multiculturalism and globalism.* Some multicultural lessons should be designed to advance the student along the stages of ethnic identity development from the lower stages of "ethnic psychological captivity" and "ethnic encapsulation" to the higher stages of "multiethnicity/reflective nationalism" and "globalism" in James Banks' Stages of Ethnic Identity or advance the student's development along the stages of Bennett's Model of Stages of Intercultural Sensitivity.

③ *A well-designed multicultural curriculum includes learning experiences and lessons that increase the student's interpersonal contact and the quality of interracial and intercultural relationships with diverse persons.* Some multicultural lessons should increase students' interpersonal contacts and the quality of their relationships with peers and adults of other cultural/ethnic groups and persons who are different by age, gender, physical condition, sexual orientation, etc. These types of lessons should (a) develop tolerance for and acceptance of diversity, (b) develop interpersonal skills to relate to persons who differ, (c) include constructive ways to resolve conflicts, and (d) increase students' understanding of racism, prejudice, stereotyping, discrimination, etc.

④ *A well-designed multicultural curriculum contains learning experiences and lessons that increase the students' knowledge of their own culture and the cultures of others.* Some multicultural lessons should advance students' knowledge of their and others' "surface" and "deep" culture, particularly of those cultural, ethnic, and other groups who have historically been omitted in Eurocentric and androcentric curricula. These lessons focus on "multicultural content" and include the historical contributions and perspectives of various cultures and other groups such as women and gay and lesbian persons in the areas of literature, music, dance, architecture, art, science, mathematics, politics, technology, social studies, spirituality, and other areas of human endeavor. This strand of learning experiences in a multicultural curriculum corresponds primarily to the contribution, additive, and, to a lesser degree, to the transformation levels of multicultural curriculum described by Banks (1988a, 1993) or to that type of curriculum called "multicultural education" by Sleeter and Grant (1988a, 1994).

⑤ *A well-designed multicultural curriculum contains learning experiences and lessons that enable students to examine issues, concepts, themes, and human events through the multiple perspectives of different cultures.* Some multicultural lessons should develop students' knowledge and abilities to "view concepts, issues, and themes from the perspective of diverse ethnic and cultural groups" (Banks, 1988a, p. 3). That is, some multicultural lessons should be designed at Banks' transformation level of curriculum integration.

⑥ *A well-designed multicultural curriculum contains learning experiences and lessons that enable students to apply multicultural knowledge to analyzing and solving social problems and to living a multicultural lifestyle.* Some multicultural lessons should enable students to study social problems, particularly those that result from or involve inequality, and to take actions to solve such problems. These lessons often involve student research projects to study social inequity and student projects to ameliorate social problems. These lessons enable students to apply their multicultural knowledge to real life action. Some activities in these lessons center upon living a multicultural lifestyle.

Infusing the Knowledge Base on Principles of Culturally Responsive Curriculum Development

Teacher educators who are synthesizing the literature on multicultural curriculum development theory and who are collecting materials to teach principles of multicultural curriculum development in courses for preservice and inservice teachers will find an abundance of available resources. The four-level model of multicultural curriculum integration developed by Banks (1988a, 1993), the five-type model of multicultural curriculum described by Sleeter and Grant (1988a, 1994), and the model for global and multicultural perspectives in curriculum developed by Christine L. Bennett (1995) are essential introductory pieces of the knowledge base on designing and developing culturally inclusive curriculum. Another instructive model for developing nonsexist, multicultural curriculum is advocated by Theresa Mickey McCormick (1994). Perhaps one of the most comprehensive guides to assist preservice and inservice teachers in developing multicultural curricula is *Planning and Organizing for Multicultural Instruction* by Gwendolyn C. Baker (1994), a resource that provides a step-by-step method for developing multicultural curricula and sample lesson plans for a variety of subject areas. Sample lesson plans illustrative of the six principles of culturally responsive curriculum presented above are also found in such publications as: *Turning on Learning: Five Approaches for Multicultural Teaching Plans for Race, Class, Gender, and Disability* by Sleeter and Grant (1988b), *Multicultural Teaching: A Handbook of Activities, Information, and Resources* by Tiedt and Tiedt (1995), and *Teaching the Diverse Classroom: Learner-Centered Activities That Work* by Tonya Huber-Bowen (1993). Although works that provide sample multicultural lesson plans are too numerous to review here, other starter sources that merit mention include publications by Elliot (1992), Schniedewind and Davidson (1983), King (1990), and The National Conference (1994).

Chapter 8

Knowledge Base 7: *Effective Strategies for Teaching Minority Students*

> It is a deadly fog formed when the cold mist of the bias and ignorance meets the warm vital reality of children of color in many of our schools.
>
> — Lisa Delpit, *Other People's Children*

An important knowledge base for training teachers for culturally diverse classrooms is what is known about effective strategies for teaching African American, Asian American, Hispanic American, Native American, and other minority and poor White students. Currently much of this knowledge base about effective strategies is found in the (a) effective teaching research, (b) effective schools research, (c) the cooperative learning research, (d) the craft wisdom research, (e) the resilient-child research, and (f) the parental involvement research. Some of these bodies of research have been increasingly emphasized in some teacher education textbooks and teacher education curricula during the past five years, at least more so than they were previously. However, the presentation of these bodies of research on effective strategies is often over-generalized across all students as if we know for certain that the research findings are applicable universally to all ethnic/cultural groups of minority students.

Knowledge Base 7 serves two primary purposes in a culturally responsive teacher education program. The foremost and most obvious purpose is to provide preservice and inservice teachers a repertoire of teaching methods and approaches that have proven effectiveness with minority students and that constitute a cluster of methods that will enable teachers to substitute *culturally contextualized instructional variability* for traditional didactic teaching methods. If research has shown anything at all, it has shown that dull didactic instruction consisting only of teacher talk and seatwork is not effective with most minority students. A second important purpose for including Knowledge Base 7 in teacher education programs is that part of its research base provides the scientific evidence needed to counteract negative beliefs and attitudes many preservice and inservice teachers have about most minority students. The experience of most teacher educators confirms what much of the research documents about preservice teachers' beliefs about minority students, particularly African American students. For example, despite the fact that most preservice teachers have had almost no firsthand experience with African American students, they already have firmly established negative preconceptions that African American students cannot achieve at levels equal to their White counterparts; that they are talkative, unruly, undisciplined, and unmotivated; that they come from deficient, impoverished homes and neighborhoods that make learning impossible; and that they come from families who simply do not value education.

All five of the bodies of research that undergird the knowledge base on effective strategies, however, contradict these negative perceptions. The effective teaching research, the effective schools research, and the craft wisdom research provide evidence that African American students can and do achieve well under specified instructional and school environment conditions. The cooperative learning research provides evidence that most minority students from most cultural groups achieve when teachers use culturally compatible learning strategies that tap into cultural interpersonal and relational needs of students. The resilient-child research provides evidence that African American and minority children from other ethnic groups do indeed manifest self-reliance, problem-solving abilities, motivation attributes, and personal and cultural strengths which can be and often are directed toward school achievement. Similarly, the parental involvement research shows that minority parents are concerned about their children's education and will work in concert with the school if culturally appropriate methods of inviting and communicating with parents are utilized.

Synthesizing the Theory and Research on Effective Strategies for Teaching Minority Students

Several points need to be made regarding effective strategies for teaching minority students as a distinct, separate knowledge base for inclusion in teacher education programs. First, there is a clear relationship between effective strategies for teaching minority students as a knowledge base and other knowledge bases previously discussed in this book, particularly Knowledge Base 3: Cultural and Cognitive Learning Style Theory and Research and Knowledge Base 6: Principles of Culturally Responsive Teaching and Culturally Responsive Curriculum Development. Second, major reasons for separate treatment of these knowledge bases are that each has a separate history of development as a field of study in education, each has evolved through the works of a distinctly different groups of writers, scholars, and researchers, and each is supported by different bodies of research literature. Third, only recently have these three knowledge bases begun to merge in the scholarly literature of teacher education. For example, Irvine (1990) was one of the first writers to draw clear connections between the literature about culturally responsive teaching and the research literature on cooperative learning, learning styles, and effective schools; and Gay (1994) has recently written about the connections between culturally responsive pedagogy and cultural

learning styles in her discussion of culturally contextualized teaching. Fourth, far more theory and research exist on effective strategies for African American and Hispanic American students than for other ethnic, racial, and cultural groups.

Fifth, in general, much of the present research indicates that effective strategies for minority students—except for the deadly combination of didactic teacher talk (lecturing, asking simple questions, and giving instructions) and pencil-paper seatwork—are also effective strategies for most White middle class students. The difference between minority students and White students seems to be that there are sufficient numbers of White students who, because of middle-class cultural emphasis on "doing a job whether you like it or not," endure and learn in spite of the deadly routine Goodlad (1984) found to be characteristic of teaching in most schools across the United States. The bottom line on *effective strategies*, as Irvine (1990) has noted, seems to be that *culturally contextualized instructional variability* holds the most promise for the academic success of minority students as well as mainstream White students.

What, then, are the bodies of research on effective strategies that should constitute the curriculum of a teacher education program that prepares preservice and inservice teachers to teach successfully culturally diverse students? The answer to this important question is not simply "the same bodies of research on effective strategies as are found in generic teacher education programs." The answer to this question should be "the same bodies of research on effective strategies *as they relate to African American, Hispanic American, Asian American, Native American, and other historically disenfranchised and educationally underserved students.*"

...dull didactic instruction consisting only of teacher talk and seatwork is not effective with most minority students.

Thus, the elements missing most of all from the traditional, generic curriculum of teacher education programs are the multiple perspectives of minority scholars who describe the causes of and solutions to the undereducation of minority students.

Teacher educators will find that several minority scholars have already synthesized and interpreted these relatively well-known bodies of theory and research as they apply to minority student populations. In *Black Students and School Failure*, a publication suitable for use as a text in teacher education courses, Irvine (1990) identifies effective strategies for African American students that emerge from four bodies of theory and research: (a) the Afrocentric instructional research, (b) the teaching effectiveness research, (c) the effective schools research, and (d) the parental involvement research. Defining Afrocentric instructional strategies as those that are compatible with cultural retentions of African American students, Irvine draws upon and synthesizes the works of Hale-Benson (1986), Boykin (1986), Cureton (1978), Slaughter (1969), the National Alliance of Black School Educators (1984), Brandt (1986), Houlton (1986), Longstreet (1978), and Fordham and Ogbu (1986). Irvine has also extracted the relevant findings regarding successful teaching strategies for African American and other minority students from the effective teaching research (Brophy, 1982; Hawley, et al., 1984a; Cruickshank, 1985; Wiggens, 1988; Gersten & Keating, 1987) and notes important contradictory findings based on her own observations and on the research of Lomotey and Brookins (1988). Irvine has also synthesized research findings from studies that show positive effects of cooperative learning strategies on the achievement of African American students (Slavin, 1980, 1982, 1987a, 1987b) and on social outcomes for African American students (Schofield, 1982; Slavin & Madden, 1979).

Irvine's summary of findings from the literature on the characteristics of effective schools for low-income African American children includes those from research conducted by Edmonds (1979), those from a comprehensive review of 1,200 research studies done by Clark, Lotto, and McCarthy (1980), and those from the review of effective school literature conducted by Glenn (1981). Edmond's well-known findings from his seminal

research found that characteristics of effective schools included principals who were strong instructional leaders; principals and teachers who emphasized reading and mathematics skills; frequent, systematic monitoring of student progress; orderly, safe school environments; and teachers who had high expectations for students. Similarly Clark, Lotto, and McCarthy organized their findings regarding the achievement of urban children into six clusters of variables: leadership, teaching personnel, finances, resources and facilities, curriculum and instruction, and community resources. Those variables most related to the *knowledge base on effective instructional strategies* included specifically focused inservice programs designed to modify teaching strategies, reduced teacher-student ratios, clearly stated goals and objectives expressed as a mission, structured learning environments, and individualized instruction. Significant non-instructional variables including parental involvement in school activities were also found. Irvine (1990) succinctly captures the essence of the effective school research in her summary of findings from the review conducted by Glenn:

> Glenn (1981) in a publication of the Center for Law and Education at Harvard, summarized the findings of effective schools research and concluded that effective schools have teachers and other adults who are committed to teaching poor and black children. There is a belief by these adults that black children can be taught to read, write, and compute. The curriculum is focused on reading, writing, and mathematics with systematic testing of students' mastery. Teachers have high expectations, and principals are strong leaders who maintain an orderly school environment. Parents are involved in the children's education. (p. 103).

Other extensive ready-to-use reviews that synthesize the literature on effectively teaching minority students include those done by King (1994), Foster (1994), and Garcia (1994). All of these reviews can be found in *Teaching Diverse Populations: Formulating and Knowledge Base* by Hollins, King, and Hayman (1994). The reviews by King and Foster center primarily upon effective school strategies for African American students, and the review by Garcia extracts research findings on effective strategies for linguistic minority students. King reviews four bodies of literature that have emerged from five different research perspectives which, in turn, are aligned with different views regarding the purpose of education for African American students: (a) *culture centered research*, (b) *culturally congruent research*, (c) *cultural difference research*, and (d) *cultural deficit research*. In addition, King asserts that findings from these four research perspectives constitute knowledge bases that should be included in teacher preparation programs. Foster's review of literature uniquely centers upon what teacher education has learned about effective teaching strategies from the study of effective African American teachers. Garcia's review of the effective schools research for linguistic minority students covers both instructional strategies and non-instructional variables.

Other books that merit mention as having relevance to the knowledge base on effective strategies for teaching minority students include *From Rage to Hope: Strategies for Reclaiming Black & Hispanic Students* by Kuykendall (1992), *High Impact Teaching: Strategies for Educating Minority Youth* by Brown (1988), and *Effective Strategies for Teaching Minority Students* by Hill (1989). Whereas none of these books are scholarly reviews of research literature, the authors provide advice, principles, and strategies for effective teaching practices that are based upon theory and research. Because each of these three books are brief and can be read easily by preservice and inservice teachers in a single day, they are suitable resources for introducing the knowledge base of effective strategies for minority students, particularly if teacher educators supplement them with the appropriate reviews of theory and research discussed in this chapter.

Another element of the knowledge base on effective strategies for teaching minority students is the body of theory and research on craft wisdom. As defined here, craft wisdom refers to insights and learnings derived from the teaching experiences of classroom teachers. Because craft wisdom historically and traditionally has been based upon teachers' reflections about their experience rather than upon a strong quantitative research base, what many

teachers have learned from experience about successfully teaching minority students has not been considered a "legitimate" knowledge base by some professional teacher educators. However, Shulman (1987a) suggests that "wisdom of practice" derived from expert teachers is a legitimate knowledge base for teacher education. Teachers' knowledge about teaching as a knowledge base, Shulman (1987b) insists, includes what expert pedagogues do in the classroom, the thinking that undergirds their pedagogical decisions, and the context in which their teaching occurs.

Clearly, a distinct knowledge base of craft wisdom about successfully teaching minority students has been emerging since the mid-1980s that should be studied by preservice and inservice teachers. Most of the evolving theory on the contextualized teaching of minority students has evolved from research studies, largely ethnographic, on teachers whose classroom practices are exemplary models of culturally responsive teaching. That is, beginning with teachers who have recognized reputations for being effective teachers of minority students, a number of ethnographic researchers have investigated what these exemplary teachers of minority students actually do in their classrooms that differs from less successful teachers. Although the body of emerging literature that centers upon insights gained from craft wisdom seemingly began and evolved as a separate trend, there is a relationship between this knowledge base and the one previously described as *principles of culturally responsive teaching and culturally responsive curriculum development.*

Whereas craft wisdom is often defined as the insights and learnings derived from the teaching experiences of expert teachers, at a deeper level the content of craft wisdom is shaped by enduring cultural wisdoms as perceived and felt, often, by persons native to the culture of the pupils they are teaching. That is, some African American and Native American teachers, for example, have been found to have "intuitive cultural knowledge about what works in the classroom," particularly with students from the same cultural heritage as theirs. Building on the idea of putting "education into culture rather than continuing the practice of putting culture into education," Pewewardy (1994) defines this deeper level of craft wisdom:

Teachers of Indian students should be knowledgeable, sensitive, and comfortable in working with Indian students' languages, code switching, style of presentation, and tribal community values. Whether Indian students come from reservation areas or urban settings, the element of obtaining "craft wisdom" is critical to maximizing learning for all students. Obtaining craft wisdom many times takes years to acquire. Some teachers have almost a natural instinct in adapting and working successfully with diverse populations, while others may take a lifetime.

Craft wisdom comes from acquiring the element of being "street smart," "reservation smart," and/or the ability to adapt to culturally diverse populations and geographical locations. It also brings together all the personal qualities of classroom leadership. Like "OJT" (on the job training), classroom leadership is something to be learned over time, not simply by completing a teacher training program. Basic leadership is an art—more tribal than scientific. It's more a weaving of relationships than an amassing of information, and in that sense encompasses all the elements of craft wisdom. (pp. 82-83)

Thus far, minority scholars in the field of education have used the terms "practice wisdom" and "craft wisdom" somewhat interchangeably but almost always in reference to applying *intuitive cultural wisdom* to the effective education of children from non-White cultures. Thus, within the recent trend in teacher education to build theory from practice rather than to apply theory to practice, much of the research base for "practice wisdom" and "craft wisdom" consists of studies that have examined how exemplary African American teachers teach African American children or how Native American teachers teach Native American children. Most of these studies have been based on the premise that by studying how exemplary culture-centered teachers teach children from their

own culture a knowledge base about effective practice for culturally diverse students can be built, one that will inform teacher educators how teachers who come from "outside" the culture can be trained to be better teachers of culturally diverse pupil populations. This nascent research base has revealed a good deal about exemplary African American teachers but has not yet developed sufficiently to address whether or not, for example, White teachers can internalize culture-based craft wisdom at deep enough levels to replicate the culturally responsive practices of teachers from cultures different from their own. Despite the questions not yet answered, the knowledge base about craft wisdom, including the theory and research, merits inclusion in teacher education programs.

At present, teacher educators must assemble their own synthesis of theory and research in formats appropriate for infusing information about craft wisdom into the teacher education programs. Some of the research has already been synthesized but remains outside the mainstream teacher education literature. The review of 36 studies that examined the effects of teacher race and student race on teachers' expectations for African American students conducted by Irvine (1988) is part of this research base. Irvine (1990) has also provided a review of these studies and other related research in *Black Students and School Failure: Policies, Practice, and Prescriptions* and has found that "the data do seem to imply...White teachers had more negative expectations for Black students than did Black teachers" (p. 59), but ultimately concluded that both White and African American teachers can be effective teachers of African American students. Irvine writes:

> Do the conclusions of this paper suggest that all White teachers are ineffective teachers of Black children or that all Black teachers are effective teachers of Black children? Certainly not. What is suggested is that as a group, White teachers are more likely than Black teachers to hold negative expectations for Black children and that White teachers are more likely than Black teachers to be out of cultural sync with the Black students they teach. These conclusions do not ignore the fact

that some White teachers are excellent teachers of Black children or that some Black teachers are ineffective with Black children, treating them with disdain and hostility.(p. 61)

Michelle Foster, Gloria Ladson-Billings, and Lisa Delpit are three African American scholars whose research and scholarship should be included in the knowledge base on craft wisdom. The works of Foster and Ladson-Billings have contributed considerably to those aspects of the knowledge base that have been extracted from the practices of effective teachers of African American students. Through examining the research literature on effective black teachers and through her own research on effective Black teachers who were selected by "community nomination," Foster (1989, 1990, 1991a, 1991b, 1991c, 1991d, 1993, 1994) has been able to identify several attributes of effective Black teachers of Black students that seem to derive more from culture-centered craft wisdom than from any training received in teacher education programs. In brief, Foster found effective African American teachers to possess cultural solidarity with the African American community, felt a kinship identity with African American culture, often employed a teaching style that resembled an authoritative parenting style, linked classroom content to students' cultural and community experiences, focused on development of the whole child rather than just upon cognitive development, used familiar cultural patterns to organize instruction and incorporated culturally compatible communication and interaction patterns. Beyond these findings, however, the point being made here is that the literature review and theory building done by Foster should be part of the knowledge base studied by preservice and inservice teachers in teacher education programs that profess to prepare teachers for culturally diverse classrooms.

Similarly, the research and scholarship of Gloria Ladson-Billings should be studied by preservice teachers and inservice teachers, particularly at the junctures where the knowledge base on culturally responsive teaching and culture-centered craft wisdom cross. Ladson-Billings (1994b) has noted the relationships between craft wisdom and culturally relevant teaching and has written one of the best

synthesis of research studies that supports the notion that culture-centered craft wisdom is a legitimate knowledge base for teacher education. Much of Ladson-Billings' scholarship and research has been discussed under Knowledge Base 6: Culturally Responsive Teaching; however, her book, *The Dreamkeepers: Successful Teachers of African American Children* (1994a), is an additional rich resource for assembling the knowledge base emerging from culture-centered craft wisdom.

Much of the research base on culture-centered craft wisdom consists of naturalistic and ethnographic studies. Consequently, what is known that would inform teacher educators about how to restructure teacher education programs to train teachers effectively for culturally diverse classrooms has been revealed through teachers' voices. Furthermore, the study of these voices seems imperative if preservice and inservice teachers are to grasp the significance and complexity of deep reflection about their craft. However, the important point is that preservice and inservice teachers must experience the voices of teachers from different races and cultures. It is important for preservice and inservice teachers to understand how teachers from cultures different from their own think about the craft of teaching. Thus, in addition to the previously mentioned resources for constructing a viable knowledge base on craft wisdom, teacher educators ought to include the works of Lisa Delpit (1986, 1990, 1991) including *Other People's Children: White Teachers, Students of Color and Other Cultural Conflicts* (1995). Other sources that contain the voices of Hispanic and African American teachers are teachers' narratives as found in popular books and film versions of popular books such as *Stand*

> *It is important for preservice and inservice teachers to understand how teachers from cultures different from their own think about the craft of teaching.*

and Deliver and *The Marva Collins Story.* Some teacher educators are, in fact, presently using these resources in conjunction with teacher educators' analyses of Jaime Escalante's teaching by Irvine (1990) and Marva Collins' teaching by Hollins (1982) to introduce preservice and inservice teachers to the knowledge base emanating from the craft wisdom of effective minority teachers.

Teacher educators who are synthesizing the theory and research for the Knowledge Base on Effective Strategies for Teaching Minority Students should also include the bodies of literature on resiliency of minority students and effective programs for culturally diverse and minority parents. Imbedded in these bodies of literature are implications for both effective classroom instructional strategies and effective school-community strategies. Key starter sources (Bernard, 1991; Garmezy, 1991; McIntyre, Wait, & Yoast, 1990; Rutter, 1990; and Winfield, 1991) for synthesizing the resiliency literature have been discussed under Knowledge Base 2. The resilient child literature clearly provides evidence that cross-age peer teaching and role modeling are effective strategies that are significant factors in the lives of minority students who have overcome the odds to become successful academic achievers. The body of literature on minority parent involvement also provides strong evidence that parental participation in the child's school life is a correlate to the academic achievement of minority pupils. The rationale for including the literature on resiliency and parental involvement in Knowledge Base 7 should be obvious since the general philosophy of traditional teacher education programs and textbooks often continues to reflect the negative legacy from the views of Coleman (1966) and Jencks, et al. (1972) regarding the hopelessness of overcoming "deficient" home environments. Both the resiliency literature and minority parental involvement literature contradict Coleman and Jencks' conclusions and produce the evidence necessary for preservice and inservice teachers to shed negative assumptions about minority achievement and minority home environments.

The general literature on parent involvement is vast, but the literature most needed in culturally responsive and responsible teacher education programs is the alternative literature of more limited scope on developing parental involvement programs among multiracial, multicultural, and multilingual parent populations. *Building Communities of Learners: A Collaboration Among Teachers, Students, Families and Community* by McCaleb (1994) is one of the best already existing syntheses of literature that challenges the premises of traditional parent involvement programs and enables preservice and inservice teachers to review the alternative research literature about effective minority parent involvement. Another important part of the research base on parental involvement programs is the review of 29 controlled studies on school parent programs by Walberg (1984a) in which he found parent involvement in the students' education twice as predictive of academic learning as socioeconomic status. Moreover, teacher educators who are just beginning to synthesize the theory of research on parental involvement will find no shortage of literature reviews.

In addition to McCaleb's publication, starter resources include the sensitive analysis of the rift between parents and schools by Lightfoot (1978) and the extensive literature reviews by Bempechat (1990), Chavkin (1989), Williams and Chavkin (1989), Epstein (1987), and Liontes (1992). Another genre of literature centers upon culture-specific parental involvement such as publications about African American parent involvement (Clark, 1983; Comer, 1986), Southeast Asian parent involvement (Morrow, 1989) and Puerto-Rican family-school relationships (Torrez-Guzman, et al., 1994). *Families and Schools in a Pluralistic Society* by Chavkin (1993), an edited volume, is a comprehensive resource that includes not only much of the current research from Stanford University's Center for the Study of Families Children, and Youth, The John Hopkins University's Center for Research on Elementary and Middle Schools, the Southwest Educational Development Laboratory, and the National Catholic Education Association but also strategies for working with Asian American, Native American, Hispanic American, African American and other minority group families. In addition, descriptions of model parent involvement programs and research literature have been provided in special thematic issues of educational journals. The 1988 issue (Vol. 57, No. 3) of the *Journal of Negro*

Education is illustrative of this genre of literature. Three thematic issues of the journal, *Equity and Choice*, also merit mention as resources for parent involvement literature. These thematic issues of *Equity and Choice* include the spring 1993 issue (Vol. IX, No. 3), subtitled *New Directions in Family Involvement*; the fall 1993 issue (Vol. X, No. 1), subtitled *Circles of Change: Parent-Teacher Action Research*; and the Winter 1994 issue (Vol. X, No. 2), subtitled *Race-Ethnicity-Family-Community-Student Success*.

In conclusion, Irvine (1992), Hilliard (1988b), and Garibaldi (1992) as well as others insist that teacher education programs must be restructured to include emphasis on effective strategies for teaching minority students. Once the teacher education faculty members have synthesized the theory and research on effective strategies for teaching minority students, they will learn that effective teachers of minority students utilize many of the same strategies as do effective teachers of mainstream, White middle-class students but that there are also fine discernable differences between effective teachers of minority students, and successful teachers of White students. Irvine (1992), for example, notes that "effective teachers of at-risk students, compared to effective teachers of privileged students, more often use interactive rather than didactic methods" and "often ignore and sometimes violate the principles of effective teaching" (p. 82) when they culturally contextualize their teaching. These observations are, of course, important points to be considered when colleges of education infuse Knowledge Base 7 into the teacher education curriculum.

CHAPTER 9
Knowledge Base 8: *Foundations of Racism*

There is a physical difference between the White and Black races which I believe will forever forbid the two races living together on terms of social and racial equality, and in as much as they cannot so live, while they do remain together there must be the position of superior and inferior and I was as much as any other man in favor of having the superior position assigned to the White race.

— Abraham Lincoln

No teacher should graduate from a teacher preparation program without having thoroughly studied th*e foundations of racism.* As a knowledge base, the foundations of racism should *minimally* consist of (a) the history of prejudice, discrimination, and racism in the United States, (b) the theory and research from interdisciplinary fields of study (i.e. psychology, sociology, anthropology and other behavioral sciences) on how racist attitudes, stereotypes and prejudices are learned and integrated into one's self-image, personality structure, and ethnic identity, and (c) the effects of racism on members of the dominant White culture and on members of minority cultures. In addition to these "minimal components" of the knowledge base described as the *foundations of racism*, preservice and inservice teachers should (a) study the literature of theory and research on "changing racial attitudes and attitudes towards diversity," (b) review a variety of attitudes scales and instruments that purport to measure racism and/or attitudes towards diversity, and (c) examine a variety of antibias and antiracist curricula that have been developed for use in the K-12 school curriculum.

A formal study of the components of this knowledge base is necessary if schools, colleges, and departments of education expect graduates to be comfortable discussing racism among racially diverse peers and teaching about racism in the classroom. A formal study of this knowledge base is

also necessary to provide an informed factual context within which preservice and inservice teachers can examine their own attitudes toward members of diverse races, cultures, social classes, genders, and sexual orientations.

Synthesizing the Knowledge Base on Racism for Teacher Education Programs

What to include among the essential elements of a knowledge base on racism and how to present and teach the material to preservice and inservice teachers are exacerbated by several factors. First, the body of literature that has accumulated over the last half century is enormous. Second, a historical silent conspiracy to omit the formal study of racism and the tendency to deny the existence of racism have resulted in preservice and inservice teachers' having very little prior knowledge about racism, limited experience in discussing racism, and even less experience in examining their own attitudes toward people who differ from themselves. A third factor affecting the content and process of this knowledge base centers on the individual teacher educator's knowledge about racism and level of comfort as the instructional facilitator. What is recommended here is a head-on, thorough treatment of racism as a fundamental knowledge base in teacher education programs since the courses teacher education students typically take outside the school, college, or department of education usually do not provide sufficient treatment of the topic.

There exist many sources for academic definitions of key terms such as *prejudice, discrimination,* and *personal* and *institutional racism,* but locating a single source that provides sufficient introduction to the history of racism in the United States is a greater challenge. *Think about Racism* (Mizell, 1992) is one recommended text that contains both basic definitions and a history of racism. Written for an audience with a below college reading level, Mizell's text is a quick-read that provides the opportunity to fill in gaps in preservice and inservice teachers' knowledge about the history of racism in the Americas and the United States from 1492 to about the 1980s.

A recommended college-level text for remediating preservice and inservice teachers' lack of knowledge about the history of racism in the United States is *A Different Mirror: A History of Multicultural America* (Takaki, 1993). Retelling the history of the United States throuh the voices of African Americans, Asian Americans, Latinos, Native Americans, and others, Takaki's *A Different Mirror* provides numerous examples of prejudice, discrimination, and personal and institutionalized racism that have a powerful effect on the views and attitudes of undergraduate and graduate students in teacher education programs.

There is a rich extensive legacy of literature on the element of this knowledge base that centers upon theory and research regarding how and to what degree racial attitudes and prejudices are learned and integrated into the self-image, personality structure, and identity of Whites and persons of color. This literature includes the earlier classic works generated during the 1950s by Allport (1954) and Adorno, et al. (1950), perhaps in an effort to understand how the shocking atrocities of the Holocaust during World War II could have occurred. A more contemporary source that provides a synthesis and reinterpretation of the early literature and new literature is *Impacts of Racism on White Americans* (Bowser & Hunt, 1996). Several contributing authors of this edited volume synthesize literature on theoretical models of racism and research studies that examine racism as pathological and in the context of a mental illness continuum.

Since many preservice and inservice teachers perceive racism as "normal," the value of their studying the literature on racism as mental illness is obvious. Classic research studies that document racial attitudes and behavior in U.S. society are also an important part of the knowledge base on racism that preservice and inservice teachers must study. Perhaps the most comprehensive review of empirical evidence from survey research from 1940 to 1986 on White-Black racial attitudes available for teacher educators to use in their classes is provided in *Common Destiny: Blacks and American Society* (Jaynes & Willians, 1989). A more contemporary study of inter-group relations and beliefs among European Americans, Asian Americans, Latino Americans, and African Americans that is representative of the type of research preservice and inservice teachers should study is *Taking America's Pulse* (National Conference, 1994).

Some of the theory and research on changing racial attitudes and attitudes toward diversities other than race harkens back to literature reviewed in the chapter on Knowledge Base 2, particularly the literature on ethnic identity development (Banks, 1988c, 1992; Bennett, 1986). This previously reviewed literature can be expanded through such sources as *Preventing Prejudice: A Guide for Counselors and Educators* (Ponterotto & Pederson, 1993). Other literature on changing the racial attitudes and attitudes toward diversity of preservice and inservice teachers is discussed under Knowledge Base 12. However, a considerable body of "attitude-change"

> *Most instruments used to measure change in racial attitudes and behavior...are of a "homemade" variety developed by researchers for a specific research study...*

literature outside the field of teacher education on the U.S. population at-large and other samples exists in the behavioral science fields.

Three chapters in the *Handbook of Research on Multicultural Education* (Banks & Banks, 1995) that present reviews of the research literature on modifying racial and gender role attitudes and promotive positive intergroup relations are exceptionally suitable for teacher educators to use as required readings in teacher education courses. Perhaps the best existing review of research studies on modifying K-12 students' racial and gender role attitudes is the chapter by J.A. Banks (1995), "Multicultural Education: Its Effects on Students' Racial and Gender Role Attitudes." Banks' treatise is an exceptional instructional aid for teacher educators because it presents a historical review of studies from 1929 to the present and a balanced critique of research studies that have examined the effects of curriculum units and courses, curriculum materials, and teaching methods on the racial and gender role attitudes of K-12 students. A chapter by Slavin (1995) reviews and synthesizes research studies that have examined the effects of cooperative learning on modifying racial attitudes and cross-racial and cross-ethnic social relationships. A chapter by Schofield (1995) reviews strategies on the structural and policy levels that foster positive relations among many different racial and ethnic groups. Although Schofield's chapter is not intended to be a review of research studies, it is a significant review of research-based theory that should be read by preservice and inservice teachers.

Teacher educators searching for attitude scales and instruments that measure racial attitudes and behaviors or that measure attitudes toward diversity to have preservice and inservice teachers review or to use in research will find this aspect of Knowledge Base 8 least available and in most need of development. Most instruments used to measure change in racial attitudes and behavior or attitudes toward diversity are of a "homemade" variety developed by researchers for a specific research study or are often adapted versions of the Social Distance Scale developed by Bogardus (1939). An exception is the *Diversity Awareness Profile* (Grote, 1991), a published instrument with reliability literature but no published validity literature as yet. A second exception is the *Multicultural Efficacy Scale* (Guyton

& Wesche, 1996), an instrument designed specifically to measure the multicultural efficacy of preservice teachers A...along with multicultural teacher education dimensions of intercultural experiences, minority group knowledge, attitudes about diversity and knowledge of teaching skills in multicultural settings (p.1)." An instrument designed to measure cross-cultural adaptability beliefs and behaviors in training environments is the Cross-Cultural Adaptability Inventory (CCAI) developed by Kelly and Meyers (1993). The CCAI does have a research base supportive of reliability and some forms of validity. However, as yet, as far as the author knows, no comprehensive measurement handbook has been developed that provides an extensive list of instruments designed to measure attitudes toward diversity and describes the reliability and validity literature for each instrument.

Teacher educators who are just beginning to collect anti-bias curricula for demonstration purposes and for preservice and inservice teachers to examine and evaluate will find abundant resources. These resources include commercially developed curriculum kits and professionally developed curriculum programs for students from preschool ages through adulthood. *Anti-Bias Curriculum: Tools for Empowering Young Children* (Derman-Sparks, 1989), *Educator's Guide to Strait Talk About America* (The National Conference, 1994), *The Multicultural Caterpillar: Children's Activities in Cultural Awareness* (Matiella, 1990), *Words Can Hurt You: Beginning A Program of Anti-Bias Education* (Thompson, 1993), *A World of Difference Institute: Elementary Study Guide* (Mattenson, Batiste, & Berman, 1994); *Different and the Same* (Family Communications, 1995), and a multitude of similar curriculum resources distributed by Educators for Social Responsibility are illustrative of this genre of curriculum resources.[2] In addition, teacher educators who are building the curriculum library resources on antiracist education will find such programs regularly reviewed in *Multicultural Education, Multicultural Review*, and *Teaching Tolerance*.[3]

Several special references cut across some of the essential elements of this knowledge base and are useful in teacher education courses to stimulate preservice and inservice teachers' self-reflection about their racial attitudes and their assumptions about the distribution of power. Among these are "White Racism" by Sleeter (1994), "The Silenced Dialogue: Power and Pedagogy in Educating Other People's Children" by Delpit (1990), and "Whites in Multicultural Education: Rethinking Our Role" by Howard (1993). Perspectives presented in these articles have instructive relevance to both White and minority preservice and inservice teachers.

Similarly, some extraordinary personal narratives written by White females and males about their personal growth from ethnocentric attitudes toward open multicultural attitudes constitute another genre of literature with exceptional instructive value to preservice and inservice teachers, particularly those of European American heritage. Recommended personal narratives include *The Education of a WASP* by Stalvey (1970), "White Privilege: Unpacking the Invisible Knapsack" by McIntosh (1990) "Paths for Multiculturalism: One Perspective" by McGinnis (1994), and quotations of monocultural graduates in a study conducted by Fuller (1994). References that provide useful college-level activities for teaching about racism and bias against diversity include *Hate, Prejudice, and Racism* by Kleg (1993) and *Multicultural Teaching in the University* by Schoem et al. (1993). These references can also provide perspectives that enable preservice and inservice teachers to understand how personal and institutional racism are translated into school policy and practice described in Knowledge Base 9.

In the final analysis, teacher educators who infuse the knowledge base on foundations of racism into the teacher education curriculum must address racism's relationship to other forms of bigotry. Logical relationships between the foundations of racism and other types of bigotry addressed in other knowledge bases have implications for curriculum design. After all, racism is but one manifestation of the larger problem of bigotry in the United States. Bigotry is bigotry—whether it is based on social class, gender, sexual orientation, or any other characteristic that marks one as different. In Knowledge Base 9, manifestations of classism, institutional racism, and other forms of bigotry are addressed in the context of policies and practices that perpetuate inequities in the educational system for minority, poor, female, handicapped, and gay and lesbian students. Sexism and homophobia are addressed in Knowledge Base 12. Curriculum designers at some institutions may find treatment of all forms of bigotry in a single course or unit of study the most effective organization for sequencing curriculum content in the teacher education program. Others may find that various forms of bigotry are best treated in different courses as discreetly separate but related curriculum strands.

CHAPTER 10

Knowledge Base 9: *Effects of Policy and Practice on Culture, Race, Gender, and Other Categories of Diversity*

An educator in a system oppression is either a revolutionary or an oppressor.

— Lerone Bennett

A study of the theory and research about the differential effects of policy and practice on culture, race, class, gender, and other categories of diversity should be a major knowledge base in teacher education programs. The major purpose of this knowledge base is to expose preservice and inservice teachers to policies and practices that (a) perpetuate inequity and unfairness in the education system, particularly for minority, poor, female, handicapped, and gay and lesbian students; (b) result in meritocratic rather than democratic schooling; (c) and permeate the education system from kindergarten through higher education and are traceable to federal, state, district, school building, and classroom levels of origin. This knowledge base also consists of a study of the connections between policies and practices that have harmful effects on traditionally excluded and disenfranchised minority and low SES student populations and the inequitable distribution of economic resources and political power among these groups in the larger American society. More specifically, the content of this knowledge base centers upon the effects of such policies and practices as (a) ability grouping and curriculum tracking; (b) segregated schools by race and social class; (c) school choice, privatization and vouchers; (d) inequitable school funding; (e) disciplining students, (f) teacher expectations and teacher-student interactions; and (g) standardized

testing. In addition, this knowledge base includes the research studies on the effects of integrated schooling on public school students.

Much of the research literature of this knowledge base is summarized in textbooks published for use in sociology of education courses at the graduate level such as Ballantine's *Sociology of Education* (1993) and, to some extent, some textbooks written for use in undergraduate foundations of education courses. However, there seems to be no single source, a textbook or a "ready-made" publication, that includes all of the related sub-parts of this knowledge base as it is conceptualized here. The presentation of the research base for this knowledge base is, more often than not, scattered throughout various textbooks and is not organized into an impressive, stand-alone knowledge base that forces preservice and inservice teachers to delve intensively into an examination of policies and practices that are detrimental to the education of most minority students. Preservice teachers need to be able to see how the policies and practices examined in this knowledge base interact with each other and collectively work in concert to support an educational system that disproportionately favors middle-class White students but mitigates against high-quality education for most poor children and children of color. Thus, the case being made here is that the theory and research for this knowledge base must be packaged to form a single unit of study in the teacher education curriculum.

Preservice and inservice teachers need to address such questions as the following: Do these policies and practices constitute a deliberate conspiracy perpetrated by those who have power in the society to preserve privilege for themselves and exclude historically disenfranchised groups? Why? Why not? If specific policies and practices are known to have negative effects on equity for some racial groups, females, poor students, physically challenged students, and gay and lesbian students, why are they continued? Why are they not changed? What are the political forces in the society that support retention of policies that have inequitable results for minorities? What political forces and groups in the society support reform and elimination of such policies and practices? How are conservative and liberal ideologies related to policies of exclusion?

Synthesizing the Knowledge Base on Educational Policies and Practices That Are Harmful to Diverse Student Populations

The organization and presentation of Knowledge Base 9 in teacher education programs should be accomplished in a manner that enables preservice and inservice teachers to gain the academic skills necessary to increase their critical literacy and develop a critical understanding of power and patterns of cultural reproduction. As noted above, examples of organizing the content of Knowledge Base 9 in a manner that causes preservice teachers and inservice teachers to question school policies and practices that mitigate against equality are "Chapter 3: Education and the Process of Stratification" and "Chapter 4: Sex, Race, and Attempts to Achieve Equality of Educational Opportunity" in *The Sociology of Education: A Systematic Analysis* by Ballantine (1993). In these two chapters, Ballantine provides a compact, thorough synthesis of the literature on ability grouping and curriculum tracking, choice policies and practices, and segregated schools. Another reference that is suitable for use as a text in teacher education courses is *Choosing Equality: The Case for Democratic Schooling* by

Bastian, et al. (1986). Although somewhat dated, this book aptly synthesizes some of the research on deleterious effects of policies and practices on minority students in the context of conservative power and its influence to insure that meritocratic education rather than democratic education remains the preferred model for education in the United States.

Ability Grouping and Curriculum Tracking. Teacher educators who are assembling their own resources to support Knowledge Base 9 will find no shortage of articles and books that summarize research studies documenting the deleterious effects of ability grouping and curriculum tracking on females, minority, and low SES students. Illustrative classic studies and extensive reviews of research literature that constitute the research base on ability grouping and curriculum tracking and that should be studied by preservice and inservice teachers include the works of Rist (1973), Oakes (1985, 1986, 1990), Slavin (1990), Wheelock (1992), Hallinan and Sorensen (1986), and Hallinan (1990). Another important source is the excellent synthesis provided by Irvine (1990) of historical evidence that homogenous tracking is the "one educational practice that seems to contribute most to the miseducation and nonachievement of Black children" (p. 9).

With regard to the research base for documenting the negative impact of ability grouping and curriculum tracking on Hispanic students, preservice and inservice teachers should be exposed to the results of the extensive study conducted by Meier and Stewart (1991). Using OCR data from surveys for 1968 to 1982, the 1984 survey, and the 1986 survey, Meier and Stewart examined grouping and discipline practices and concluded:

> Three distinct educational patterns emerge. The education experiences for Mexican Americans follow the classic pattern found for Black students. Mexican Americans are disproportionately assigned to lower academic groups and kept out of higher academic groups. They are punished more frequently and are less likely to finish high school. The pattern for Puerto Ricans is different. Puerto

Ricans are not disproportionately grouped in lower academic group classes and are not disproportionately punished or suspended. They do not get access to gifted classes, however, and are expelled in greater numbers. The end result is similar to that for Mexican Americans—high dropout rates and low high school graduation rates. Only Cuban Americans avoid the general pattern. While Cuban Americans also do not get access to gifted classes, they are not assigned disproportionately to lower academic group classes, they are not excessively punished, and they finish high school more often than their classmates.

The patterns of access to educational opportunity reflect, in part, the social class differences among the Hispanic communities. Cuban American educational patterns mirror the advantages of middle-class status except for access to gifted classes. Mexican American patterns and, to a lesser extent Puerto Rican patterns, are also consistent with their lower-socioeconomic class status. (pp. 137-138)

Other important syntheses of research studies on the effects of ability grouping and curriculum tracking by ethnicity, race, gender, and social class

> *One genre of theory and research literature that should be introduced to preservice and inservice teachers centers upon the long history of scientific racism associated with the measurement of intelligence in the United States.*

are discussed further in Knowledge Base12: Gender and Sexual Orientation.

School Segregation, Desegregation, and Integration. The literature on school segregation, desegregation, and integration should be studied by preservice and inservice teachers in far greater depth than is presently the case in most traditional teacher education programs. Most foundations textbooks devote little more than 10 pages to these topics and therefore, do not force teacher education students to confront how their personal lifestyle choices and the lifestyle choices of previous generations have complemented educational policies that have maintained a racially segregated society. Further-more, the more in-depth preservice and inservice teachers study this body of literature the more likely teacher educators will have to deal with university students, particularly, conservative White students, who find the subject matter unsavory. Nevertheless, the essential elements of this body of literature include (a) classic court cases such as *Brown v. Board of Education, Board of Education of Oklahoma City Public Schools v. Dowell, Freeman v. Pitts*, etc.; (b) research studies that document White flight, White resistance to achieving full integration of schools, and the current status and effectiveness of such desegregation programs as busing, magnet schools, and other voluntary and involuntary plans (Coleman, et al., 1966, 1990; Orfield, 1983, 1992; Orntstein, 1991; Green and Pettigrew, 1976; Wilson, 1985; Crain, Mahard, and Narot, 1982; Smock and Wilson, 1991); and (c) research studies that document the effects of desegregated school environments on achievement, interracial relation-ships, and self-esteem (Braddock II, Crain, and McPartland, 1984; Sage, 1978; Patchen, 1982; Wortman, 1983; Alejandro and Wilson, 1976; Hauser and Anderson, 1991; McPartland, Dawkins, Braddock II, Crain, and Strauss, 1985; Grant, 1984; Blank, 1984; Rossell, 1990; Doyle and Levine, 1984; and Rosenberg and Simmons, 1971). With regard to a historical treatment of studies on the effects of desegregated school environments on interracial relationships and attitudes, teacher educators will also want to read "Schools and Opportunities for Multicultural Contact" by Marrett, Mizuno and Collins (1992).

Several important recent references will help teacher educators to update themselves on the contemporary theoretical advances and the results of recent studies on the effects of desegregation. Two such references are *School Desegregation Research: New Directions in Situation Analysis* edited by Prager, et al. (1986) and *Desegregation Analysis Report* by Trent (1991). An important literature review by Wells and Crain (1994) is helpful to teacher educators for identifying the parameters of research on the long-term effects of desegregation, a body of literature that should be included in teacher education programs. Their review is couched in Braddock's (1980) perpetuation theory and organizes studies into three topical categories—occupational aspirations and expectations, occupational attainment and educational levels, and adult social networks. In brief, they concluded that African American students who attended desegregated schools, when compared to their counterparts who attended segregated schools, set occupational aspirations at higher levels, had occupational levels that were more realistically related to their educational aspirations, attain higher educational levels, work in desegregated employment environments, work more often in white-collar and professional jobs than government or blue-collar jobs. One excellent article that summarizes most of the research studies from 1980 to 1994 on the effects of desegregation on the lives of students is *The Continuing Significance of Desegregation: School Racial Composition and African American Inclusion in American Society* by Dawkins and Braddock (1994).

A second suitable synthesis of research studies on the effects of desegregation that can be used as an assigned reading in teacher education courses is "Review of Research on Desegregation's Impact on Elementary and Secondary School Students" by Schofield (1995), a chapter in *Handbook of Research on Multicultural Education* (Banks & Banks, 1995). Schofield's extant review examines the effects of desegregation on academic achievement, dropout and suspension rates, educational and occupational outcomes, and self-esteem of African American, Hispanic American, White, and selected other racial and ethnic groups.

The research and scholarship of Gary Orfield and his colleagues in the Harvard Project on School Desegregation often provide the most recent analyses of data and conclusions regarding national trends in desegregating schools. *Dismantling Desegregation: The Quiet Reversal of Brown v. Board of Education* by Orfield, Eaton, & the Harvard Project on School Desegregation (1996) is an outstanding starter reference work for teacher educators and graduate students to educate themselves about this element of Knowledge Base 9. An excellent shorter report to use by teacher educators as an assigned reading for undergraduates is *Deepening Segregation in American Public Schools* by Orfield, Bachmeier, James & Eitle (1997). This report provides data to show that presently the Northern states are more segregated than the Southern states and the Southern states are more segregated now than they were in the 1980s. Other essential findings include trends of accelerated segregation of African American and Latino students, a strong relationship between segregation by race and segregation by poverty, and the impact of recent conservative court decisions that have been reversing the *Brown* decision.

School Choice, Privatization, and Vouchers. Related to the literature on the effects of segregation and desegregation on minority learners is the literature on the effects of school choice, privatization, and voucher plans on minority students' access to quality education. Presently, this literature is far more theoretical than research-based and consists of rational arguments for and against these three related policies and practices. In general, conservative writers support school choice, privatization, and vouchers as "democratic" policies aimed at improving education for all students. In contrast, liberal, progressive educators criticize these policies as disguised methods of social control to maintain a meritocratic educational system that drains resources from the public schools and that resegregates school populations by race and social class. A few writers, however, argue in favor of choice programs from a liberal perspective. Because choice, privatization, and voucher programs are new, research studies that assess the effects of these programs are few. The limited studies that have been conducted, however, tend to support the criticism of liberal theorists that choice programs give the White middle class *first* choice and do not improve schooling for low-income and minority youth.

Teacher educators who are compiling resources for infusing a unit of study on choice, privatization, and voucher policies will want to examine a number of starter resources. Works illustrative of theoretical arguments in support of choice and vouchers are *Politics, Markets, and America's Schools* by Chubb and Moe (1990) and *Education by Choice: The Case for Family Control* by Coons and Sugarman (1978). Chubb and Moe argue in favor of choice from a conservative perspective; Coons and Sugarman argue in favor of choice from a liberal perspective. Diverse perspectives on choice issues are presented in *Public Dollars for Private Schools: The Case of Tuition Tax Credits* by James and Levin (1983), *Choice and Control in American Education* by Clune and Witte (1990), and *Choice in Education: Potential and Problems* by Boyd and Walberg (1990). Liberal theoretical arguments critical of choice, privatization, and voucher policies are presented in *False Choices: Why School Vouchers Threaten Our Children's Future* edited by Lowe and Miner (1992) and parts of *Savage Inequalities: Children in America's Schools* by Kozol (1991). Starter sources for identifying the limited but emerging research base on choice policies include works by Manski (1992), Glenn (1993), Bauch (1993), Bridge and Blackman (1978), Catterall (1983), Levy (1986), Maddaus (1988), and the survey of choice initiatives, *A Special Report: School Choice*, conducted by the Carnegie Foundation for the Advancement of Teaching (1992).

Inequitable School Financing. To be literate regarding practices and policies that mitigate against high quality education for poor and minority students, preservice and inservice teachers need to experience a well-designed unit of study that documents unequal school financing methods. Although some textbooks such as *Those Who Can, Teach* by Ryan and Cooper (1992) written for Foundations of Education courses provide rudimentary coverage on the topic of school financing, most preservice and too many inservice teachers doubt that gross inequities within and across school districts favor the children of the elite wealthy and White middle class and disfavor the children from most poor and minority backgrounds. Minimally, the essential elements of school financing as a unit of study in teacher education programs ought to include (a) profiles of data that show U.S. per-pupil expenditure as ranking low compared to many industrialized nations (Nelson, 1991; *Shortchanging Education*, 1990); (b) graphic profiles of unequal distribution of funds for schools within and across U.S. districts (Kozol, 1991); (c) case studies and profiles of court cases regarding unconstitutional school-funding formulas in Alaska, Connecticut, Indiana, Kentucky, New Jersey, Michigan, Minnesota, North Dakota, Oregon, Tennessee, Texas, and other states (*Rich Schools, Poor Schools*, 1989); and (d) case studies of political influence in school finance (Timar and Shimasaki, 1993).

Discipline. Preservice and inservice teachers should also study the research literature that documents disproportionate and discriminatory discipline practices on students of color, particularly African American and Hispanic American students. Excellent reviews of this research literature have already been conducted. Irvine (1990) and Meier, Stewart, and England (1989) have conducted extensive reviews of the effects of disproportionate suspension, expulsion, and corporal punishment on African American students. In addition, Meier and Stewarts' *The Politics of Hispanic Education: Un paso pa'lante y dos pa'tras* (1991), a landmark study of second-generation discrimination patterns in the educational experiences of Mexican Americans, Cuban Americans, and Puerto Rican Americans, is perhaps the most extensive examination of not only discipline procedures but also many other policies and practices such as segregated schools, ability grouping, and curriculum tracking that are described as parts of Knowledge Base 9.

Teacher Expectations and Teacher-Student Interactions. The theory and research literature on the differential effects of teacher expectations and types of teacher-student interactions on minority, female, and lower social class students is an essential element of the knowledge base on bad classroom practice that preservice and inservice teachers should study in a culturally responsive teacher education program. Both the teacher expectation research and the teacher-student interaction research have a long history of criticism, praise, interpretation, reinterpretation, and sometimes contradictory findings; but a clear best-evidence set of patterns has emerged. In fact, a good many textbooks used currently in traditional teacher education programs include fairly comprehensive summaries of both of these bodies of literature that document negative patterns in the education system for too many minority, female, and low social class students. The purpose of including these two bodies of research in teacher education is obvious. Without studying the research on teacher expectations and teacher-student interactions, preservice and inservice teachers are not likely to have the knowledge necessary to identify a key problem of inequality for historically undereducated students and to support the moral reasoning to take a reconstructionist approach to eliminating inequality in their own classrooms and the school districts where they work. Although the research base cited in this section includes some findings regarding gender as a variable in the teacher expectancy and teacher-student interaction literature, the greater emphasis is on race and social class. The research base on gender is addressed more comprehensively in the discussion on Knowledge Base 12.

Teacher Expectations. The effects of low teacher expectations in creating a self-fulfilling prophecy of low achievement for students of color is well-documented and should be studied by preservice and inservice teachers if the historical under-education of most minority students is to be reversed. Despite the existence of at least two decades of theory and research regarding the detrimental effects of low teacher expectations, there is little evidence that the curriculum of teacher preparation programs has had much success in changing low teacher expectations for students, particularly minority students and low SES minority ethnic and White students.

The research base regarding bias in teachers' expectations overlaps considerably with the research base on teacher-student interactions since both expectations and interactions frequently have been studied concomitantly. Generally, the research

indicates that, throughout the educational pipeline from preschool through high school, both preservice and inservice teachers have higher expectations for White middle class students than African American, Hispanic American, and working class and low SES White students. The weight of the evidence also indicates that White teachers have lower expectations for African American students than do African American teachers. Teacher educators who wish to create their own organization of research literature on teacher expectations regarding African American students will find numerous studies (Gottlieb, 1964; Meyer & Lindstrom, 1969; Brown, et al., 1970; Williams, 1970; Howe, 1971; Woodward & Salzer, 1971; Braxton & Bullock, 1972; Byers & Byers, 1972; Coates, 1972; Byalick & Bersoff, 1974; Word, et al., 1974; Eaves, 1975; Harvey & Slavin, 1975; Peck et al., 1977; Hillman & Davenport, 1978; Lietz & Gregory, 1978; Barnes, 1978; Bennett, 1979; Feldman & Orchowsky, 1979; Taylor, 1979; Beady & Hansell, 1980; Cornbleth & Korth, 1980; Griffen & London, 1980; Scott & Ntegeye, 1980; Washington, 1980; Aloia, Maxwell, & Aloia, 1981; Aaron & Powell, 1982; Washington, 1982; Simpson & Erickson, 1983; L. Grant, 1984).

Although the research literature on teacher expectations for Hispanic students and low SES White students is not as voluminous as for African American students, a research base does exist for infusion into teacher education programs. Preservice and inservice teachers should be introduced to a number of studies on teacher expectations for Hispanic students (U.S. Civil Rights, 1974; Jensen & Rosenfeld, 1974; Figueroa & Gallegos, 1978; Wilkerson, 1980; Campos, 1983; and Matute-Bianchi, 1986), as well as studies that document bias in teacher expectations for low SES White students (Rist, 1973; Harvey & Slavin, 1975; Adams & Cohen, 1976; Ogbu, 1978; Bennett, 1979; Metheny, 1979; Smith, 1979; Reck, 1982; and Reck, et al., 1987).

Some special references and already existing syntheses of teacher expectancy research merit the attention of teacher educators who are organizing their own literature reviews. *Teacher Expectancies,* edited by Dusek (1985), is an excellent general reference. Two literature reviews on teacher expectations and African American students are those conducted by Baron, Tom, and Cooper (1985) and by Irvine (1990), both of which conclude that race is an operative factor in the teacher expectancy research.

Teacher-Student Interactions. The findings of Sadker and Sadker (1987) summarize a trend of repeated consistency found in research on teacher-student interaction conducted by other researchers. In general, teacher-student interactions decrease in quality and quantity in descending order for White males, minority males, White females and minority females, although a number of studies indicate that Black females receive more positive teacher-student intellectual interactions than do Black males who typically experience frequent but negative interactions with teachers. More specifically, the research literature documents the following findings:

■ Teachers praise White students more than African American students and most Hispanic students.

■ Teachers criticize African American and Mexican American students more than White students.

■ Teachers direct more questions to White students than to African American, Native American, and Hispanic students.

■ Teachers respond to more questions asked by White students than asked by African American and Native American students.

■ Teachers discipline and verbally criticize working class White students more than middle class students.

■ Teachers are more authoritarian and less democratic or open with African American students than with White students.

■ Teachers direct more questions to male students than to female students but are likely to direct more questions to

White females than to African American and Native American males.

■ When teachers praise African American students, the praise is likely to be routine rather than for a specific achievement or behavior. Praise for African American students is more often qualified than for White students.

■ White teachers demonstrate more concern for White female students' academic work than African American females' academic work and demonstrate more concern for African American females' behavior.

The research base to support the above findings for infusion into the teacher education curriculum is extensive (Datta, et al., 1969; Leacock, 1969; St. John, 1971; Rubovitz & Maehr, 1973; Brophy and Good, 1974; Byalick & Bersoff, 1974; Jackson & Cosca, 1974; U.S. Commission on Civil Rights, 1974; Appleford, et al, 1976; Dweck & Bush, 1976; Friedman, 1976; Persell, 1977; Laosa, 1977; DeMeis & Turner, 1978; Hillman & Davenport, 1978; Marwit, et al, 1978; McGhan, 1978; Guilmet, 1979; Huffine, et al, 1979; Safilios-Rothschild, 1979; Brophy and Evertson, 1981; Scritchfield & Picou, 1982; Smith, 1982; Tobias, et al., 1982; Buriel, 1983; Dusek & Joseph, 1983; Hamilton, 1983; Simpson & Erickson, 1983; Tobias, et al., 1983; L. Grant, 1984; Damico & Scott, 1985; L. Grant 1985; Muñoz-Hernández & Santiago Santiago, 1985; and Woolridge & Richman, 1985).

Teacher educators who are searching for already existing syntheses of research literature on teacher-student interaction to include in teacher education programs are directed to the works of Irvine (1990), Meier, et al. (1989), Meier and Stewart (1991) and Grossman and Grossman (1994). Irvine's review is one of the most comprehensive contemporary examinations of teacher interactions with African American students and, unlike many reviews, organizes the findings of studies by lower elementary, upper elementary, and junior-high grade levels to develop profiles of the different experiences of

African American female and male students as they progress through the educational system. In addition, her review examines both student-initiated interactions and public response opportunities in classrooms. Meier, et al. (1989) synthesize the research literature on teacher-student interactions as part of their own study of such second-generation discrimination factors as discipline, ability grouping, and curriculum tracking in the educational experiences of African American students. Meier and Stewart (1991) briefly review the research literature on teacher-student interaction in a corresponding study of second-generation discrimination in the educational experiences of Hispanic students. Grossman and Grossman (1994) focus their review of teacher-student interaction studies in the context of both gender and ethnicity.

Standardized Testing. Another important part of Knowledge Base 9 consists of the theory and research on the disproportionate and discriminatory effects of standardized testing on many ethnic minority, female, and poor White students. Minimally, preservice and inservice teachers ought to study (a) test-score profiles that show differences in mean scores by ethnicity/race, gender, and socioeconomic status on I.Q. tests, tests used for ability grouping and curriculum tracking, college admissions, awarding academic scholarships, graduate and professional school admissions, and teacher certification; (b) profiles of elimination rates by ethnicity/race, gender, and socioeconomic status; (c) the validity and lack of validity literature on the major tests used in the kindergarten through higher education system; and (d) research studies that document the discriminatory effects of using standardized tests to allocate educational opportunity. The academic content and theory and research regarding standardized testing are discussed in more detail in the following section on Knowledge Base 10 where assessment and test use are treated as a stand-alone separate knowledge base.

Thus, standardized testing is mentioned here in Knowledge Base 9 only in its close relationship to ability grouping and curriculum tracking and as one of several policies and practices that have damaging discriminatory effects on historically disenfranchised groups of students.

In summary, the power of Knowledge Base 9 to increase the critical literacy and change the views of preservice and inservice teachers is dependent upon their understanding of how a cluster of many policies and practices work in concert to mitigate against democratic education. If teacher educators are to employ a critical pedagogy that challenges students and teachers to empower themselves to teach social activism for justice and to advance democracy and equality, the subcomponents of Knowledge Base 9 must be integrated and presented as a single unit of study in teacher education programs. Suitable treatises to include in instructional packets of readings for preservice and inservice teachers to facilitate the application of critical pedagogy include "Inequality and Access to Knowledge" by Linda Darling-Hammond (1995) and "Research on Racial Issues in Higher Education" by C. Bennett (1995). Darling-Hammond's examination of institutionally sanctioned discrimination in access to education provides research-based information to enable preservice and inservice teachers to craft and answer questions regarding funding inequality; access to good teaching, access to courses, curriculum materials, and equipment; and the discriminatory effects of testing and curriculum tracking. Bennett's analysis of racism and discrimination in higher education grounds the teacher education curriculum in the lives of preservice and teachers as higher education students. *Rethinking Our Schools: Teaching for Equity and Social Justice* (Bigelow, Christenson, Karp, Miner & Peterson, 1994) is recommended as an excellent resource to introduce preservice teachers to examples of teaching for social justice in K-12 classroom.

CHAPTER 11

Knowledge Base 10: *Culturally Responsive Diagnosis, Measurement, and Assessment*

A significant segment of society...has experienced and continues to experience testing as a hostile gatekeeper: although tests open gates of opportunity for some, they slam them shut for many others.

— National Commission on Testing and Public Policy

The knowledge base on culturally responsive diagnosis, measurement, and assessment that challenges conventional psychometry is seldom studied by preservice and inservice teachers. This knowledge base consists of (a) a fairly well-defined body of literature of both theory and research in the field of tests and measurements regarding culturally skewed diagnosis, measurement, and assessment of cultural and ethnic minority groups; (b) the validity literature on specific intelligence tests, achievement tests, and aptitude tests; (c) the literature that questions use of testing to allocate educational opportunity in the educational system, K through higher education, of a democratic society; and (d)

> *If preservice and inservice teachers were to study the research and theory that constitute the knowledge base on culturally responsive assessment, they would have good reason to question many current testing practices.*

the growing body of literature on alternative and authentic assessment. Generally, a recurring theme that cuts across the subtopics of this knowledge base is that standardized testing is an antiquated concept and practice in culturally diverse democratic societies.

Historically, preservice teachers have studied only the traditional or "conventional" knowledge base of theory and research regarding testing and its uses and, therefore, enter the classroom with unquestioned acceptance of the value of standardized testing. In contrast, if preservice and inservice teachers were to study the research and theory that constitute the knowledge base on culturally responsive assessment, they would have good reason to question many current testing practices. They also would understand that there are at least four decades of research to show that standardized testing is the least effective means for identifying talents, skills, abilities, and potential across cultures. Furthermore, preservice teachers and inservice teachers who studied the research and specific samples of the data that document the lack of predictive validity for most standardized instruments would understand that, more often than not, standardized tests are screening devices used to confer educational privilege to the already privileged and do little to break up the established social order to enable upward mobility for most poor White students and most students of color. In short, if preservice and inservice teachers are not exposed to this knowledge base, they will not have the knowledge to support the moral reasoning necessary to reject testing as a method of exclusion and to initiate testing reforms. This knowledge base is a critical part of the education of teachers if they are to develop a preference for democratic education over meritocratic education.

Synthesizing the Theory and Research on Culturally Responsive Diagnosis, Measurement, and Assessment

Much of Knowledge Base 10 is found in the "outlaw" literature on testing that has accumulated over the last four decades. In fact, the enormity of this body of literature exceeds the space that can be devoted in this chapter to its identification. However, for teacher educators who need guidance in assembling and synthesizing relevant theory and research for infusion into teacher preparation programs, some key starter references are discussed.

One genre of theory and research literature that should be introduced to preservice and inservice teachers centers upon the long history of scientific racism associated with the measurement of intelligence in the United States. *The Mismeasure of Man* by Gould (1981) provides an excellent historical treatment of scientific racism in the measurement of human abilities. Gould's book and similar books are the sort of literature to which preservice and inservice teachers are seldom exposed and, therefore, must read to have the foundational knowledge to reject contemporary examples of scientific racism and unsupported claims about genetics and intelligence as are found in *The Bell Curve* by Herrnstein and Murray (1994). A thematic issue of *American Behavioral Scientist*, subtitled *The Bell Curve: Laying Bare the Resurgence of Scientific Racism* and edited by Newby (1995), is an excellent collection of eight articles suitable to use as a supplementary text of readings for undergraduate and graduate students. This collection debunks Herrnstein and Murray's spurious reasoning and scholarship in several historical and contemporary contexts that include the measurement of intelligence, the political economy, and racist knowledge construction. Of

particular relevance to Knowledge Base 10 is an article by Nunley (1995) in this collection which argues that neither the concept of intelligence nor its measurement have withstood a cross-cultural test.

Other resources that synthesize the research on both historical and contemporary scientific racism in the measurement of intelligence are *The IQ Mythology: Class, Race, Gender, and Inequality* by Mensh and Mensh (1991) and *The Science and Politics of IQ* by Kamin (1974). The reinterpretation of theory and data regarding heritability and malleability of intelligence by Locurto (1991) in *Sense and Nonsense About I.Q.: The Case for Uniqueness* is also part of this knowledge base.

Several publications that examine the disproportionately damaging effects of standardized testing on Hispanic populations are illustrative of the type of resources that should be introduced to preservice and inservice teachers as part of the research base for Knowledge Base 10. Figueroa and Garcia (1994) have discussed briefly most of the topics identified as constituting essential elements of this knowledge base on culturally responsive assessment and have provided a bibliography that is a starter source for teacher educators who are organizing the theoretical tenets and supportive research studies for classroom instruction in teacher preparation programs. No doubt, more in-depth treatment of the topics in Knowledge Base 10 will be provided in the forthcoming book, *Bilingualism and Psychometrics: A Special Case of Bias* by Valdes and Figueroa (in press). A broad range of issues

> *Very little of the literature of theory or research addresses whether or not alternative or authentic assessments are any less free of bias than are traditional methods of assessment.*

related to the use of standardized tests to block access to higher education and to the teaching profession are treated in *Assessment and Access: Hispanics in Higher Education*, edited by Keller, Deneen and Magallan (1991).

One of the best sources for identifying the existing syntheses of literature and for reading the literature that challenges conventional psychometric theory and practice is *Testing African American Students* edited by Hilliard (1991), a book that is also suitable for use as a text in teacher education programs. Contributing authors describe a broad range of tests—I.Q. tests, developmental inventories, minimum competency tests for students and teachers, aptitude tests, personality inventories and college entrance exams. In addition, the technical inadequacies of existing pen and pencil standardized tests and the misuse of such tests to allocate educational opportunity are addressed in ways that are understandable to preservice and inservice teachers.

Another publication that presents part of Knowledge Base 10 is *From Gatekeeper to Gateway: Transforming Testing in America*, a report published by the National Commission on Testing and Public Policy (1990). Also suitable for use as a text in teacher education courses, this publication presents the commission's eight recommendations regarding testing to which preservice and inservice teachers should be exposed. The extant research base for this report is found in two edited volumes by Gifford (1989a, 1989b), both of which are suitable for the study of this knowledge base at graduate and advanced levels. The second volume in the series by Gifford, *Test Policy and Test Performance: Education, Language, and Culture* (1989b), provides exceptional exposure through chapters by contributing authors to research studies regarding language and cultural factors in testing.

Teacher educators who are assembling the theory and research literature on the emerging part of Knowledge Base 10 that centers on *alternative* and *authentic assessment* so that it can be included in teacher preparation programs are aware, no doubt, of the multitude of articles that have been published in the mainstream professional literature during recent years. Much of this literature is diversity-blind, but some is not. Very little of the literature of theory or research addresses whether or not alternative or authentic assessments are any less free of bias than are traditional methods of assessment. An early classic in this genre of literature on assessment is *Toward a New Science of Educational Testing and Assessment* (Berlak, et al., 1992). Arguing for replacing the conventional psychometric paradigm with a new contextual paradigm for assessment, Berlak and his co-writers draw on much of the theory and research relevant to Knowledge Base 10. Additional sources for constructing a solid body of theory and research for Knowledge Base 10 include works in the area of gifted education such as *Critical Issues in Gifted Education: Defensible Programs for Cultural and Ethnic Minorities* edited by Maker and Schierer (1989). A treatise by Tellez (1996) examines authentic assessment in the context of teacher education programs and teacher evaluation, discusses important emerging differences in definitions regarding authentic, alternative, and traditional assessment, but does not examine such contextual factors as culture, race, ethnicity, gender, and social class. Another diversity-blind treatment of "alternative" assessment is *A Practical Guide to Alternative Assessment* (Herman, Aschbacher, & Winters, 1992). Although this how-to-book makes the point that assessment tasks should not "...reflect variables over which educators have no control, such as a child's culture, sex, or socioeconomic background (p. 78)," no specific guidelines are offered to assure fair and unbiased assessment. In contrast, *Authentic Assessment in Action: Studies of Schools and Students at Work* by Darling-Hammond, Ancess, and Falk (1995) presents case studies of five schools that serve substantial populations of multiracial, multilingual, immigrant low-income, working class, and middle-class students.

Studying Knowledge Base 10 and learning that such screening tests as the ACT, SAT, and GRE, and others have so little predictive validity often shock preservice and inservice teachers. Studying Knowledge Base 10 also enables preservice and inservice teachers, particularly those of middle-class European American heritage, to see for the first time how they have benefitted from privileged societal status and from testing practices that disproportionately favor them and disfavor persons of color and lower socioeconomic status in the educational system.

CHAPTER 12

Knowledge Base 11: *Sociocultural Influences on Subject-Specific Learning*

> Culture influences the way people see things and understand concepts.... If culture determines the way we see a camel, and the number of colors that exist, and how accurate our perception of a certain concept is, may it not also determine the way we think, the way we prove things, the meaning of contradiction, and the logic we use?

— Munir Fasheh

There is a growing knowledge base of theory and research on how sociocultural factors influence subject-specific learning that has not been well integrated as a legitimate knowledge base in most teacher education programs. The theoretical and research literature of this knowledge base centers upon (a) cultural belief systems, values, and expectations that influence a *non-White* ethnic child's learning and achievement in specific subject areas such as standard English, mathematics, science, other languages, reading, art, etc., and (b) linguistic factors of non-native English-speaking groups that influence how students master skills in such specific subjects as mathematics. This knowledge base, perhaps, also includes the body of literature that defines what is known about cultural and social mind-sets and expectations regarding achievement of female and minority students in science, mathematics, and technology. At first glance, this knowledge base appears to be nothing more than a part of some of the previously defined knowledge bases. Clearly dimensions of this knowledge base are related to other knowledge bases, but what distinguishes it as a stand-alone knowledge base is its emphasis upon *subject-specific learning*. That is, a considerable number of scholars have begun to synthesize research and/or theorize about how culture influences learning mathematics as found,

for example, in Cocking and Mestre's *Linguistic and Cultural Influences on Learning Mathematics* (1988) or Orr's *Twice as Less* (1989) which discusses the author's thinking about how Black English influences the way some African American children conceptualize mathematical concepts and relationships.

At this time the knowledge base defined as *cultural influences on subject-specific learning* must be described as emerging and as having some aspects more developed than others, particularly compared to some of the other more fully developed knowledge bases. However, teacher educators, particularly instructors of courses in methods of teaching mathematics or science, would do well to infuse this knowledge base into their courses. Preservice

> *...a considerable number of scholars have begun to synthesize research and/or theorize about how culture influences learning mathematics...*

teachers who have studied this knowledge base in its present evolution of development should be expected, minimally, to understand that there are complex aspects of culture that appear to define circumstances for learning some specific subjects that differ from the cultural and linguistic circumstances of White middle-class, native English-speaking children.

Synthesizing the Theory and Research on Sociocultural Influences on Subject-Specific Learning

Much of this emerging knowledge base about the sociocultural influences on subject-specific learning focuses upon the school subjects of language arts, science, and mathematics. At this time, the literature about sociocultural influences on learning other academic subjects is either non-existent or scanty at best. Most of the literature about sociocultural influences on learning language arts as a subject area has been discussed in the section on Knowledge Base 4. Although much has been written on the contributions from various cultural groups to music, art, dance and other fine and performing arts subjects, little has been written about how students from various cultures learn and achieve in these subjects. A considerable body of literature, however, exists on sociocultural influences on learning science and mathematics.

One of the early attempts to pull scholars together to describe the sociocultural influences on learning specific subjects resulted in *Teaching Academic Subjects to Diverse Learners*, edited by Kennedy (1991). Kennedy requested contributing authors to identify two domains—what teachers should know about the academic subjects of mathematics, science, history, and writing, and what teachers should know about students' knowledge, how they learn, and how their cultural backgrounds affect learning. Many authors fell woefully short of the editor's charge; that is, many authors either wrote only about what teachers should know about the academic subject or wrote only about how culture influences learning "in general" but not necessarily about how students of a particular culture learn specific academic subjects. When authors did try to address all elements of the

charge, cultural influences on subject-specific learning was the most thinly treated topic. Few of the contributing authors directly addressed the question: What does research say about cultural influences on learning mathematics or other specific subjects? However, Grant (1991) addressed what teachers should know about the cultures of their students generally and McDiarmid (1991) made the following recommendations:

① Teachers need to know how school knowledge is perceived in their learners' cultures—their peer, family, and community cultures. Resistance to school authority and knowledge among poor, working-class, minority youngsters is well documented.

② Teachers need to know what kind of knowledge, skills, and commitments are valued in the learners' cultures. Such knowledge is critical to developing representations of subject matter that either bridge or confront the knowledge and understandings that learners bring with them.

③ Teachers need to know about students' prior knowledge of and experience with the subject matter. The frameworks of understanding, based on prior experience, that learners use to make sense out of new ideas and information are also critical if teachers are to represent their subject matter in ways that help students understand. (p.262)

A more successful attempt to have a group of scholars address cultural influences on learning mathematics resulted in the edited volume, *Linguistic and Cultural Influences on Learning Mathematics* by Cocking and Mestre (1988). Contributing authors in this seminal work place greater emphasis upon linguistic influences of language minority students on learning mathematics than upon non-linguistic cultural variables; but this volume does provide a good synthesis of research studies on minority students' access to mathematics instruction, and cultural influences on the higher-order cognitive and reasoning skills needed to learn mathematics.

Similarly, Orr (1987) hypothesizes that Black English function words, such as prepositions, conjunctions, and relative pronouns, interfere with understanding and conveying specific quantitative ideas in mathematics instruction. Baugh (1994), however, refutes Orr's thesis. Both of these perspectives constitute an important part of the knowledge base on linguistic and cultural influences on learning mathematics.

In addition to the previously mentioned references, teacher educators will find three resources to be invaluable in their efforts to assemble the theory and research literature for Knowledge Base 11. Two of the resources treat both mathematics and science. One centers on ethnomathematics. The first is the *Annotated Bibliography of Multicultural Issues in Mathematics Education* by Wilson, Padron, Strutchens, and Thomas (1994). The second is *Multicultural Education: Inclusion of All*, edited by Atwater, Radzik-Marsh, and Strutchens (1994). Within the latter edited book several chapters merit mention as having particular relevance to sociocultural influences on learning mathematics and science. For example, Secada (1994) synthesizes the literature on mathematics teacher's knowledge, beliefs, and decisions about diverse student populations. Wilson and Padron (1994) define *culture-inclusive mathematics education* and review literature on the philosophy and sociology of mathematics, mathematics as sociocultural product and process, and female and minority access to mathematics education. Kahle (1994) synthesizes research literature on gender factors affecting achievement and retention levels of females in science. Frankenstein (1994) defines *critical mathematics education* as a promising, developing strand of this knowledge base. Strutchens (1994) synthesizes literature on theories about general achievement of African American students, factors related specifically to mathematics achievement of African American students, and parental involvement in mathematics achievement.

A third resource is *Ethnomathematics*, a collection of essays edited by Powell and Frankenstein (1997). Intended primarily for mathematicians and math educators, this resource defines ethnomathematical knowledge, challenges

Eurocentrism in mathematics education, uncovers distorted and hidden history of mathematical knowledge, and redefines what should be called mathematical knowledge. Throughout the book, various authors propose that culture shapes one's spatial concepts, logic, ways of knowing, ways of thinking, and many other factors, which, in turn, determine how members of those cultures understand and use mathematics.

In the final analysis, the emerging knowledge base on how culture influences the learning of specific school subjects is less well developed than the other knowledge bases treated in this book. It is difficult to predict either the directions or the pace the theory and research development for Knowledge Base 11 will take. At present, the school subjects are perceived, organized, and presented to students in Western paradigms. Very little in the current literature clarifies precisely how teachers in Western nations can translate what is presently known into practical classroom practice. It is conceivable, eventually, that research related to this knowledge base will reveal more definitively the finite ways cultures with non-Western roots conceptualize, create, and use non-Western patterns of thinking and organization and how these elements influence student understanding in most school subjects—art, music, literature, composition, social studies, mathematics, and science. In truth, much is not known. The important point being made here, however, is that far more is known, particularly in mathematics and science, than most teacher educators probably know. Ultimately, depending on future developments, this knowledge base would appear presently to hold considerable promise for better preparing teachers to teach culturally diverse students.

...there is as great a need to eliminate gender bias and sexual orientation bias from the education system as there is need to eliminate cultural and racial bias.

CHAPTER 13

Knowledge Base 12: *Gender and Sexual Orientation*

Women are simply not endowed by nature with the same measures of single-minded ambition and the will to succeed in the fierce competitive world of Western capitalism.

— Pat Buchanan, G.O.P. presidential primary speech, 1996

Every day I go to work, I'm there to teach integrity.
But how can I teach anything with a closet door in front of me?
`Cause when I look at the faces, one or two see through the lies.
And when I look right back at them, I see the pain of my own youth in their eyes.
It breaks my heart, and makes me feel so ashamed to wear this mask each day from 8 to 3.
I can't reach out to the ones who need a friend, so I must pretend to be one of the enemy.

— Ron Romanovsky, "One of the Enemy," 1991

The two quotations which begin this chapter speak partially to the rationale for including well-defined knowledge bases on gender and sexual orientation in progressive teacher preparation programs. Pat Buchanan's statement is a stark

> *The modern teacher cannot be considered well educated nor prepared for classrooms without having read widely in the feminist literature that challenges traditional male-centered theories of human growth and development.*

reminder that the belief systems of even our educated political leaders are sometimes little more than pronouncements of bigotry. The verse from Romanovsky's song, "One of the Enemy," reminds teacher educators that bigotry and discrimination based on sexual orientation often force gay and lesbian educators, out of fear, into silence, a silence that supports the oppression of gay and lesbian people in our society at large and that results too often in teachers' ignoring the educational, psychological, and emotional needs of gay and lesbian high school students. Thus, distinct bodies of theory and research on gender and sexual orientation constitute knowledge bases that must be infused into modern culturally responsive teacher education programs that profess to prepare teachers to educate today's highly diverse student populations. Indeed, according to research conducted by Sadker and Sadker (1986) on gender equity and by Sears (1992) on attitudes toward gay and lesbian students, there is as great a need to eliminate gender bias and sexual orientation bias from the education system as there is need to eliminate cultural and racial bias.

Gender

Much of what has been written about teacher education and culture can also be said about teacher education and gender. The modern teacher cannot be considered well educated nor prepared for classrooms without having read widely in the feminist literature that challenges traditional male-centered theories of human growth and development. Neither can teachers be considered well educated if they have not studied "the voices of women." It is as important for a teacher to be well grounded in the theory and research that describes how feminists describe school failure, its causes, and its solutions as it is to be well educated in the theory and research that describes how scholars and researchers of color have described the historical undereducation of various ethnic and minority populations. It is as important to understand sexism and sex discrimination as it is racism and race discrimination. It is also as important for the modern teacher to understand the dangers of gender-blind perspectives as it is to understand race-blind or culture-blind perspectives. Furthermore, it is as important to understand gender-sensitive pedagogy as it is to understand culturally responsive pedagogy.

The essential elements of a teacher education knowledge base on gender should include minimally (a) important terms related to the study of gender-inclusive education such as *nonsexist education, gender-free education, gender-sensitive education, nonsexist and culturally inclusive education, feminism, androcentrism, sexism, sex discrimination*, etc; (b) the history of sexism in the United States and a more inclusive accurate history of women's lives and contributions to society; (c) the theory and research on principles of human growth and development, gender identity, and moral development that challenge male-as-norm models; (d) the theory and research literature that documents sex discrimination against females in the education system (teacher-student interaction, testing, learning style and communication style preferences, gender-oppressive language, etc.; (e) principles of nonsexist-

culturally inclusive curriculum development, and principles of establishing gender-sensitive learning environments; and (f) knowledge about the wide array of new regular and supplementary textbooks and materials designed for gender and culture inclusive elementary, middle, and secondary school curricula.

All of the above essential elements of a knowledge base on gender have been organized and synthesized in *Creating a Nonsexist Classroom: A Multicultural Approach* by Theresa Mickey McCormick (1994). Written for use in teacher education programs, McCormick's textbook not only provides a logical organization for a knowledge base on gender but also highlights important points of intersection between gender and such diversity variables as race, culture, and social class. Teacher educators who prefer to develop their own organizational structure for an expanded knowledge base on gender will find McCormick's reference section and recommended readings invaluable.

Written as a textbook to be used in teacher education programs, *Gender Issues in Education* by Grossman and Grossman (1994) presents a somewhat different but logical organization of the essential elements of a teacher education knowledge base on gender. Grossman and Grossman organize theory and research studies to support such relevant topics as gender differences, biological and sociocultural origins of gender differences, philosophical positions about gender equity and gender differences, accommodation of gender differences in

> *Most preservice and inservice teachers are woefully undereducated and underprepared by traditional teacher education programs to deal with educational issues related to sexual orientation.*

educational settings, and reduction of gender-stereotypical behavior in school settings. Within this topical organization, Grossman and Grossman address theory and research regarding teachers' expectations, teachers' evaluations, teacher-student interactions, students' reactions to bias, learning and communication styles, ability grouping, curriculum tracking, discipline, and other significant gender-related topics. Admitting up front that more gender-difference research exists on European American middle-class students than on other ethnic, cultural and social class groups, Grossman and Grossman have, however, presented one of the most comprehensive contemporary compilations of gender-difference research on ethnic groups and socioeconomic classes to be found in the literature. The authors take special care to note what is and is not known through research about gender differences among African American, Hispanic American, Asian American, Native American, European American, recent immigrant groups, and middle-class and working-class groups.

In addition to McCormick's and Grossman and Grossman's textbooks, teacher educators will want to examine the works of Banner (1974), Tavris (1992), and Tavris and Offir (1977) for historical perspectives on sexism and women's history; the works of Matlin (1987), Chodorow (1978, 1989), and Gilligan (1977, 1982) on female identity and moral development; the work of Sadker and Sadker (1987) on teacher-female student interaction; the works of Warren (1989) and Jeanne Brady Giroux (1989) on feminist pedagogy; and the work of Sadker and Sadker (1982) on sex equity in the classroom. Perhaps the most comprehensive single source that presents the work of Sadker and Sadker (1995) and their conception of key elements of a knowledge base on gender is *Failing at Fairness: How Our Schools Cheat Girls*. Appropriate to use as a textbook in teacher preparation courses, this publication centers upon such relevant topics as the hidden messages for females in the traditional school curriculum, the history of woman's education, teacher-student interaction patterns that discriminate against females, female identity and self-esteem, discrimination against females based on the use of standardized tests to allocate educational opportunity, and the miseducation of males.

Curriculum resources and lesson plan idea books suitable for kindergarten through grade 12 that parallel elements of the knowledge base on gender and that should be examined by preservice and inservice teachers are too numerous to list here. However, notable sources from which such materials can be ordered include the National Women's History Project and the Women's Educational Equity Act Publishing Center (WEEA). Curriculum materials from these and other sources suitable for the curriculum library collections are periodically reviewed in *Multicultural Education* and *The Multicultural Review*. These two publications also regularly review printed resources and films suitable for use by teacher educators to present the gender knowledge base in college-level teacher education courses.

Sexual Orientation

Most preservice and inservice teachers are woefully undereducated and underprepared by traditional teacher education programs to deal with educational issues related to sexual orientation. The topics of scholarship and research that have emerged in this field of study over the last two decades suggest that the minimal essential elements of a teacher education knowledge base on sexual orientation ought to include (a) foundation knowledge about human sexuality including gay, lesbian, and bisexual identity development and personal empowerment; (b) the unique psychological, emotional, and educational needs of gay, lesbian, and bisexual students, including research studies on internalized homophobia, alienation, and other psychosocial aspects of peer, family, and societal rejection and acceptance; (c) contemporary survey profiles and literature that present public attitudes regarding homosexuality; (d) a study of the personal lives and voices of gay, lesbian, and bisexual teachers and students; (e) an examination of gay and lesbian sexual orientation in a variety of cultural contexts, i.e., African American, Hispanic American, Asian American, Native American, European American, etc. and in the context of other diversity variables such as social class, gender, and religion; (f) a history of case law on gay and lesbian teacher dismissal and credential revocation and on gay and lesbian students; and (g) examination of and knowledge about curriculum and school materials suitable for instruction about the historical contributions to society of notable gay and lesbian persons, instruction for developing self-acceptance among gay and lesbian students and peer acceptance and tolerance for gay and lesbian classmates, and instruction in HIV education.

Where can teacher educators locate the theory and research to construct a knowledge base on sexual orientation suitable for inclusion in a culturally responsive teacher education program? As is the case with several of the other knowledge bases, teacher educators must go to several sources to develop a comprehensive synthesis of theory and research on sexual orientation. *Coming out of the Classroom Closet: Gay and Lesbian Students, Teachers, and Curricula*, edited by Harbeck (1992) is perhaps the first and best current single-source volume that attempts to synthesize empirical studies for most but not all of the essential elements described above. The research and scholarship of James Sears (1987, 1988a, 1988b, 1989a, 1989b, 1990, in press) including *Growing Up Gay in the South: Race, Gender and Journeys of the Spirit* (1991), have been a major impetus in shaping the parameters of a knowledge base on sexual orientation for the field of education. The chapter by Sears (1992) in Harbeck's book, for example, provides an excellent review of research on the attitudes toward homosexuality of prospective teachers, administrators, counselors, and members of other helping professions.

In addition, several chapters in Harbeck's book provide teacher educators with insights on racial, cultural, gender, social class, and religious dimensions of sexual orientation identity development. Additional theory and research on sexual orientation identity development can be found in such psychology and counseling books as *Lesbian and Gay Psychology: Theory, Research, and Clinical Applications* edited by Greene and Herek (1994). Teacher educators will also find "Gay/Lesbian/Queer Studies" (1994), a special thematic issue of *Radical Teacher*, and the annotated bibliography titled "Roundup of Recent Releases on Gay and Lesbian Experience" by Azzolina (1993) to be excellent resources for developing a knowledge base on sexual orientation that is suitable for the undergraduate and graduate teacher education curricula.

Three books are especially good resources to

introduce preservice and inservice teachers to important issues in the personal and professional lives of gay and lesbian teachers. *Lesbian Teachers: An Invisible Presence* by Madiha Didi Khayatt (1992) is based on an ethnographic study of 19 lesbian elementary and secondary teachers in Canada. One of the best resources for teacher educators to use to introduce preservice teachers to the voices of gay and lesbian teachers and to provide support for gay and lesbian college students who are entering the teaching profession is *One in Ten Teachers* (Jennings, 1995). Although not research-based, this publication is a collection of powerful personal stories about the struggles and victories of gay and lesbian teachers from most regions of the United States. *The Last Closet: The Real Lives of Lesbian and Gay Teachers* by Kissen (1996), an accomplished qualitative researcher and teacher educator, is perhaps the most suitable publication to use as a text in undergraduate- and graduate-level courses in teacher education programs. Kissen's book is based on interviews with over 100 gay and lesbian elementary and secondary teachers and informs readers about several of the above elements listed in a well-designed knowledge base on sexual orientation: the complexity of establishing an authentic identity, homophobia and bigotry, gay and lesbian identity in the context of race and culture, and political and legal issues. Kissen's book is also inspirational and provides teachers suggestions for living and teaching as social reconstructionists who are committed by action to ideals of social justice and equity.

There are a variety of classroom resources for both teacher educators to introduce the knowledge base on sexual orientation to preservice and inservice teachers and for classroom teachers to use with their pupils. Although a deliberate effort has been made not to include film and video resources for other knowledge bases, such resources are so few and new in the area sexual orientation that several merit mention. *It's Elementary: Talking about Gay Issues in School*, produced by Cohen and Chasnoff (1996), is an excellent video for teacher educators to use to disabuse cautious preservice and inservice teachers of the belief that sexual orientation is an inappropriate topic for elementary and secondary students. *School's Out: Gay and Lesbian Youth* (Scagliotti & Spalding, 1993) presents youth-oriented discussions among multiracial gay and lesbian students at Harvey Milk School, an alternative high school that operates under the auspices of the New York City Board of Education. *Sticks, Stones, and Stereotypes* (Equity Institute, 1994) with its accompanying teacher's guide is another film that will sensitize preservice and inservice teachers to gay/lesbian experiences, identity and self-image development, pain caused by taunts and ridicule, and parallels between racism and homophobia through interviews with a group of multiracial gay and lesbian students.

Teacher educators who are searching for school curriculum materials of the type to which preservice and inservice teachers should be introduced are directed to *The Gay Teen: Educational Practice and Theory for Lesbian, Gay, and Bisexual Students* (Unks, 1995), a resource that critiques curricula in a number of secondary subject areas such as literature, sex education, sports, and social studies. *Out with It: Gay and Straight Teens Write about Homosexuality* (Kay, Estapa, & Dessetta, 1996) includes over 100 essays by multiracial teenagers on a variety of issues

related to a knowledge base on sexual orientation. Curriculum materials illustrative of the type to which teacher education students in Social Studies and English Education should be introduced include such series as *Issues in Gay and Lesbian Life* and *Lives of Notable Gay Men and Lesbians* edited by Duberman (1993a, 1993b) published by Chelsea House Publishers for students, ages 14 and older, and such literature anthologies as *Growing Up Gay, Growing Up Lesbian: A Literary Anthology* edited by Singer (1994).

Other excellent resources for synthesizing and organizing the knowledge bases on gender and sexual orientation exist, but the points being made here are that sufficient resources exist and schools, colleges and departments of education must infuse these knowledge bases into the preservice and inservice curricula. Another important point is that teacher education programs have the responsibility to require teacher education students to take general education and major and minor subject area courses from Women's Studies and Gay and Lesbian Studies programs in order to broaden their background knowledge.

CHAPTER 14
Knowledge Base 13: *Experiential Knowledge*

But something can be done to empower some teachers... to reflect upon their own life situations, to speak out in their own voices about the lacks that must be repaired, the possibilities to be acted upon in the name of what they deem decent, human, and just..

— Maxine Greene, *Landscapes of Learning*

The experiential knowledge base most relevant to preparing teachers for culturally diverse classrooms consists of those learnings about diversity that have been extracted from the teacher candidate's life experiences and supervised clinical experiences. These experiences include (a) personal cross-cultural and multicultural lifestyle experiences (informal and planned cross-cultural experiences for teacher candidates) and (b) supervised demonstration of culturally responsive teaching (pre- and student teaching experiences) in clinical school settings with culturally diverse student populations. The assumption here, of course, is that teacher candidates with a rich background of multicultural lifestyle experiences and a rich background of clinical teaching experiences in culturally diverse settings will be better prepared to teach culturally diverse students *than* those teacher candidates who have lived insulated, monocultural lifestyles and who have had no clinical experiences in culturally diverse classroom settings.

Enabling teacher candidates to construct their own personal knowledge base about diversity from life experience compels teacher education programs to structure unique educational experiences that require teacher education candidates to explore interracial and intercultural interactions with people different from themselves. Minimally, a teacher education program that has a strong experiential knowledge-base component should expect

preservice teachers, upon graduation, to have bonded in friendship with a variety of people from racial, cultural, social class, and sexual orientation backgrounds different from their own and (2) to have experienced a variety of cross-cultural events and activities that expanded their knowledge of and enhanced their sensitivity to other cultural groups. Ideally, a well-designed experiential knowledge-base component would result in preservice teachers who

> *Enabling teacher candidates to construct their own personal knowledge base about diversity...compels teacher education programs to structure unique educational experiences that require teacher education candidates to explore interracial and intercultural interactions with people different from themselves.*

prefer to live multicultural lifestyles rather than monocultural lifestyles and who, therefore, have progressed as a result of their higher education experiences to advanced stages of interracial and intercultural sensitivity as described in Bennett's model of "stages of developing intercultural sensitivity" (Bennett, 1986) or Banks' model of "stages of ethnic identity" (Banks, 1992).

A strong experiential knowledge base component in a modern teacher education program should place preservice and inservice teachers' primary emphasis upon the experiences with U.S. cultural groups *but also* provide opportunities for some teacher education students and inservice teachers to participate in international travel-study programs and internship experiences in other countries. At this time in the history of teacher education, internships in other countries are often cost prohibitive and, therefore, cannot likely be required of all teacher education students. However, such options for international student teaching experiences should be made easily available, and teacher education programs should work toward establishing scholarships that enable more preservice and inservice teachers to participate in international internships.

Teacher education programs that stimulate teacher candidates to construct a personalized, experiential knowledge base consisting of learnings from personal experiences in culturally diverse settings have several common characteristics. First, the best programs are developmental. That is, after formally studying stages of development that progress from ethnocentrism to ethnorelativism or multiculturalism, teacher education students assess their own level of development. Second, students design or select cross-cultural and interracial experiences they believe will advance their own development in cultural knowledge, awareness, and sensitivity. Third, the best programs often include journal writing, interviewing, structured and open-ended observation forms, and classroom debriefing sessions. The results and products of these strategies are included in the teacher education student=s portfolio. Finally, the best programs usually provide some culminating experience near the end of a two-year teacher education program that requires preservice teachers to reflect on their portfolio record of growth regarding their personal attitudes toward cultural diversity.

The teacher education student's experiential knowledge base must also be expanded in teacher education programs through supervised pre- and student teaching *clinical experiences with culturally diverse student and family populations.* Well-designed clinical experience programs are also usually developmental and begin with such pre-student teaching experiences as working in a community agency that serves low-income and racially diverse client populations and completing a case study on a child from a cultural or social background different from that of the preservice teacher, advance to serving for a specified number of clock hours as a teacher's assistant in a culturally diverse classroom and to planning and teaching a single lesson or a series of lessons in a culturally diverse classroom, and lead ultimately to a full-term or full-year internship as a student teacher in a culturally diverse school setting. In communities where the schools are not well racially integrated, single-race classrooms where the children come from racial and cultural backgrounds different from that of the intern are substituted for culturally diverse classroom placements. The better designed clinical experiences are grounded in the context of formal course work related to teaching culturally diverse students. For example, preservice teachers who have made a formal study of Black English as a sociolinguistic system, perhaps through using Dandy's *Black Communications* as a textbook, engage in guided clinical experiences in which knowledge gained from formal course work in teacher education courses is used as a basis for teaching language arts or reading lessons at the

The better-designed clinical experiences are grounded in the context of formal coursework related to teaching culturally diverse students.

clinical site. As with cross-cultural, life-experience learning activities, the objective of formal clinical experiences is to assist preservice teachers in constructing their own experiential knowledge base of learnings from observations and supervised classroom teaching experiences with culturally diverse students.

Synthesizing the Research on the Effectiveness of Culturally Diverse Experiences

Despite the fact that the NCATE standards require teacher education programs to provide internship experiences in culturally diverse classroom settings, the research base for designing such programs is in a developmental stage. There does exist an emerging body of research findings on the effectiveness of *planned informal experiences* and *formal clinical experiences* (both pre-student teaching and student teaching) on changing the attitudes and teaching behaviors of preservice and inservice teachers. However, the definitive synthesis of these empirical findings has not yet been written. One problem, of course, is that many studies are unable to separate the effects of formal academic learning in the university classroom from the effects of real-life interactions and clinical experiences with culturally diverse people and classroom students.

Grant and Secada (1990) conducted an extensive review of the literature on preparing teachers for diversity that examined both studies on the effects of multicultural course work and the effects culturally diverse field experiences. After winnowing 500 journal and 700 ERIC citations from 1964 to June 1988, as well as several other sources, Grant and Secada found only 16 studies on preservice teacher education and seven on inservice teacher education. In general, they found that modest and sometimes, but rarely, dramatic changes can be made in teachers' attitudes and behaviors regarding diversity. Grant and Secada also concluded from their review of empirical studies that "experiences with representatives from diverse populations are worthwhile for teachers ....and positive results... seem predicated on the students' and the teachers' having support mechanisms and some contexts within which to interpret their experiences" (p.418). With regard to

multicultural content, Grant and Secada concluded that the bulk of empirical evidence tends to indicate that the "more intense the exposure and the more time spent learning the content, the more likely learning will be successful" (p. 418).

Perhaps the most extensive recent review of literature regarding Knowledge Base 13 has been conducted by Gomez (1993) who examined the effects of teacher education efforts to change teacher candidates' beliefs positively toward culturally different "others." She organized the reviewed studies into three types: (a) teacher education programs focusing on diversity (Gomez and Tabachnick, 1991, 1992; Noordhoff and Kleinfeld, 1990, 1991); (b) single courses, focusing on diversity with and without a brief field experience component (Ahlquist, 1991; Ladson-Billings, 1991a; and Beyer, 1991); and (c) field experiences focusing on diversity (Cooper, Beare, and Thorman, 1990; Larke, 1990; Larke, Wiseman, and Bradley, 1990; Mahan 1982a, 1982b; and Murrell, 1992). Teacher education programs designed to prepare teachers for culturally diverse classrooms consisted of a combination of coordinated courses, seminars, and field experiences.

Gomez concluded generally that year-long, two-or-more semester-long, and labor-intensive "combination" programs can produce in "prospective teachers...substantial reconsideration of the ideas about diverse learners they held when they entered the program " (p.465). In general, Gomez

> *...many studies are unable to separate the effects of formal academic learning in the university classroom from the effects of real-life interactions and clinical experiences with culturally diverse people and classroom students.*

concluded that single courses with and without a brief field experience component produced limited to moderate changes in preservice teachers' beliefs about diversity. Finally, from her review of studies focused on culturally diverse field experiences, Gomez concluded that (a) out-of-area (geographical) intense, immersion field experience programs in which primarily White teacher candidates are placed in Native American, Latino, or inner-city communities, (b) field experience programs where preservice teachers become "the minority" or "other," and (c) field experience programs "combined with seminars and other ongoing conversations guiding students' self-inquiry and reflection about teaching and working with persons different from themselves" hold the most promise "for challenging and changing preservice teachers' perspectives" (p. 468).

Other reviews of theory and research regarding field experiences, multicultural course content, or a combination of both provide guidance for restructuring teacher education experiences that enable preservice and inservice teachers to construct their own experiential knowledge bases about diversity. These reviews have resulted in conclusions that generally concur with the conclusions of Grant and Secada and Gomez. Teacher educators who wish to inform their efforts to restructure teacher education for diversity are directed to Sleeter's review of research studies on preservice teachers (1985) and inservice teachers (1992) and to the research and extensive review of literature conducted by Adeeb (1994). In addition, teacher educators will want to examine new studies (Colville-Hall, MacDonald, & Smolen, 1995; Deering & Stanutz, 1995; Finney &

Orr, 1995; Greenman & Kimmel, 1995; Hood and Parker, 1994; Jordan, 1995; McCall, 1995; Reed, 1993; and Tran, Young & DiLella, 1994) not included in the extant reviews cited above.

Numerous resources exist to help teacher educators plan comprehensive, developmental field experience programs for better preparing teachers for culturally diverse classrooms. One source of ideas, of course, is the collective body of numerous research studies referenced above as the research base for Knowledge Base 13. A second type of resource, particularly for "ready-made" action research projects that immerse preservice teachers in culturally diverse communities and schools, is the extensive array of textbooks written specifically for multicultural teacher education courses. Referenced in the discussion of Knowledge Base 1, many of these textbooks include a "suggested learning activities" section. For example, *Turning on Learning* (Grant & Sleeter, 1989) includes several recommended action research activities suitable for field experience programs. A third source of ideas is textbooks written specifically for field experience courses. For example, perhaps the most comprehensive, single resource is *Field Experience: Strategies for Exploring Diversity* (Powell, Zehm, & Garcia, 1996). Designed as a text for preservice and inservice teachers, this book not only presents a model developmental field experience program, it also includes many ready-made action research projects. Most importantly, this publication correlates field experience activities to most of the 13 knowledge bases discussed in this book.

CHAPTER 15
A Final Word: *Justice*

The arc of a moral universe is long, but it bends toward justice.

— Martin Luther King, Jr.

The overarching purpose of this book has been to advance the profession=s thinking about what teachers need to know and experience to be more effective in culturally diverse classrooms. An effort has been made to push teacher educators to clarify and become more concrete in their thinking by describing 13 knowledge bases that hold promise for preparing teachers to meet the needs of increasingly diverse and underserved student populations in the United States. Each of the 13 knowledge bases has been broadly defined by its essential content elements or, in some cases, such as the knowledge base on experiential knowledge, its process elements. In the main but not exclusively, this book has addressed only the knowledge bases related to underserved student populations that are most often omitted from teacher education programs. For example, knowledge bases relevant to preparing regular teachers for teaching special education students have not been addressed because most teacher education programs already require at least one course regarding the needs of special students.

Another important knowledge base that has been omitted, however, is the one on international and global education. Clearly, the absence of a well-organized, integrated knowledge base on international and comparative education in most teacher education programs contributes to the provincialism of most teachers in the United States (Gutek, 1997). Thus, the 13 described knowledge bases do not represent all that should be included in a teacher's education; rather, they are knowledge bases recommended for integration with other existing knowledge bases commonly found in most teacher education programs.

In addition, this book has attempted to identify the literature of theory and research that supports each of the 13 knowledge bases. More often than not, treatment of the literature for each knowledge base focused on informing teacher educators where they can find the relevant literature rather than what the literature says. Extraction of the actual theoretical constructs, concepts, research findings, principles and practices has been left largely to the teacher educators who bear the responsibility for the curriculum content and design of teacher education programs at their unique institutions. From these efforts, no doubt, the actual content of the theory and research will be clarified more definitively as new textbooks are written.

> *...this book has addressed only the knowledge bases related to underserved student populations that are most often omitted from teacher education programs.*

The identification and advocacy of any set of knowledge bases for teacher education present several predictable problems. First, defining the term knowledge base is itself problematic, so problematic, in fact, that there is little consensus within the profession of teacher education regarding what constitutes a knowledge base and how one might go about constructing one. Knowledge base is a term used so frequently in the literature that we teacher educators have come to assume we know its meaning. Yet, we have only to read the fall 1993 issue of the *Review of Educational Research* to think otherwise. This particular issue of the *Review of Educational Research* contained the ambitious effort of Wang, Haertel, and Walberg to use meta-analysis to define "a knowledge base for school learning" and eight critiques by respected scholars. Wang, Haertel and Walberg (1993) presented the following definition of a knowledge base for school learning:

> ...A knowledge base of school learning should include the learners' contexts, as well as the characteristics of learners themselves. It should not represent a particular philosophy, such as behaviorism or pragmatism. Rather, it should include theories explaining the influences on school learning, empirical results distilled from research studies, and expert judgements about influences on school learning.
>
> Psychological, sociocultural, and instructional theories of learning and schooling should be included in such a knowledge base. Empirical results in a knowledge base for school learning should contain

several types of information, including the identification of specific variables affecting school learning and their relative influence. A wide range of variables would have to be considered, including student abilities, preferences, and prior achievement; teacher characteristics and classroom behaviors; instructional materials and practices; amount of time devoted to learning; curriculum content; classroom climate; characteristics of the school, home, and community; district and state educational policies; and demographic information characterizing students, schools, communities, and states. Experts would then be able to confirm or refute empirical findings based on their experience as practitioners and researchers.

> Theories, empirical results, and expert judgements are needed to establish a valid knowledge base. In this article, then, the term knowledge base is used to represent the distillation of understandings from experts, narrative reviews, and meta-analysis of variables that influence school learning. (pp. 222-223)

Ultimately, Wang, Haertel, and Walbert concluded that distal variables such as demography, policy, and organization have little influence on school learning; whereas proximal variables such as individual psychology, classroom instruction, and home environment have the greater influence. Although several of the eight scholars who responded to Wang, Haertel, and Walberg's effort couched their critiques in questions regarding the methodology used to derive a knowledge base, others expressed grave skepticism about defining a knowledge base for school learning and whether identifying such a knowledge base is even possible or useful (Kerdeman & Phillips, 1993; Peterson, 1993; Palincsar & McPhail, 1993; Levin, 1993; Hedges & Waddington, 1993; and Singer, 1993). Kliebard (1993) expressed his skepticism in the title of his critique, "What Is a Knowledge Base, and Who Would Use It If We Had One?" Elmore (1993) echoed similar skepticism in his critique, "What Knowledge Base?"

> *...identifying knowledge bases is exacerbated by the evolving and changing nature of knowledge and its relationship to truth.*

Second, in addition to problems related to defining the term *knowledge base*, identifying knowledge bases is exacerbated by the evolving and changing nature of knowledge and its relationship to truth. The integrity of any knowledge base for teacher education ought to rest largely on the strength of truth, as validated by the best available research produced in the social sciences during a given historical era. However, the ethereal nature of truth poses problems for anyone who prescribes what truths ought to constitute a universe of knowledge most appropriate to be studied by those who are training for the professional role of teacher. Truth, after all, is relative—relative over time and historical era, relative to the social beliefs of the day, relative to new research, relative to cultural setting, and, yes, relative even to the perceiver. If we have learned anything at all in the social sciences, we have learned that "past truth" has often been rendered completely false in subsequent historical eras, a fact that is particularly true about our "knowledge" regarding women and people of color.

We have also learned that "past truth," which turned out later to be false, has often done tragic damage to disenfranchised, oppressed groups. Teacher educators need only to read Stephen Jay Gould's *The Mismeasure of Man* (1981) to sense the depth of tragedy resulting from basing our knowledge about race and gender on false sciences and the products of scientific racism. Over the course of history, particularly in Europe and the United States from the 1700s to the present, Gould notes that the "sciences" and scientific instruments of craniometry, phylogeny, and modern I.Q. testing have generated false knowledge, knowledge that has been taught to subsequent generations as valid and used to justify the exclusion of this or that group—sometimes women and almost always people of African, Native American, and other non-Caucasian origins of descent. Thus, not only must we be cognizant of how knowledge changes, we must also be wary of the relativity of its truth. Even more important, we must understand that "validated" knowledge as well as false knowledge can be misused.

Third, advocating any set of knowledge bases for teacher preparation can be problematic because we teacher educators disagree so much and, in fact, enjoy argumentation. Since most of the knowledge bases described in this book rest heavily on the belief that culture influences the way human beings go about learning, they are certain to elicit considerable disagreement. Not everyone accepts this belief. There are those researchers, educators, scholars, and members of the public who suspect that cultural differences are relatively insignificant and disappear when social class factors are controlled. As James Banks (1988b) has noted, Wilson (1978) and Gordon (1964) are two such voices that argue that social class is a more powerful factor than ethnicity in determining behavioral patterns.

Wilson, for instance, posits that the importance of race has declined in the United States and that class stratification has created deep divisions within the African American community. Gordon argues "with regard to cultural behavior, differences of social class are more important and decisive than differences of ethnic group. This means that people of the same social class tend to act alike and to have the same values even if they have different ethnic backgrounds" (as cited in Banks, 1988b, p. 454).

In truth, there is much that we do not yet know about how culture influences learning. There is much that we do not yet know about teaching African American, Hispanic American, Native American, and other students of non-European descent. For that matter, it can be argued that there is much we do not yet know about teaching middle-class European American students who are presently the group best served by the educational system. We are just beginning to learn more about the degree to which cultural differences are influenced by such variables as gender, social class, sexual orientation, region, religion, and perhaps a number of new aspects of diversity. The variables receiving most attention presently seem to be race, class, and gender. For example, Grant and Sleeter (1986) reviewed the results of 71 studies about variables of race, class, and gender that appeared in the *American Educational Research Journal*, the *Harvard Educational Review*, the *Review of Educational Research*, and the *Teachers College Record* from 1973 through 1983. They concluded that most researchers examined only one or two of the variables and only a few researchers integrated all three factors in their research designs and data analyses. They further argued that the lack of integration of race, gender, and socioeconomic status oversimplifies analysis and understanding of student behavior in the educational system. Others have echoed similar arguments. Reyes and Stanic (1985) have argued that research on race-related and cultural differences must consider socioeconomic differences to avoid confounding the two variables and, therefore, drawing inaccurate conclusions about racial differences. In addition, there is much we do not yet know about intragroup diversity. Another aspect of the complexities and difficulties of conducting research studies that support knowledge bases predicated largely on cultural differences is described by Banks (1988b):

> With regard to cultural behavior, ethnicity continues to influence the behavior of members of ethnic groups with certain characteristics when social mobility occurs. This means that while people of the same social class from different ethnic groups will exhibit some similar behaviors, they will have some significant behavioral differences caused by the persistence of ethnicity.

> When studying race, class, and ethnicity, social scientists need to examine generational middle-class status as a variable. There are often important behavioral and attitudinal differences between a Black individual who grew up poor and became middle class within his or her adulthood and a Black who is fourth-generation middle class. Many of the middle-class Afro-Americans and Mexican Americans described in existing research studies are probably first-generation middle class. Such individuals are sometimes compared with Whites who have been middle class for several generations. Generational social-class status needs to be varied systematically in research studies so that we can learn more about the tenacity of ethnicity across generations. (p. 464)

Thus, there is much we do not know about the knowledge bases described in this book and even these 13 knowledge bases will change as new research is conducted. It is the nature of knowledge bases to evolve, to change, perhaps even to disappear as new knowledge renders them irrelevant. Clearly, the knowledge bases advocated for the preparation of teachers in the 1960s and 1970s have changed. In light of new evidence and new theory development, knowledge bases based on the cultural deficit paradigm have given way to knowledge bases based on the cultural difference paradigm. Even now, the cultural difference paradigm is undergoing changes that involve broader definitions of diversity. The danger of advocating the 13 knowledge bases described in this book is that someone may want to canonize them into rigid taxonomies rather than let them remain organic. The knowledge bases described here are not offered as absolutes, as the final word. They are offered only as those knowledge bases of today that hold promise for better educating tomorrow's teachers for diversity.

The identification of specific teacher education knowledge bases for diversity and their undergirding bodies of theory and research is just the beginning. Some steps must follow.

① **Accreditation standards for teacher education programs must be revised to state more explicitly the knowledge bases for diversity that evaluation teams expect to find in programs that profess to prepare preservice teachers for diverse student populations.** More prescriptive standards that require more specifically described *knowledge bases for diversity* will be a necessary, important impetus for reforming teacher education programs, whether the knowledge bases identified in the new standards parallel those described in this book or some other conceptualization of knowledge bases for diversity. Schools, colleges, and departments of education should not be equivocating about whether or not they should prepare teachers for culturally diverse populations. In a multiracial, culturally, and linguistically diverse nation where stark socioeconomic contrasts exist, archaic teacher preparation programs that choose to ignore diversity should simply not be approved to carry accredited status.

② **Textbooks for teacher education programs must be revised to include the theory and research that is most relevant to preparing teachers to be effective with diverse student populations.** The truth is that diversity-blind textbooks, more often than not, define knowledge bases for most teacher education programs more than do the teacher educators themselves. Enormous opportunities await those teacher educators who step forward to rewrite a new genre of textbooks that better prepare preservice and inservice teachers to serve diverse students.

The knowledge bases described in this book, alone, are not likely to make great differences in teachers' abilities to be effective with diverse students unless the knowledge bases are integrated well and placed within the framework of a social reconstructionist teacher preparation program. If the overarching mission statement, goals, and objectives of the teacher preparation program do not reflect a commitment to reconstructing a more fair and just democratic society, these knowledge bases will likely have little impact. Similarly, if the

The reform of teacher education programs must be much more than merely substituting the rote memorization of one set of truths for another.

knowledge bases for diversity are not treated within the context of a critical pedagogy that challenges the status quo of inequities, includes critical dialogue, utilizes multiple perspectives, and ultimately empowers teachers to take social action in their personal and classroom lives to correct social injustices, impact will likely be minimal. The reform of teacher education programs must be much more than merely substituting the rote memorization of one set of truths for another.

Finally, the identification of teacher educator knowledge bases for diversity must be followed by steps taken by teacher educators as individuals. Over the long term, what teacher educators teach may not be nearly as powerful as what they model. It is likely that long after teacher education students have forgotten many of the specific facts, the formal theories, and bodies of research in the knowledge bases for diversity that are described in this book, what they will remember most of all is how teacher educators lived their personal lives.

So it is important that teacher educators not only develop thorough expertise in the knowledge bases for diversity but that they also model a multicultural and multiracial lifestyle. It is important for students to see teacher educators having interracial and intercultural friendships. It is important for preservice and inservice teachers to see that not only do teacher educators believe that a racially integrated education is superior to a segregated education but that teacher educators send their children to racially and socially integrated schools. And, most important of all, teacher education students must see teacher educators not merely as paying lip service to diversity, but they must see them actively engaged in their communities fighting racism and other forms of bigotry and trying to correct social injustice.

Martin Luther King, Jr. was correct to suggest that the arc of a moral universe appears long, particularly through the eyes of the oppressed and the marginalized, but the final word is that it will bend more visibly if teacher educators can break the cycle of producing generation after generation of monocultural teachers who are underprepared to be effective teachers of diverse student populations.

References

Aaron, R., & Powell, G. (1982). Feedback practices as a function of teacher and pupil race during reading groups instruction. *Journal of Negro Education, 51*(1), 50-59.

Aaronson, D., & Ferrer, S. (1987). The impact of language differences on language processing: An example from Chinese-English bilingualism. In Homel, P., Palij, M., & Aaronson, D. (Eds.), *Childhood bilingualism: Aspects of linguistic, cognitive, and social development* (pp.75-119). Hillsdale, NJ: Lawrence Erlbaum Associates.

Aboud, R. E., & Doyle, A. (1993). The early development of ethnic identity and attitudes. In M. E. Bernal and G. P. Knight (Eds.), *Ethnic identity: Formation and transmission among Hispanics and other minorities* (pp. 47-59). Albany, NY: State University of New York Press.

Adams, G., & Cohen, A. (1976). An examination of cumulative folder information used by teachers in making differential judgements of children's abilities. *Alberta Journal of Educational Research, 22*(3), 216-225.

Adeeb, P. M. (1994). A quasi-experimental design to study the effect of multicultural coursework and culturally diverse field placements on preservice teachers' attitudes toward diversity. Unpublished Dissertation. University of North Florida.

Adler, S. (1993). *Multicultural communication skills in the classroom.* Needham Heights, MA: Allyn & Bacon.

Adorno, T. W., Frenkel-Brunswick, E., Levinson, D. J., & Sanford, R. N. (1950). *The authoritarian personality.* New York: Harper & Row.

African Americans in science, mathematics, medicine, and invention. (1993). Rochester, NY: Rochester City School District (Distributed by Peoples Publishing Group, Inc., 230 West Passaic St., Maywood, NJ 07607).

Ahlquist, R. (1991). Position and imposition: Power relations in a multicultural foundations class. *Journal of Negro Education, 60*(2), 158-169.

Alejandro, P., & Wilson, K. L. (1976). Black-White differences in educational attainment. *American Sociological Review, 41*(3), 414-431.

Allport, G. W. (1954). *The nature of prejudice.* Reading, MA: Addison-Wesley.

Aloia, G., Maxwell, J., & Aloia, S. (1981). Influence of a child's race and the EMR label on initial impressions of regular classroom teachers. *American Journal of Mental Deficiency, 85*(6), 619-623.

Ambert, A. M. (Ed.). (1988). *Bilingual education and English as a second language: A research handbook, 1986-1987.* New York: Garland.

Ambert, A. M. (Ed.). (1991). *Bilingual education and English as a second language: A research handbook, 1988-1990.* New York: Garland.

American Association of Colleges for Teacher Education. (December, 1987). *Teacher education policy in the states: A 50-state survey of legislative and administrative actions.* Washington, DC: Author.

American Association of Colleges for Teacher Education. (1987). *Teaching teachers: Facts and figures, 1987.* Washington, DC: Author.

American Association of Colleges for Teacher Education. (1990). *AACTE/Metropolitan Life survey of teacher education students.* Washington, DC: Author.

Anderson, J. A. (1988). Cognitive styles and multicultural populations. *Journal of Teacher Education, 39*(1), 2-9.

Appleford, B., Fralick, P., & Ryan, T. J. (1976). Teacher-child interactions as related to sex, socioeconomic status, and physical appearance. (ERIC Document Reproduction Service No. ED 138 869)

A salute to Black scientists and inventors (1985). Chicago, IL: Empak Publishing Company.

Asante, M. K. (1990). African elements in African-American English. In J. E. Holloway (Ed.), *Africanisms in American culture* (pp. 19-33). Bloomington, IN: Indiana University Press.

Atkinson, D. R., Morten, & Sue, D. W. (Eds.). (1979). *Counseling American minorities: A cross-cultural perspective.* Dubuque, IA: William C. Brown.

Atwater, M. M., Radzik-Marsh, K., & Strutchens, M. (Eds.). (1994). *Multicultural education: Inclusion of all.* Athens, GA: University of Georgia.

Au, K. H., & Jordan, C. (1981). Teaching reading to Hawaiian children: Finding a culturally appropriate solution. In H. Trueba et al. (Eds.), *Culture and the bilingual classrooms: Studies in classroom ethnography* (pp. 139-152). Rowley, MA: Newbury House.

Au, K. H., & Kawakami, A. J. (1994). Cultural congruence in instruction. In E. R. Hollins, J. E. King, & W. C. Hayman (Eds.), *Teaching diverse populations: Formulating a knowledge base* (pp. 5-23). Albany, NY: State University of New York Press.

Augenbraum, H., & Stavans, I. (Eds.). (1993). *Growing up Latino: Memoirs and stories.* New York: Houghton Mifflin.

Azzolina, D. S. (1993). Roundup of recent releases on the gay and lesbian experience. *Multicultural Review, 2*(4), 22-27.

Baker, G. C. (1994). *Planning and organizing for multicultural instruction* (2nd. ed.). New York: Addison & Wesley.

Ballantine, J. H. (1993). *The sociology of education* (3rd ed.). Englewood Cliffs, NJ: Prentice Hall.

Banks, J. A. (1988a). Approaches to multicultural curriculum reform. *Multicultural Leader, 1*(22), 1-3.

Banks, J. A. (1988b). Ethnicity, class, cognitive, and motivational styles: Research and teaching implications. *Journal of Negro Education, 57*(4), 452-466.

Banks, J. A. (1988c). *Multiethnic education: Theory and practice* (2nd ed.). Boston: Allyn & Bacon.

Banks, J. A. (1992). The stages of ethnicity. In P. A. Richard-Amato & M. A. Snow (Eds.), *The multicultural classroom: Readings for the content-area teachers* (pp. 93-101). White Plains, NY: Longman.

Banks, J. A. (1993). Approaches to multicultural curriculum reform. In J. A. Banks & C. A. Banks (Eds.), *Multicultural education: Issues and perspectives* (pp. 195-214). Boston: Allyn & Bacon.

Banks, J. A. (1993). Multicultural education as an academic discipline. *Multicultural Education, 1*(3), 8-11, 39.

Banks, J. A. (1994). *An introduction to multicultural education.* Boston: Allyn & Bacon.

Banks, J. A. (1997). *Teaching strategies for ethnic studies* (6th ed.). Boston: Allyn & Bacon.

Banks, J. A., & Banks, C. A. (Eds.). (1993). *Multicultural education: Issues and perspectives.* Boston: Allyn & Bacon.

Banks, J.A., & Banks, C. A. (Eds.). (1995). *Handbook of research on multicultural education.* New York: Macmillan.

Banks, J. A., & Lynch, J. (Eds.). (1986). *Multicultural education in Western societies.* New York: Holt Rinehart & Winston.

Banner, L. W. (1974). *Women in modern America: A brief history.* New York: Harcourt Brace Jovanovich.

Baptiste, H. P., & Archer, C. (1994). A comprehensive multicultural teacher education program: An idea whose time has come. In M. M. Atwater, K. Radzik-Marsh, & M. Strutchens (Eds.), *Multicultural education: Inclusion of all* (pp. 63-90). Athens, GA: The University of Georgia.

Baratz, J., & Baratz, S. (1972). Black culture on Black terms: A rejection of the social pathology model. In T. Kochman (Ed.), *Rappin' and stylin' out* (pp. 3-16). Urbana, IL: University of Illinois Press.

Baratz, J., & Shuy, R. (1969). *Teaching Black children to read.* Washington, DC: Center for Applied Linguistics.

Barba, R. H. (1995). *Science in the multicultural classroom: A guide to teaching and learning.* Boston: Allyn & Bacon.

Barbe, W. B., & Swassing, R. H. (1979). *Teaching through modality strengths: Concepts and practice.* Columbus, OH: Zaner-Bloser.

Barnes, W. J. (1978). Student-teacher dyadic interaction in desegregated high school classrooms. *Western Journal of Black Studies, 2*(2), 132-137.

Baron, D. E. (1975). Nonstandard English, composition, and the academic establishment. *College English, 37*(2),176-183.

Baron, R. M., Tom, D. Y., & Cooper, H. M. (1985). Social class, race and teacher expectations. In J. B. Dusek (Ed.), *Teacher expectancies* (pp. 251-269). Hillsdale, NJ: Lawrence Erlbaum Associates.

Bartlet, G., Jasper, S. P., & Hoffer, B. (Eds.). (1982). *Essays in Native American English.* San Antonio, TX: Trinity University Press.

Bastian, A., Frucher, N., Gittel, M., Greer, C., & Haskins, K. (1986). *Choosing equality: The case for democratic schooling.* Philadelphia: Temple University Press.

Bauch, P. A. (1993). Improving education for minority adolescents: Toward an ecological perspective on school choice and parent involvement. In N. F. Chavkin (Ed.), *Families and schools in a pluralistic society* (pp. 121-146). Albany: State University of New York Press.

Baugh, J. (1994). New and prevailing misconceptions of African American English for logic and mathematics. In E. R. Hollins, J. E. King, & W. C. Hayman (Eds.), *Teaching diverse populations: Formulating a knowledge base* (pp. 191-205). Albany, NY: State University of New York Press.

Beady, C. H., & Hansell, S. (1980). Teacher race and expectations for student achievement. (ERIC Document Reproduction Service No. ED 200 695)

Beardon, R., & Henderson, H. (1993). *A history of African-American artists from 1792 to the present.* New York: Pantheon Books.

Bempechat, J. (1990). The role of parent involvement in children's academic achievement: A review of the literature. Trends and Issues No. 14. ERIC Clearinghouse on Urban Education, Institute for Urban and Minority Education. Teachers College, Columbia University, New York. (ERIC Document Reproduction Service No. ED 322285)

Bennett, C. (1995). *Comprehensive multicultural education: Theory and practice* (3rd ed.). Boston: Allyn & Bacon.

Bennett, C. (1995) Research on racial issues in higher education. In J. Banks and C. Banks (Eds.), *Handbook of research on multicultural education* (pp.663-682). New York: Macmillan.

Bennett, C. L. (1979). The effects of student characteristics on teacher expectations and attributions. *Dissertation Abstracts International, 40,* 978-980-B.

Bennett, M. J. (1986). A developmental approach to training for intercultural sensitivity. *International Journal of Intercultural Relations, 10,* 179-196.

Benson, C. S., Medrich, E. A., & Buckley, S. (1980). A new view of school efficiency: Household time contributions to school achievement. In J. Guthrie (Ed.), *School finance policies and practices. The 1980s: A decade of conflict* (pp. 169-204). Cambridge, MA: Ballinger.

Berlak, H., Newmann, F. M., Adams, E., Archbald, D. A., Burgess, T., Raven, J., & Romberg, T. A. (1992). *Toward a new science of educational testing and assessment.* Albany, NY: State University of New York Press.

Berliner, D. C. (1984). The half-full glass: A review of research on teaching. In P. L. Hosford (Ed.), *Using what we know about teaching* (pp. 51-77). Alexandria, VA: Association for Supervision and Curriculum Development.

Bernal, M. E., & Knight, G. P. (Eds.). (1993). *Ethnic identity: Formation and transmission among Hispanics and other minorities.* Albany, NY: State University of New York Press.

Bernal, M. E., Knight, G. P., Ocampo, K. A., Garza, C. A., & Cota, M. K. (1993). Development of Mexican American identity: Formation and transmission among Hispanics and other minorities. In M. E. Bernal & G. P. Knight (Eds.), *Ethnic identity: Formation and transmission among Hispanics and other minorities.* (pp. 31-46). Albany, NY: State University of New York Press.

Bernard, B. (1991). *Fostering resilience in kids: Protective factors in the family, school, and community.* Portland, OR: Northwest Regional Educational Laboratory.

Berry, G. L., & Asamen, J. K. (Eds.). (1989). *Black students: Psychosocial issues and academic achievement.* Newbury Park, CA: Sage.

Beyer, L. E. (1991). Teacher education, reflective inquiry, and moral action. In B. R. Tabachnick & K. M. Zeichner (Eds.), *Inquiry-oriented practice in teacher education* (pp. 113-129). New York: Falmer Press.

Bigelow, B., Christenson, L., Karp, S., Miner, B., & Peterson, B. (1994). *Rethinking our schools: Teaching for equity and social justice.* Milwaukee, WI: Rethinking Schools, Ltd.

Billingsley, A. (1968). *Black families in White America.* Englewood Cliffs, NJ: Prentice Hall.

Blank, R. K. (1984). The effects of magnet schools on the quality of education in urban school districts. *Phi Delta Kappan, 66*(4), 270.

Bobo, S. A., & Thompson, P. M. (1990). *Teaching English to speakers of ESD, ESL and EFL.* New York: University Press of America.

Bogardus, E. (1939). A social distance scale. *Sociology and Social Research, 3,* 265-271.

Bowers, C. A. (1974). *Cultural literacy for freedom.* Eugene, OR: Elan.

Bowers, C. A., & Flinders, D. J. (1990). *Responsive teaching: An ecological approach to classroom patterns of language, culture, and thought.* New York: Teachers College Press.

Bowser, B. P., & Hunt, R. G. (Eds.). (1996). *Impacts of racism on White Americans* (2nd edition). Newbury Park, CA: Sage.

Boyd, W. L., & Walberg, H. (Eds). (1990). *Choice in education: Potential and problems.* Berkeley, CA: McCutchen.

Boyer, J. (1994). Teacher education and schools of the future: Issues of race, class, and gender. Unpublished manuscript. Manhattan, KS: Kansas State University.

Boykin, A. W. (1979). Psychological/behavioral verve: Some theoretical explorations and empirical manifestations. In A. W. Boykin, A. J. Franklin, & J. F. Yates (Eds.), *Research directions of Black psychologists* (pp. 351-367). New York: Russell Sage Foundation.

Boykin, A. W. (1982). Task variability and the performance of Black and White schoolchildren: Vervistic explorations. *Journal of Black Studies, 12*(4), 469-485.

Boykin, A. W. (1983). The academic performance of Afro-American children. In J. Spence (Ed.), *Achievement and Achievement Motives.* San Francisco: W. Freeman.

Boykin, A. W. (1986). The triple quandary and the schooling of Afro-American children. In U. Neisser (Ed.), *The school achievement of minority children* (pp. 57-92). Hillsdale, NJ: Lawrence Erlbaum Associates.

Boykin, A. W. (1994). Afrocultural expression and its implications for schooling. In E. R. Hollins, J. E. King, & W. C. Hayman (Eds.), *Teaching diverse populations: Formulating a knowledge base* (pp. 105-127). Albany, NY: State University of New York Press.

Boykin, A. W., & Allen, B. (1988). Rhythmic-movement facilitated learning in working-class Afro-American children. *Journal of Genetic Psychology, 148,* 335-347.

Boykin, A. W., & Toms, F. (1985). Black child socialization: A conceptual framework. In H. McAdoo & J. McAdoo (Eds.), *Black children* (pp. 33-51). Newbury Park, CA: Sage.

Braddock, J. H. (1980). The perpetuation of segregation across levels of education: A behavioral assessment of the contact-hypothesis. *Sociology of Education, 53,* 178-186.

Braddock II, J. H., Crain, R. L., & McPartland, J. M. (1984). A long-term view of school desegregation: Some recent studies of graduates as adults. *Phi Delta Kappan, 66*(4), 259-264.

Brandt, G. L. (1986). *Cultural diversity in the primary school.* London: B.T. Balsford, Ltd.

Brandt, G. L. (1986). *The realization of anti-racist teaching.* London: Taylor & Francis.

Braxton, M. V., & Bullock, C. S. (1972). Teacher partiality in desegregation. *Integrated Education, 10,* 42-46.

Bridge, R. G., & Blackman, J. (1978). *A study of alternatives in American education, Vol. IV: Family choice in schooling.* (Report R-2170/4-NIE, Santa Monica, CA: Rand.

Bronstein, P. A., & Paludi, M. (1988). The introductory psychology course from a broader human perspective. In P. A. Bronstein & K. Quina (Eds.), *Teaching a psychology of people: Resources for gender and sociocultural awareness* (pp. 21-36). Washington, DC: American Psychological Association.

Brophy, J., & Evertson, C. M. (1981). *Student characteristics and teaching.* New York: Longman Press.

Brophy J., & Good, T. (1974). *Teacher-student relationships: Causes and consequences.* New York: Holt, Rinehart & Winston.

Brophy, J. E. (1982). Successful teaching strategies for the inner-city child. *Phi Delta Kappan, 63*(8), 527-530.

Brown, T. J. (1988). *High impact teaching: Strategies for educating minority youth.* Lanham, MD: University Press of America.

Brown, W., Payne, L., Lankowich, L., and Cornell, J. (1970). Praise, criticism, and race. *Elementary School Journal, 70,* 373-377.

Bullivant, B. M. (1981). *Race, ethnicity, and curriculum.* Melbourne: Macmillan.

Bullivant, B. M. (1981). *The pluralist dilemma in education: Six case studies.* Sydney: George Allen & Unwin.

Burgess, B. J. (1978). Native American learning styles. In L. Morris, G. Sather, & S. Scull (Eds.), *Extracting learning styles from social/cultural diversity: A study of five American minorities* (pp. 41-53). Norman, OK: Southeast Teacher Corps Network. (Grant No. G007-700-119, U.S. Office of Education, Department of Health, Education, and Welfare)

Buriel, R. (1982, December). Teacher-student interactions and their relationship to student achievement: A comparison of Mexican-American and Anglo-American children. *Journal of Educational Psychology, 75,* 889-897.

Burling, R. (1973). *English in Black and White.* New York: Holt, Rinehart & Winston.

Byalick, R., & Bersoff, D. N. (1974). Reinforcement practices of Black and White teachers in integrated classrooms. *Journal of Educational Psychology, 66,*(4), 473-480.

Byers, P, & Byers, H. (1972). Non-verbal communication in the education of children. In C. Cazden, V. John, & D. Hymes (Eds.), *Function of language in the classroom* (pp. 3-31). New York: Teachers College Press.

California State Department of Education, Bilingual Education Office. (1986). *A handbook for teaching Pilipino-speaking students.* Sacramento, CA: Author.

California State Department of Education, Bilingual Education Office. (1987). *A handbook for teaching Japanese-speaking students.* Sacramento, CA: Author.

California State Department of Education, Bilingual Education Office. (1989). *A handbook for teaching Cantonese-speaking students.* Sacramento, CA: Author.

California State Department of Education, Bilingual Education Office. (1989). *A handbook for teaching Portuguese-speaking students.* Sacramento, CA: Author.

California State Department of Education, Bilingual Education Office. (1992). *A handbook for teaching Korean-American students.* Sacramento, CA: Author.

Campbell, D.E. (1996). *Choosing democracy: A practical guide to multicultural education.*Englewood Cliffs, NJ: Merrill.

Campos, F. (1983). The attitudes and expectations of student teachers and cooperating teachers toward students in predominantly Mexican American schools: A qualitative data perspective. (ERIC Document Reproduction Service No. ED 234 026)

Carnegie Foundation for the Advancement of Teaching. (1992). *A special report: School choice.* Princeton, NJ: Author.

Catterral, J. S. (1983). *Tax tuition credits: Fact and fiction.* Bloomington, IN: Phi Delta Kappa Educational Foundation.

Cazden, C., & Leggett, E. (1981). Culturally responsive education: Recommendations for achieving Lau remedies. In H. Trueba et al. (Eds.), *Culture and the bilingual classroom* (pp. 69-86). Rowley, MA: Newbury House.

Cazden, C. B., & Mehan, H. (1989). Principles from sociology and anthropology: Context, code, classroom, and culture. In M. C. Reynolds (Ed.), *Knowledge base for the beginning teacher* (pp. 47-57). New York: Pergamon.

Chan, J. P., Chin, F., Inoda, L. F., & Wong, S. (Eds.). (1991). *The big aiiieeeee! An anthology of Chinese American and Japanese American literature.* New York: Meridian Books.

Chavkin, N. F. (1989). Debunking the myth about minority parents. *Education Horizons, 67*(4), 119-123.

Chavkin, N.F. (Ed.). (1993). *Families and schools in a pluralistic society.* Albany, NY: State University of New York Press.

Chinn, P. C., & Plata, M. (1986). Perspectives and educational implications of Southeast Asian students. In Kitano, M. K., & Chinn, P. C. (Eds.), *Exceptional Asian children and youth* (pp. 12-28). Reston, VA: The Council for Exceptional Children.

Christiansen, K. M., & Delgado, G. L. (Eds.). (1993). *Multicultural issues in deafness.* White Plains, NY: Longman.

Chodorow, N. (1978). *The reproduction of mothering.* Berkeley: University of California Press.

Chodorow, N. (1989). *Feminism and psychoanalytic theory.* New Haven, CT: Yale University Press.

Chu, H., & Levy, J. (1988). Multicultural skills for bilingual teachers. *NABE Journal, 12*(2), 17-36.

Chubb, J.E., & Moe, T.M. (1990). *Politics, markets, and America's schools.*Washington, DC: The Brookings Institution.

Clark, D. L., Lotto, L. S., & McCarthy, M. M. (1980). Factors associated with success in urban elementary schools. *Phi Delta Kappan, 61,* 467-470.

Clark, L., DeWolf, S., & Clark, C. (1992). Teaching teachers to avoid having culturally assaultive classrooms. *Young Children, 47*(5), 4-9.

Clark, R. M. (1983). *Family life and School achievement: Why poor Black children succeed or fail.* Chicago: University of Chicago Press.

Clune, W. H., & Witte, J. A. (Eds.). (1990). *Choice and control in American education* (2 volumes). Bristol, PA: Falmer Press.

Coates, B. (1972). White adult behavior toward Black and White children. *Child Development, 43*(1), 143-154.

Cocking, R. R., & Mestre, J. P. (Eds.). (1988). *Linguistic and cultural influences on learning mathematics.* Hillsdale, NJ: Lawrence Erlbaum Associates.

Cohen, H. & Chasnoff, D. (Producers), & Chasnoff, D. (Director). (1996). It's elementary: Talking about gay issues in school [Film]. (Available from Women's Educational Media, 21800 Bryant St., Suite 203, San Francisco, CA 94110)

Cohen, R. (1969). Conceptual styles, culture conflict and nonverbal tests of intelligence. *American Anthropologist, 71,* 828-856.

Collier, C., & Hoover, J. J. (1987). *Cognitive learning strategies for minority handicapped students.* Lindale, TX: Hamilton Publications.

Collier, J. P. (1985). University models for ESL and bilingual teacher training. In National Clearinghouse for Bilingual Education. *Issues in English Language Development* (pp. 81-90). Rosslyn, VA: Editor.

Coleman, J. S. (1966). *Equality of educational opportunity.* Washington, DC: U.S. Office of Education.

Coleman, J. S. (1990). *Equality and achievement in education.* Boulder, CO: Westview Press.

Colville-Hall, S. MacDonald, S., & Smolen, L. (1995). Preparing preservice teachers for diversity in learners. *Journal of Teacher Education, 4*(4), 295-303.

Comer, J. P. (1980). *School power: Implications of an intervention project.* New York: Free Press.

Comer, J. P. (1986). Parent participation in the schools. *Phi Delta Kappan, 67*(6), 442-446.

Comer, J. P. (1988). Educating poor minority children. *Scientific American, 259*(5), 42-49.

Comer, J. P. (1989). The school development program: A psychosocial model of school intervention. In G. L. Berry & J. K. Asamen (Eds.), *Black students: Psychosocial issues and academic achievement* (pp. 264-285). Newbury Park, CA: Sage.

Comer, J. P., & Haynes, N. M. (1987). Dimensions of children's self-concept as predictors of social competence. *Journal of Social Psychology, 127*(3), 321-329.

Contreras, A. (1988). Multicultural attitudes and knowledge of education students at a midwestern university. In C. A. Heid (Ed.). *Multicultural education: Knowledge and perceptions* (pp. 63-78). Bloomington, IN: Indiana University, Center for Urban and Multicultural Education.

Coons, J. E., & Sugarman, S. D. (1978). *Education by choice: The case for family control.* Berkeley: University of California Press.

Cooper, A., Beare, P., & Thorman, J. (1990). Preparing teachers for diversity: A comparison of student teaching experiences in Minnesota and South Texas. *Action in Teacher Education, 12*(3), 1-4.

Cornbleth, C., & Korth, W. (1980). Teacher perceptions and teacher-student interaction in integrated classrooms. *Journal of Experimental Education, 48,* 259-263.

Cortes, C. (1978). Chicano culture, experience and learning. In L. Morris, G. Sather, & S. Scull (Eds.), *Extracting learning styles from social/cultural diversity: A study of five American minorities* (pp. 29-53). Norman, OK: Southwest Teacher Corps Network. (Grant No. G007-700-119, U.S. Office of Education, Department of Health, Education, and Welfare)

Crain, R. L., Mahard, R. E., & Narot, R. E. (1982). *Making desegregation work.* Cambridge, MA: Ballinger.

Cross, W. E., Jr. (1991). *Shades of Black: Diversity in African American identity.* Philadelphia: Temple University Press.

Crouse, J., & Trusheim, D. (1988). *The case against the SAT.* Chicago: The University of Chicago Press.

Cruickshank, D. R. (1985). Profile of an effective teacher. In F. Schultz (Ed.), *Education 87-88* (pp. 216-221). Guilford, CT: Dushkin Publishing.

Cureton, G. O. (1978). Using a Black learning style. *The Reading Teacher, 31*(7), 751-756.

Damico, S. B., & Scott, E. (1985, March). Comparison of Black and White females' behavior in elementary and middle schools. Paper presented at the Annual Meeting of the American Educational Research Association, Chicago.

Dandy, E. B. (1991). *Black communications: Breaking down the barriers.* Chicago, IL: African American Images.

Darling-Hammond, L., Ancess, J., & Falk, B. (1995). *Authentic assessment in action: Studies of schools and students at work.* New York: Teachers College Press.

Darling-Hammond, L. (1995). Inequity and access to knowledge. In J. Banks & C. Banks (Eds.), *Handbook of research on multicultural education* (pp.465-483). New York: Macmillan

Datta, L., Schaefer, E., & Davis, M. (1968). Sex and scholastic aptitude as variables in teachers' ratings of adjustment and classroom behaviors of Negro and other seventh-grade students. *Journal of Educational Psychology, 59,* 94-101.

Dawkins, M. & Braddock, J. (1994). The continuing significance of desegregation: School racial composition and African American inclusion in society, *Journal of Negro Education, 63*(3), 394-405

Deering, R.E. & Stanutz, A. (1995). Preservice field experience as a multicultural component of a teacher education program. *Journal of Teacher Education, 46*(5), 390-394.

Delpit, L. D. (1986). Skills and other dilemmas of a progressive Black educator. *Harvard Educational Review, 57,* 379-385.

Delpit. L. D. (1990). The silenced dialogue: Power and pedagogy in educating other people's children. In N. M. Hidalgo, C. L. McDowell, & E. V. Siddle (Eds.), *Facing racism in education* (pp. 84-102). Cambridge, MA: Harvard Educational Review.

Delpit, L. D. (1991). Teachers' voices: Rethinking teacher education for diversity. Paper presented at the Annual Meeting of the American Association of Colleges for Teacher Education, Atlanta.

Delpit, L. D. (1995). *Other people's children: White teachers, students of color, and other cultural conflicts in the classroom.* New York: The New Press.

DeMeis, D. K., & Turner, R. H. (1978). Effects of students' race, physical attractiveness, and dialect on teachers' evaluations. *Contemporary Educational Psychology, 3*(1), 77-86.

Derman-Sparks, L., & The A.B.C. Task Force (1989). *Anti-bias curriculum: Tools for empowering young children.* Washington, DC: National Association for the Education of Young Children.

Development Associates. (1984, December). Final report: Descriptive study phase of the national longitudinal evaluation of the effectiveness of services for language minority limited English proficient students. Arlington, VA: Author.

Diaz, C. (1989). Hispanic cultures and cognitive styles: Implications for teachers. *Multicultural Leader, 2*(4), 1-4.

Dillard, J. L. (1972). *Black English: Its history and usage in the United States.* New York: Vintage House.

Dillard, J. L. (1977). *Lexicon of Black English.* New York: Seabury Press.

Dilworth, M. E. (1990). *Reading between the lines: Teachers and their racial/ethnic cultures.* Washington, DC: ERIC Clearinghouse for Teacher Education, American Association of Colleges for Teacher Education. (ERIC Document Reproduction Service No. ED 322 148).

Dilworth, M. E. (1992). *Diversity in teacher education: New expectations.* San Francisco: Jossey-Bass.

Doyle, D. P., & Levine, M. (1984). Magnet schools: Choice and quality in public education. *Phi Delta Kappan, 66*(4), 268.

Duberman, M. (Ed.). (1993a). *Issues in gay and lesbian life* (series of 25 vols.). Broomall, PA: Chelsea House Publishers.

Duberman, M. (Ed.). (1993b). *Lives of notable gay men and lesbian woman* (series of 30 vols.). Broomall, PA: Chelsea House Publishers.

Ducette, J.P., Sewell, T. E., & Shapiro, J. P. (1996). Diversity in education: Problem and possibilities. In F. B. Murray (Ed.), *The teacher educator's handbook: Building a knowledge base for the preparation of teachers.* San Francisco: Jossey-Bass.

Dunn, R., & Dunn, K. (1978). *Teaching students through their individual learning styles.* Reston, VA: Preston Co.

Dunn, R. (1983). Learning style and its relation to exceptionality at both ends of the spectrum. *Exceptional Children, 49*(6), 496-506.

Dunn, R., Beaudry, J., & Klavas, A. (1989). Survey of research on learning styles. *Educational Leadership, 46*(6), 50-58.

Duran, R. R., Emight, M. K., & Rock, D. A. (1985). Language factors and Hispanic freshman's student profile. *College Board Report #85-3,* ETSRR #85-44, New York.

Dusek, J. B. (Ed.). (1985). *Teacher expectancies.* Hillsdale, NJ: Lawrence Erlbaum Associates.

Dusek, J. B., & Joseph, G. (1983). The bases of teacher expectancies: A meta-analysis. *Journal of Educational Psychology, 75,* 327-346.

Edmonds, R. (1979). Effective schools for the urban poor. *Educational Leadership, 37*(1), 15-23.

Elmore, R. F. (1993). What knowledge base? *Review of Educational Research, 63*(3), 314-318.

Dweck, C. S., & Bush, E. S. (1976). Sex differences in learned helplessness: Differential debilitation with peer and adult evaluators. *Developmental Psychology, 12*(2), 147-156.

Eaves, R. C. (1975). Teacher race, student race, and behavior problem checklist. *Journal of Abnormal Child Psychology, 3*(1), 1-9.

Eller-Powell, R. (1994). Teaching for change in Appalachia. In E. R. Hollins, J. E. King, & W. C. Hayman (Eds.), *Teaching diverse populations: Formulating a knowledge base* (pp. 61-74). Albany, NY: State University of New York Press.

Elliot, R. (1992). *We: Lessons on equal worth and dignity.* Minneapolis: United Nations Association of Minnesota. (1929 S. 5th St., Minneapolis, MN 55454)

Epstein, J. L. (1987). Parent involvement: What research says to administrators. *Education and Urban Society, 19*(2), 119-136.

Equity Institute. (1994). Sticks, stones, and stereotypes. [Film]. (Available from Equity Institute, Inc., 6400 Hollis St., Suite 15, Emeryville, CA 94608)

Evans, E., Torrey, C., & Newton, S. (1997). Multicultural education requirements in teacher certification. *Multicultural Education, 4* (3), 9-11.

Family Communications, Inc. (1995). *Different and the same.* Pittsburgh, PA: Author.

Feldman, R. S., & Orchowsky, S. (1979). Race and performance of students as determinants of teacher nonverbal behavior. *Contemporary Education Psychology, 4*(4), 324-333.

Figueroa, R. A., & Gallegos, E. A. (1978). Ethnic differences in school behavior. *Sociology of Education,* 51(4), 289-298.

Figueroa, R. A., & Garcia, E. (1994). Issues in testing students from culturally and linguistically diverse backgrounds. *Multicultural Education, 2*(1), 10-19.

Fillmore, L. W., & Valadez, C. (1986). Teaching bilingual learners. In M. C. Wittrock (Ed.), *Handbook of research on teaching* (3rd ed., pp. 648-685). New York: Macmillan.

Finney, S. & Orr, J. (1995). I've really learned a lot, but...": Cross-cultural understanding and teacher education in a racist society. *Journal of Teacher Education, 46*(5), 327-333.

Florio-Ruane, S. (1989). Social organization of classes and schools. In M. C. Reynolds (Ed.), *Knowledge base for the beginning teacher* (pp. 163-172). New York: Pergamon.

Fordham, S., & Ogbu, J. U. (1986). Black students; school success: Coping with the "burden of acting White." *The Urban Review, 18*(3), 176-206.

Foster, H. L. (1974). *Ribbin', jivin', and playin' the dozens: The unrecognized dilemma of inner city schools.* Cambridge, MA: Ballinger Publishing.

Foster, M. (1989). It's cookin' now: A performance analysis of the speech events of a Black teacher in an urban community college. *Language in Society, 18*(1), 1-29.

Foster, M. (1990). Some things change, most stay the same: Examining the pedagogical practice of African American women teachers. Paper presented at the American Anthropological Association Conference, Washington, DC.

Foster, M. (1991a). Constancy, change and constraints in the lives of Black women teachers: Some things change, most stay the same. *NWSA Journal, 3*(2), 233-261.

Foster, M. (1991b). The politics of race: Through African teachers' eyes. *Journal of Education, 172*(3), 123-141.

Foster, M. (1991c). African-American teachers and the politics of race. In K. Weiler (Ed.), *What schools can do: Critical pedagogy and practice.* Buffalo, NY: State University of New York Press.

Foster, M. (1991d). Just got to find a way: Case studies of the lives and practice of exemplary Black high school teachers. In M. Foster (Ed.), *Readings on equal education. Volume 11: Qualitative investigations into schools and schooling* (pp. 273-309). New York: AMS Press.

Foster, M. (1993). Educating for competence in community and culture: Exploring the views of exemplary African American teachers. *Urban Education, 27*(4), 370-394.

Foster, M. (1994). Effective Black teachers: A literature review. In E. R. Hollins, J. E. King, & W. C. Hayman (Eds.), *Teaching diverse populations: Formulating a knowledge base* (pp. 225-241). Albany, NY: State University of New York Press.

Frankenstein, M. (1994). Critical mathematics education: Bringing multiculturalism to the mathematics classroom. In M. M. Atwater, K. Radzick-Marsh, & M. Strutchens (Eds.), *Multicultural education: Inclusion of all* (pp. 167-189). Athens, GA: The University of Georgia.

Friedman, P. (1976). Comparison of teacher reinforcement schedules for students with different social class backgrounds. *Journal of Educational Psychology, 68*(3), 286-293.

Frosch, M. (1994). *Coming of age in America: A multicultural anthology.* New York: W. W. Norton.

Fuller, M. L. (1994). The monocultural graduate in the multicultural environment: A challenge for teacher educators, *Journal of Teacher Education, 45*(4), 269-277.

Garcia, E. E. (1990). Educating teachers for language minority students. In W. R. Houston, M. Haberman, & J. Sikula (Eds.), *Handbook of research on teacher education* (pp. 717-729). New York: Macmillan.

Garcia, E. E. (1994). Attributes of effective schools for language minority students. In E. R. Hollins, J. E. King, & W. C. Hayman (Eds.), *Teaching diverse populations: Formulating a knowledge base* (pp. 93-103). Albany, NY: State University of New York Press.

Gardner, H. (1983). *Frames of mind.* New York: Basic Books.

Garmezy, N. (1991). Resiliency and vulnerability to adverse developmental outcomes associated with poverty. *American Behavioral Scientist, 34*(4), 416-430.

Gary, L. E. (Ed.). (1981). *Black men.* Newbury Park, CA: Sage.

Gay, G. (1977a). Changing conceptions of multicultural education. *Educational Perspectives, 16*(4), 4-9.

Gay, G. (1977b). Curriculum for multicultural teacher education. In F. H. Klassen & D. M. Gollnick (Eds.), *Pluralism and the American teacher: Issues and case studies* (pp. 31-62). Washington, DC: American Association of Colleges for Teacher Education.

Gay, G. (1983). Multiethnic education:Historical developments and future prospects. *Phi Delta Kappan, 64*(8),560-563.

Gay, G. (1986). Multicultural teacher education. In Banks, J. A., & Lynch, J. (Eds.), *Multicultural education in Western societies* (pp. 154-177). New York: Holt, Rinehart & Winston.

Gay, G. (1993). Building cultural bridges: A proposal for teacher education. *Education and Urban Society, 25*(3), 285-299.

Gay, G. (1994). *At the essence of learning: Multicultural education.* West Lafayette, IN: Kappa Delta Pi.

Gay, G. (1995). African American culture and contributions in American life. In C. A. Grant (Ed.), *Educating for diversity: An anthology of multicultural voices* (pp. 35-52). Boston: Allyn & Bacon.

Gay, G., & Baber, W. L. (1987). *Expressively Black: The cultural basis of ethnic identity.* New York: Praeger.

Gay/Lesbian/Queer studies. (Winter, 1994). [Thematic issue] *Radical Teacher* (No. 45). Cambridge, MA. (Order from Radical Teacher, P.O. Box 102 Kendall Square Post Office, Cambridge, MA 02142)

Gersten, R., & Keating, T. (1987). Long-term benefits from direct instruction. *Educational Leadership, 44*(6), 28-31.

Gibbs, J. T., Huang, L. N., & Associates (Eds.). (1989). *Children of color: Psychological interventions with minority youth.* San Francisco: Jossey-Bass.

Gifford, B. R. (Ed.). (1989a). *Test policy and the politics of opportunity allocation: The workplace and the law* (Vol. 1). Boston: Kluwer Academic Publishers.

Gifford, B. R. (Ed.). (1989b). *Test policy and test performance: Education, language and culture* (Vol. 2). Boston: Kluwer Academic Publishers.

Gilligan, C. (1977). In a different voice: Women's conception of self and of morality. *Harvard Educational Review, 47*(4), 481-517.

Gilligan, C. (1982). *In a different voice: Psychological theory and women's development.* Cambridge, MA: Harvard University Press.

Gilliland, H., Reyner, J., & Schaffer, R. (Eds.). (1988). *Teaching the Native American.* Dubuque, IA: Kendall/Hunt Publishing Company.

Giroux, J. B. (1989). Feminist theory as pedagogical practice. *Contemporary Education, 61*(1), 6-10.

Glenn, B.C. (1981). *What works? An Examination of effective schools for poor Black children.* Cambridge, MA: Center for Law and Education.

Glenn, C. L. (1993). Creating an irresponsible school choice program. In C. Marshall (Ed.), *The new politics of race and gender* (pp. 128-139). Washington, DC: Falmer Press.

Gollnick, D. M. (1992). Multicultural education: Policies and practices in teacher education. In C. A. Grant (Ed.), *Research & multicultural education: From margins to the mainstream* (pp. 218-239).Washington, DC: Falmer Press.

Gollnick, D. M. (1992). Understanding the dynamics of race, class, and gender. In M. E. Dilworth (Ed.), *Diversity in teacher education: New expectations* (pp. 63-78). San Francisco: Jossey-Bass.

Gollnick, D. M., & Chinn, P. C. (1998). *Multicultural education in a pluralistic society.* (5th ed.). Riverside, NY: Macmillan College Publishing Co.

Gomez, M. L. (1993). Prospective teachers' perspectives on teaching diverse children: A review with implications for teacher education and practice. *Journal of Negro Education, 62*(4), 459-474.

Gomez, M. L., & Tabachnick, B. R. (1991, April). We are the answer: Preparing preservice teachers to teach diverse learners. Paper presented at the Annual Meeting of the American Educational Research Association, Chicago, IL.

Gomez, M. L., & Tabachnick, B. R. (1992). Telling teaching stories. *Teaching Education, 4*(2), 129-138.

Good, T., & Brophy, J. (1978). *Looking in classrooms.* New York: Harper & Row.

Goodlad, J. (1984). *A place called school.* New York: McGraw-Hill.

Goodwin, M. H. (1990) *He-said-she-said: Talk as social organization among Black children.* Bloomington, IN: Indiana University Press.

Gordon, M. (1964). *Assimilation in American life.* New York: Oxford University Press.

Gottlieb, D. (1964). Teaching and students:The views of Negro and White teachers. *Sociology of Education, 37,* 345-353.

Gould, S. J. (1981). *The mismeasure of man.* New York: W. W. Norton.

Graham, S. (1994, Spring). Motivation in African Americans. *Review of Educational Research, 64*(1), 55-117.

Grant, C. A. (1991). Culture and teaching: What do teachers need to know? In M. M. Kennedy (Ed.), *Teaching academic subjects to diverse learners* (pp. 237-256). New York: Teachers College Press.

Grant, C. A. (Ed.). (1992). *Multicultural education for the twenty-first century.* Morristown, NJ: Silver Burdett Ginn, Inc.

Grant, C. A. (Ed.). (1992). *Research & multicultural education: From the margins to the mainstream.* Washington, DC: Falmer Press.

Grant, C. A. (Ed.). (1995). *Educating for diversity: An anthology of multicultural voices.* Boston: Allyn & Bacon.

Grant, C. A. & Gomez, M. L. (Eds.) (1996). *Making schooling multicultural: Campus and classroom.* Englewood Cliffs, NJ: Merrill.

Grant, C. A., & Secada, W. G. (1990). Preparing teachers for cultural diversity. In W. R. Houston, M. Haberman, & J. Sikula (Eds.), *Handbook of research on teacher education* (pp. 403-422). New York, NY: Macmillan.

Grant, C. A., & Sleeter, C. E. (1986). Race, class, and gender in educational research: An argument for integrative analysis. *Review of Educational Research, 56,* 195-211.

Grant, L. (1984). Black females' "place" in desegregated classrooms. *Sociology of Education, 57*(2), 98-111.

Grant, L. (1985). Race-gender status, classroom interaction, and childrens' socialization in elementary school. In L. C. Wilkinson and C. B. Marrett (Eds.), *Gender influences in classroom interaction* (pp. 57-77). New York: Academic Press.

Greene, B., & Herek, G. (Eds.). (1994). *Lesbian and gay psychology: Theory, research, and clinical applications.* Newbury Park, CA: Sage.

Green, R. L., & Pettigrew, T. F. (1976, February). Urban desegregation and White flight: A response to Coleman. *Phi Delta Kappan, 57*(6), 399-402.

Greenman, N.R. & Kimmel, E. B. (1995). The road to multicultural education: Potholes of resistance. *Journal of Teacher Education, 46*(5), 360-368.

Gregorc, A. F. (1979). Learning styles: Their nature and effects. *NASSP Bulletin,* 19-26.

Gregorc, A. F. (1982). *The energic model of styles.* Columbia, CT: Gregorc Associates, Inc.

Gregorc, A. F., & Butler, K. (1984, April) Learning is a matter of styles. *Vocational Education,59*(3), 27-29.

Griffeth, A. R., & London, C. B. G. (1980). Student relations among inner-city teachers: A comparative study by teacher race. *Education, 101*(2), 139-147.

Grossman, H. (1995). *Teaching in a diverse society.* Boston: Allyn & Bacon.

Grossman, H., & Grossman, S. H. (1994). *Gender issues in education.* Boston: Allyn & Bacon.

Grote, K. (1991). Diversity awareness profile. San Diego, CA: Pfieffer & Company.

Guilmet, G. M. (1979). Instructor reaction to verbal and non-verbal styles: An example of Navajo and Caucasian children. *Anthropology and Education Quarterly, 10*(4), 254-266.

Gutek, G. (1997). American education in a global society: Internationalizing teacher education (first published in 1993). Prospect Heights, IL: Waveland Press, Inc.

Guyton, E.M. & Weshe, M.V. (1996). Multicultural efficacy scale. Unpublished instrument, Department of Early Childhood Education, Georgia State University, Atlanta, Georgia.

Hale-Benson, J. E. (1982). *Black children: Their roots, culture, and learning styles* (Rev. Ed.). Baltimore, MD: Johns Hopkins University Press.

Hale-Benson, J. E. (1986). *Black children: Their roots, culture, and learning styles* (2nd ed.). Baltimore: Johns Hopkins University Press.

Hallinan, M. T. (1990). The effects of ability grouping in secondary schools: A response to Slavin's best-evidence synthesis. *Review of Educational Research, 60*(3), 501-504.

Hallinan, M. T., & Sorensen, A.B. (1986). Student characteristics and assignment to ability groups: Two conceptual frameworks. *The Sociological Quarterly, 27*(1), 1-13.

Halpern, D. R. (1986). *Sex differences in cognitive abilities.* Hillsdale, NJ: Lawrence Erlbaum.

Hamilton, S. (1983). The social side of schooling. *Elementary School Journal, 83,* 313-334.

Hanna, J.L. (1988). *Disruptive school behavior: Class, race, and culture.* New York: Holmes and Meier.

Harbeck, K. M. (Ed.). (1992). *Coming out of the classroom closet: Gay and lesbian students, teachers and curricula.* Binghamton, NY: Harrington Park Press.

Hartigon, J. A., & Wigdor, A. K. (Eds.). (1989). *Fairness in employment testing: Validity generalization, minority issues, and the General Aptitude Test Battery.* Washington, DC: National Academy Press.

Harry, B. (1992). *Cultural diversity, families, and the special education system: Communication and empowerment.* New York: Teachers College Press.

Harvey, D. G., & Slavin, G. T. (1975). The relationship between SES and teacher expectation. *School Forces, 54*(1), 140-159.

Harvey, K. D., Harjo, L. D., & Jackson, J. K. (1990). *Teaching about Native Americans* (Bulletin No. 84). Washington, DC: National Council for the Social Studies.

Hauser, R. M., & Anderson, D. K. (1991). Post-high school plans and aspirations of Black and White high school seniors: 1976-1986. *Sociology of Education, 64*(4), p. 272.

Hawley, W. D., Rosenholtz, S. J., Goodstein, H., & Hasselbring, R. (1984a). Effective teaching. *Peabody Journal of Education, 61,* 15-52.

Hawley, W. D., Rosenholtz, S. J., Goodstein, H., & Hasselbring, R. (1984b). Parent involvement and assistance. *Peabody Journal of Education, 61,* 117-24.

Hawley, W. D., Rosenholtz, S. J., Goodstein, H., & Hasselbring, R. (1984c). School leadership and student learning. *Peabody Journal of Education, 61,* 53-83.

Heath, S. B. (1982). Questioning at home and at school: A comparative study. In G. Spindler, (Ed.), *Doing the ethnography of schooling: Educational anthropology in action* (pp. 96-131). New York: Holt Rinehart & Winston.

Heath, S. B. (1983). *Ways with words: Language, life, and work in communities and classrooms.* Cambridge: Cambridge University Press.

Hedges, L. V., & Waddington, T. (1993). From evidence to knowledge to policy: Research synthesis for policy formation. *Review of Educational Research, 63*(3), 345-352.

Helms, J. E. (Ed.). (1990). *Black and White racial identity: Theory, research, and practice.* Westport, CT: Greenwood Press.

Helms, J. E. (1994). Racial identity in the school environment. In P. Pederson & J. C. Carey (Eds.), *Multicultural counseling in schools: A practical handbook* (pp. 19-37). Boston, MA: Allyn & Bacon.

Herman, J., Aschbacher, P., & Winters, L. (1991). *A practical guide to alternative assessment.* Alexandria, VA: Association for Supervision and Curriculum Development.

Henkes, R. (1993). *The art of Black American women: Works of twenty-four artists of the twentieth century.* Jefferson, NC: McFarland and Co.

Hernandez, H. (1989). *Multicultural education: A teacher's guide to content and process.* Columbus, OH: Merrill.

Herrnstein, R. J., & Murray, C. (1994). *The bell curve: Intelligence and class structure in American life.* New York: The Free Press.

Herskovits, M. J. (1935). What has Africa given America? New Republic. LXXIV, No. 1083. Reprinted in Herskovitz, F. S. (Ed.). (1966), *The new world Negro.* Bloomington, IN: Indiana University Press.

Herskovits, M. J. (1958). *The myth of the Negro past.* Boston: Beacon Press.

Hidalgo, N. M., McDowell, C. L., & Siddle, E. V. (Eds.). (1990). *Facing racism in education.* Cambridge: Harvard Educational Review.

Hill, H. D. (1989). *Effective strategies for teaching minority students.* Bloomington, IN: National Educational Service.

Hilliard, A. G. (1976). Alternatives to I.Q. testing: An approach to the identification of gifted minority children. Final report to the California State Department of Education.

Hilliard, A. G. (1988a). Psychological factors associated with language in the education of the African-American child. *Journal of Negro Education, 52*(1), 24-34.

Hilliard, A. G. (1988b). Public support for successful instructional practices for at-risk students. In Council of Chief State School Officers (Eds.), *School success for students at risk* (pp. 195-208). Orlando: Harcourt Brace Jovanovich.

Hilliard, A. G. (1988c, May). Promoting African-American student achievement. In Yount, R. & Magurn, H. (Eds.), *School/college collaboration: Teaching at-risk youth* (pp. 69-79). Conference proceedings, Council of Chief State School Officers, Baltimore, MD.

Hilliard, A. G. (Ed.). (1991). *Testing African American students.* Morristown, NJ: Aaron Press.

Hillman, S. B., & Davenport, G. (1978). Teacher-student interactions in desegregated schools. *Journal of Educational Psychology, 70*(4), 545-553.

Hirsch, E. D., Jr. (1987). *Cultural literacy: What every American needs to know.* Boston: Houghton Mifflin.

Ho, M. K. (Ed.). (1992). *Minority children and adolescents in therapy.* Newbury Park, CA: Sage.

Hollins, E. R. (1982). The Marva Collins story revisited. *Journal of Teacher Education, 33*(1), 37-40.

Hollins, E. R., King, J. E., & Hayman, W. C. (1994). *Teaching diverse populations: Formulating a knowledge base.* Albany, NY: State University of New York Press.

Homel, P., Palij, M., & Aaronson, D. (Eds.). (1987). *Childhood bilingualism: Aspects of linguistic, cognitive, and social development.* Hillsdale, NJ: Lawrence Erlbaum Associates.

Hong, M. (Ed.). (1993). *Growing up Asian American: An anthology.* New York: William Morrow.

Hood, S., & Parker, L. (1994). Minority students informing the faculty: Implications for racial diversity and the future of teacher education. *Journal of Teacher Education, 45*(3), 164-174.

Hoover-Dempsey, K. V., Bassler, O. C., & Brissie, J. S. (1987). Parent involvement: Contributions of teacher efficacy, school socioeconomic status, and other school characteristics. *American Educational Research Journal, 24,* 417-435.

Hoover, M. (1996). *Super literacy.* Benicia, CA: Onyx.

Houlton, D. (1986). *Cultural diversity in the primary school.* London: B. T. Balsford, Ltd.

Houston, W. R., Haberman, M., & Sikula, J. (Eds.). (1990). *Handbook of research on teacher education.* New York: Macmillan.

Howard, G. R. (1993, September). Whites in multicultural education: Rethinking our role. *Phi Delta Kappan,* 36-41.

Howe, F. (1971). Teacher perception toward the learning ability of students from different racial and socio-economic backgrounds. (Doctoral dissertation, Michigan State University)). *Dissertation Abstracts International, 31,* 5847A.

Huang, J., & Hatch, E. A. (1978). A Chinese child's acquisition of English. In E. M. Hatch (Ed.), *Second language acquisition.* Rowley, MA: Newbury House.

Huber, T. (1991). Culturally responsible pedagogy: Defining the concept for teacher education. Paper presented at the Annual Meeting of the American Association of Colleges for Teacher Education, Atlanta, GA.

Huber, T., & Pewewardy, C. D. (1990). A review of literature to determine successful programs for and approaches to maximizing learning for diverse learners. *Collected original resources in education (CORE), 14*(3). An International

Journal of Educational Research in Microfiche. Birmingham, West Midlands, Great Britain.

Huber-Bowen, T. (1993). *Teaching in the diverse classroom: Learner-centered activities that work.* Bloomington, IN: National Educational Service.

Huffine, S., Silverne, S. B., & Brooks, D. M. (1979). Teacher responses to contextually specific sex type behaviors in kindergarten children. *Educational Research Quarterly, 4*(2), 29-35.

Irons, C., Burnett, J., & Hoo Foon, S. W. (1993). *Mathematics from many cultures.* San Francisco, CA: Mimosa Publications.

Irvine, J. J. (1988). Teacher race as a factor in Black students' achievement. Paper presented at the Annual Meeting of the American Educational Research Association, New Orleans.

Irvine, J. J. (1990). *Black students and school failure: Policies, practices, and prescriptions.* New York: Greenwood Press.

Irvine, J. J. (1997). (Ed.) *Critical knowledge for diverse teachers & learners.* Washington, DC: American Association of Colleges for Teacher Education

Jackson, B. (1975). Black identity development. *Journal of Education Diversity, 2,* 19-25.

Jackson, G., & Cosca, G. (1974). The inequality of educational opportunity in the Southwest: An observational study of ethnically mixed classrooms. *American Educational Research Journal, 11,* 219-229.

James, T., & Levin, H. M. (Eds). (1983). *Public dollars for private schools: The case of tuition tax credits.* Philadelphia: Temple University Press.

Jaynes, G. D. & Williams, R. M. (Eds.) (1989). *A common destiny: Blacks in American society.* Washington, D.C.: National Academy Press.

Jencks, C., Smith, M., Acland, H., Bone, M. J., Cohen, D., Gintis, H., Ueyns, B., & Michaelson, S. (1972). *Inequality: A reassessment of the effect of family and schooling in America.* New York: Harper Colophon.

Jennings, K. (Ed.) (1995). *One teacher in ten.* Boston: Alyson Publications.

Jensen, M., & Rosenfeld, L. B. (1974). Influence mode of presentation, ethnicity, and social class on teachers' evaluations of students. *Journal of Educational Psychology, 66,* 540-542.

Jordan, M.L.R. (1995). Reflections on the challenges, possibilities, and perplexities of preparing preservice teachers for culturally diverse classrooms. *Journal of Teacher Education, 46*(5), 369-374.

Kagan, S. M., & Madsen, M. C. (1971). Cooperation and competition of Mexican, Mexican American, and Anglo American children of two ages under four instructional sets. *Developmental Psychology, 5*(1), 32-39.

Kagan, S. M., & Madsen, M. C. (1972). Experimental analyses of cooperation and competition of Anglo-American and Mexican children. *Developmental Psychology, 6*(1), 49-59.

Kahle, J. B. (1994). Interrelationships between gender, affect, and retention in science classrooms: A theoretical approach. In M. M. Atwater, K. Radzick-Marsh, & M. Strutchens (Eds.), *Multicultural education: Inclusion of all* (pp. 135-150). Athens, GA: University of Georgia.

Kamin, L. J. (1974). *The science and politics of I.Q.* Potomac, MD: Lawrence Erlbaum.

Kaulback, B. (1989). Styles of learning among native children. In B. R. Shade (Ed.), *Culture, style and the educative process* (pp. 137-149). Springfield, IL: Charles C. Thomas.

Keller, G. D., Deneen, J. R. & Magallan, R. J. (Eds.). (1991). *Assessment and access: Hispanics in higher education.* Albany, NY: State University of New York Press.

Kelley, C., & Meyers, J. (1993). Cross-cultural adaptability inventory. La Jolla, CA: Author (The CCAI can now be ordered from National Computer Systems, Inc., P.O. Box 1416, Minneapolis, MN 55440).

Kennedy, M. M. (Ed.). (1991). *Teaching academic subjects to diverse learners.* New York: Teachers College Press.

Kerdeman, D., & Phillips, D. C. (1993). Empiricism and the knowledge base of educational practice. *Review of Educational Research, 63*(3), 305-313.

Khayatt, M.D. (1992). *Lesbian teachers: An invisible presence.* Albany, NY: State University of New York Press.

King, E. W. (1990). *Teaching ethnic and gender awareness: Methods and materials for the elementary school* (2nd ed.). Dubuque, IA: Kendall-Hunt.

King, E. W., Chipman, M., & Cruz-Janzen, M. (1994). *Educating young children in a diverse society.* Boston: Allyn & Bacon.

King, J. E. (1994). The purpose of schooling for African American children: Including cultural knowledge. In E. R. Hollins, J. E. King, & W. C. Hayman (Eds.), *Teaching diverse populations: Formulating a knowledge base* (pp. 25-44). Albany, NY: State University of New York Press.

Kinsey, A. C., Pomeroy, M., & Martin, C. E. (1948). *Sexual behavior in the human male.* Philadelphia, PA: Saunders.

Kissen, R. M. (1996). *The last closet: The real lives of lesbian and gay teachers.* Portsmouth, NH: Heinemann.

Kleg, M. (1993). *Hate, prejudice, and racism.* Albany: State University of New York Press.

Kliebard, H. M. (1993). What is a knowledge base, and who would use it if we had one? *Review of Educational Research, 63*(3), 295-303.

Kluckhohn, F. R. (1968). Variations in value orientation as a factor in educational planning. In E.M. Bower & W. C. Hallister (Eds.), *Behavioral science frontiers in education* (pp. 289-314). New York: Riley.

Kluckhohn, F. R., & Strodtbeck, F. L. (1961). *Variations in value orientations.* Evanston, IL: Row, Peterson.

Kochman, T. (1981). *Black and White styles in conflict.* Chicago: University of Chicago Press.

Kohls, R. L. (1984a). *Survival kit for overseas living.* Yarmouth, ME: Intercultural Press.

Kohls, R. L. (1984b). *The values Americans live by.* International Connections, Washington, DC: The Washington International Center.

Kozol, J. (1991). *Savage inequalities: Children in America's schools.* NY: Crown.

Krause, M. C. (1983). *Multicultural mathematics materials.* Reston, VA: National Council of Teachers of Mathematics.

Kuykendall, C. (1992). *From rage to hope: Strategies for reclaiming Black & Hispanic students.* Bloomington, IN: National Education Service.

Labov, W. (1970). The logic of nonstandard English. In F. Williams (Ed.), *Language and poverty: Perspective on a theme* (pp. 153-189). Chicago: Markham Publishing.

Labov, W. (1972). *Language in the inner city.* Philadelphia: University of Pennsylvania Press.

Ladson-Billings, G. (1990). Culturally relevant teaching. *College Board Review, 155,* 20-25.

Ladson-Billings, G. (1991, April). When difference means disaster: Reflections on a teacher education strategy for countering student resistance to diversity. Paper presented at the Annual Meeting of the American Educational Research Association, Chicago, IL.

Ladson-Billings, G. (1991b). Like lightening in a bottle: Attempting to capture the pedagogical excellence of successful teachers of black students. *International Journal of Qualitative Studies, 3,* 335-344.

Ladson-Billings, G. (1992). Culturally relevant teaching: The key to making multicultural education work. In C. A. Grant (Ed.), *Research and multicultural education: From margins to the mainstream* (pp. 106-121). Washington, DC: Falmer Press.

Ladson-Billings, G. (1994a). *The dreamkeepers: Successful teachers of African American children.* San Francisco: Jossey-Bass.

Ladson-Billings, G. (1994b). Who will teach our children: Preparing teachers to successfully teach African American students. In E. R. Hollins, J. E. King, & W. C. Hayman (Eds.), *Teaching diverse populations: Formulating a knowledge base* (pp. 129-158). Albany, NY: State University of New York Press.

Laosa, L. M. (1977, Spring). Inequality in the classroom: Observational research on teacher-student interactions. *Aztlan, 8,* 51-67.

Larke, P. J. (1990). Cultural diversity awareness inventory: Assessing the sensitivity of preservice teachers. *Action in Teacher Education, 12*(3), 23-30.

Larke, P.J., Wiseman, D., & Bradley, C. (1990). The minority membership project: Changing attitudes of preservice teachers for diverse classrooms. *Action in Teacher Education, 12*(13), 5-12.

Larkin, J. M. & Sleeter, C.E. (Eds.). (1995). *Developing multicultural teacher education curriculum.* Albany, NY: Slate University of New York Press.

Laurendeau-Bendavid, M. (1977). Culture, schooling, and cognitive development: A comparative study of children in French Canada and Rwanda. In P. R. Dasen (Ed.), *Piagetian psychology: Cross-cultural contribution* (pp. 123-168). New York: Gardner/Wiley.

Lazear, D. (1991a). *Seven ways of knowing: Teaching for multiple intelligences* (2nd ed.). Palatine, IL: Skylight Publishing.

Lazear, D. (1991b). *Seven ways of teaching: The artistry of teaching with multiple intelligences.* Palatine, IL: Skylight Publishing.

Leacock, E. B. (1969). *Teaching and learning in city schools.* New York: Basic Books.

Leap, W. L. (Ed.). (1977). *Studies in southwestern Indian English.* San Antonio: Trinity University Press.

Leap, W. L. (1992). American Indian English. In J. Reyner (Ed.), *Teaching American Indian students* (pp. 143-153). Norman, OK: University of Oklahoma Press.

Lee, C. D. (1993). *Signifying as scaffold for literary interpretation: The pedagogical implications of an African American discourse genre.* Urbana, IL: National Council of Teachers of English.

Levin, H. M. (1987). Accelerated schools for disadvantaged students. *Educational Leadership, 44*(6), 19-21.

Levin, J. R. (1993). Estimating the value of a knowledge base for school learning. *Review of Educational Research, 63*(3), 335-343.

Levy, D. C. (Ed.). (1986). Private education: Studies in choice and public policy. New York: Oxford University Press.

Lewis, S. (1990). *African American art and artists.* Berkeley: University of California Press.

Lietz, J., & Gregory, M. (1978). Pupil race and sex determinants of office and exceptional educational referral. *Educational Research Quarterly, 3*(2), 61-66.

Lightfoot, S. L. (1978). *Worlds apart: Relationships between families and schools.* New York: Basic Books.

Liontes, L. B. (1992). *At-risk families and schools: Becoming partners.* Eugene, OR: ERIC Clearinghouse.

Lipmangay, D. (1994). *We all go together: Creative activities for children to use with multicultural folksongs.* Phoenix, AZ: Oryx Press.

Locurto, C. (1991). *Sense and nonsense about I.Q: The case for uniqueness.* New York: Praeger.

Lometey, K., & Brookins, C. C. (1988). Independent black school institutions: A cultural perspective. In D.T. Slaughter & D. J. Johnson (Eds.), *Visible now: Blacks in private schools* (pp. 163-183). Westport, CT: Greenwood Press.

Longstreet, W. C. (1978). *Aspects of ethnicity.* New York: Teachers College Press.

Lopez, T. A. (Ed.). (1993). *Growing up Chicana/Chicano.* New York: William Morrow.

Lowe, R., & Miner, B. (Eds.). (1992). False choices: Why school vouchers threaten our children's future, a special edition of *Rethinking Schools.* Milwaukee, WI: Rethinking Schools, Ltd.

Lynch, J. (1983). *The multicultural curriculum.* London: Batsford Academic and Education Ltd.

Maddaus, J. E. (1988, October). Families, neighborhoods, and schools: Parental perspectives and actions regarding choice in elementary school enrollment. *Dissertation Abstracts International, 49*(3), 477-933.

Magill, F. N. (Ed.). (1992). *Masterpieces of African American literature.* New York: Harper Collins.

Mahan, J. (1982a). Community involvement components in culturally oriented teacher preparation. *Education, 103*(2), 163-172.

Mahan, J. (1982b). Native Americans as teacher trainers: Anatomy and outcomes of a cultural immersion project. *Journal of Educational Equity and Leadership, 2*(2), 100-110.

Maker, C. J., & Schierer, S. W. (Eds.). (1989). *Critical issues in gifted education: Defensible programs for cultural and ethnic minorities.* Austin, TX: Pro-Ed.

Mallea, J. R. (1984). Cultural diversity in Canadian education: A review of contemporary developments. In R. J. Samuda, J. W. Berry, & M. Laferriere (Eds.), *Multiculturalism in Canada: Social and educational perspectives* (pp. 78-98). Toronto: Allyn & Bacon.

Mallory, B. L., & New, R. S. (Eds.).(1994). *Diversity & developmentally appropriate practices.* New York: Teachers College Press.

Manning, M. L. & Baruth, L. G. (1996). *Multicultural education of children and adolescents* (2nd ed.). Boston: Allyn & Bacon.

Manski, C. F. (1992). *Educational choice (vouchers) and social mobility.* Madison: University of Wisconsin, Institute for Research on Poverty.

Marrett, C. B., Mizuno, Y., & Collins, G. (1992). Schools and opportunities for multicultural contact. In C. A. Grant (Ed.), *Research & multicultural education: From the margins to the mainstream* (pp.203-217). Washington, DC: Falmer Press.

Martinez, J. L. (1977). *Chicano psychology.* New York: Academic Press.

Marwit, K. S., Marwit, S. J., & Walker, E. (1978, December). Effects of student race and physical attractiveness on teachers' judgments of transgressions. *Journal of Educational Psychology, 70*(6), 911-915.

Matiella, A. C. (1990). *The multicultural caterpillar: Children's activities in cultural awareness.* Santa Cruz: CA: ETR Associates.

Matlin, M. W. (1987). *The psychology of women.* Ft. Worth, TX: Holt, Rinehart and Winston.

Matsumoto, d. (1994). *People: Psychology from a cultural perspective.* Pacific Grove.

Mattenson, P. T., Batiste, D.A. & Bermon, V. S. (1994). *A world of difference institute: Elementary study guide.* New York: Anti-Defamation League.

Mattox, C. W. (1989). Shake it to the one you love best: Play songs and lullabies from Black musical traditions. El Sobrante, CA: Warren-Mattox Productions.

Matute-Bianchi, M. E. (1986). Ethnic identities and patterns of school success and failure among Mexican-descent and Japanese-American students in a California high school: An ethnographic analysis. *American Journal of Education, 95* (1), 233-255.

McAdoo, H. P. (Ed.). (1988). *Black families.* Newbury Park, CA: Sage.

McCaleb, S. P. (1994). *Building communities of learners: A collaboration among teachers, students, families, and community.* New York: St. Martin's Press.

McCall, A. L. (1995). Constructing conceptions of multicultural teaching: Preservice teachers' life experiences and teacher education. *Journal of Teacher Education, 46* (5), 340-350.

McCormick, T. M. (1994). *Creating the nonsexist classroom: A multicultural approach.* New York: Teachers College Press.

McDiarmid, G. W. (1991). What teachers need to know about cultural diversity: Restoring subject matter in the picture. In M. M. Kennedy (Ed.), *Teaching academic subjects to diverse learners* (pp. 257-269). New York: Teachers College Press.

McGhan, B. R. (1978). Teachers' use of authority and its relationship to socioeconomic status, race, teacher characteristics, and educational outcomes. (ERIC Document Reproduction Service No. ED 151 329)

McGinnis, J. R. (1994). Paths to multiculturalism: One perspective. In M. M. Atwater, K. Radzik-Marsh, & M. Strutchens (Eds.), *Multicultural education: Inclusion of all* (pp. 277-289). Athens, GA: The University of Georgia.

McIntosh, P. (1990, Winter). White privilege: Unpacking the invisible knapsack. *Independent School,* 111-115.

McIntyre, M. S. W., Wait, M. S., & Yoast, R. (1990). *Resilience among high risk youth.* Madison, WI: Wisconsin Clearinghouse.

McPartland, J. M., Dawkins, R. I., Braddock II, J. H., Crain, R. L., & Strauss, J. (1985). Three reports: Effects of employer job placement decisions and school desegregation on minority and female hiring and occupational attainment (Report 359). Baltimore: Center for Social Organization of Schools, Johns Hopkins University.

Meier, K. J., Stewart, J., Jr., & England, R. (1989). *Race, class, and education: The politics of second generation discrimination.* Madison, WI: University of Wisconsin Press.

Mensh, E., & Mensh, H. (1991). *The IQ mythology: Class, race, gender, and inequality.* Carbondale, IL: Southern Illinois University Press.

Metheny, W. (1979). The influences of grade and pupil ability levels on teachers' conceptions of reading. (ERIC Document Reproduction Services No. 182-713)

Meyer, W., & Lindstrom, D. (1969). *The distribution of teacher approval and disapproval of Head Start children.* Washington, DC: Office of Economic Opportunity.

Miller, J. G., & Bersoff, D. M. (1992). Culture and moral judgement: How are conflicts between justice and interpersonal responsiblities resolved? *Journal of Personality and Social Psychology, 62,* 156-172.

Mitzel, H. E. (1982). *Encyclopedia of educational research* (5th ed.). New York: The Free Press.

Mizell, L. (1992). *Think about racism.* New York: Walker & Co.

Mohatt, G., & Erickson, F. (1981). Cultural differences in teaching styles in an Odawa school: A socioliguistic approach. In H. Trueba, G. P. Guthrie, & K. H. Au (Eds.), *Culture and the bilingual classroom: Studies in classroom ethnography* (pp. 105-119). Rowley, MA: Newbury House.

More, A. J. (1989). Native Indian students and their learning styles: Research results and classroom applications. In B. J. Shade (Ed.), *Culture, style, and the educative process* (pp. 150-166). Springfield, IL: Charles C. Thomas.

Morris, L., Sather, G., & Scull, S. (Eds.). (1978). Extracting learning styles from social cultural diversity. Norman, OK: Southwest Teacher Corps Network. (Grant No. G007-700-119, Teacher Corps, U. S. Office of Education, Department of Health, Education, and Welfare)

Morrow, R. D. (1989). Southeast-Asian parent involvement: Can it be a reality? *Elementary School Guidance and Counseling, 23,* 289-297.

Multicultural mathematics poster and activities. (1984). Reston, VA: National Council of Teachers of Mathematics.

Multiculturalism in mathematics, science,and technology: readings and activities (1993). New York: Addison-Wesley.

Muñoz-Hernández, S., & Santiago Santiago, I. (1985). Toward a qualitative analysis of teacher disapproval behavior. In R. V. Padillo (Ed.), *Theory, technology and public policy on bilingual education* (pp. 99-112). Rosslyn, VA: National Clearinghouse for Bilingual Education.

Murrell, P., Jr. (1992, April). Deconstructing informal knowledge of exemplary teaching in diverse urban communities: Apprenticing preservice teachers as case study researchers in cultural sites. Paper presented at the Annual Meeting of the American Educational Research Association, San Francisco, CA.

Murray, F. B. (Ed.). (1996). *The teacher educator's handbook: Building a knowledge base for the preparation of teachers.* San Francisco: Jossey-Bass.

National Alliance of Black School Educators. (1984). *Saving the African American child.* Washington, DC: Author.

National Association of State Directors of Teacher Education and Certification. (1984). NASDTEC certification standards. Washington, DC: Author.

National Commission on Testing and Public Policy. (1990). *From gatekeeper to gateway: Transforming testing in America.* Chestnut Hill, MA: Author. (Order from National Commission on Testing and Public Policy, Boston College, Chestnut Hill, MA 02167)

National Conference. (1994). *Taking America's pulse: A summary report of the National Conference Survey on Inter-group Relations.* New York: Author.

National Conference. (1994). *Educator's guide to straight talk about America.* New York: Author.

Nel, J. (1993, Spring). Preservice teachers' perceptions of the goals of multicultural education: Implications for the empowerment of minority students. *Educational Horizons, 71* (3), 120-125.

Nelson, D., Joseph, G. G., & Williams, J. (1993). *Multicultural mathematics: Teaching mathematics from a global perspective.* New York: Oxford University Press.

Nelson, F. H. (1991). International comparisons of public spending on education (Research report) Washington, DC: American Federation of Teachers.

Newby, R. G. (Ed.). (1995). The bell curve: Laying bare the resurgence of scientific racism (thematic issue). *American Behavioral Scientist, 39* (1).

Nieto, S. (1992). *Affirming diversity: The sociopolitical context of multicultural education.* White Plains, NY: Longman.

Noordholf, K., & Kleinfeld, J. (1990) Shaping the rhetoric of reflection for multicultural settings. In. R. T. Clift, W. R. Houston, & M. C. Pugach (Eds.), *Encouraging reflective practice in education* (pp. 163-185). New York: Teachers College Press.

Noordhoff, K., & Kleinfeld, J. (1991, April). Preparing teachers for multicultural classrooms: A case study in rural Alaska. A paper presented at the Annual Meeting of the American Educational Research Association, Chicago, IL.

Nunley, M. (1995). The bell curve: Too smooth to be true. *American Behavioral Scientist, 39* (1), 74-83.

Oakes, J. (1985). *Keeping track: How schools structure inequality.* New Haven: Yale University Press.

Oakes, J. (1986). Tracking, inequality, and the rhetoric of reform: Why schools don't change. *Journal of Education, 168*(1), 60-80.

Oakes, J. (1990). *Multiplying inequalities: The effects of race, social class, and tracking on opportunities to learn mathematics and science.* Santa Monica, CA: Rand

Ocampo, K. A., Bernal, M. E., & Knight, G. P. (1993). Gender, race, and ethnicity: The sequencing of social constancies. In M. E. Bernal & G. P. Knight (Eds.), *Ethnic identity: Formation and transmission among Hispanics and other minorities* (pp. 11-30). Albany, NY: State University of New York Press.

O'Hair, M. J. & Odell, S. (Eds.). (1993). *Diversity and teaching: Teacher education yearbook I.* Orlando, FL: Harcourt Brace Jovanovich College Publishers.

Ogbu, J. (1978). *Minority education and caste: The American in cross-cultural perspective.* New York: Academic Press.

Ogbu, J. (1981). Schooling in the ghetto: An ecological perspective on community and home influences. Washington, DC: National Institute of Education (ERIC # ED 252270).

Ogbu, J. (1982). Cultural discontinuities and schooling. *Anthropology and Education Quarterly, 13*(4), 290-307.

Ogbu, J. (1987). Variability in minority school performance: A problem in search of an explanation. *Anthropology and Education Quarterly, 18*(4), 312-334.

Ogbu, J. (1988a). Class stratification, racial stratification, and schooling. In L. Weis (Ed.), *Class, race, and gender in American education* (pp. 163-182). Albany, NY: State University of New York Press.

Ogbu, J. (1988b). Cultural diversity and human development. In D. T. Slaughter (Ed.), *Black children and poverty: A developmental perspective* (pp. 11-28). San Francisco: Jossey-Bass.

Olson, R. (1991). Results of a K-12 and adult ESL enrollment survey—1991. *TESOL Matters, 1*(5), 4.

Orfield, G. A. (1983). *Public school desegregation in the United States, 1968-1980.* Washington, DC: Joint Center for Political Studies.

Orfield, G. A. (1992). Status of school desegregation: The next generation, Report to the National School Board Association. Alexandria, VA: National School Board Association.

Orfield, G., Backmeier, M., James, D., & Eitle, E. (1997). *Deepening segregation in American public schools.* Cambridge, MA: Harvard University, Harvard Project on School Desegregation.

Orfield, G., Eaton, S., & the Harvard Project on School Desegregation (1996). *Dismantling desegregation: The quiet reversal of Brown v. Board of Education.* New York: W. W. Norton.

Ornstein, A. C. (1991). Enrollment trends in big-city schools. *Peabody Journal of Education, 66*(4), 65-67.

Orr, E. W. (1989). *Twice as less.* New York: W. W. Norton.

Palincsar, A S., & McPhall, J. C. (1993). A critique of the metaphor of distillation in "Toward a Knowledge Base for

School Learning." *Review of Educational Research, 63*(3), 327-334.

Pasteur, A. B., & Toldson, I.L. (1982). *The roots of soul: The psychology of Black expressiveness.* New York: Anchor Press.

Patchen, M. (1982). Black-white contact in schools: Its social and academic effects. East Lafayette, IN: Purdue University Press.

Peck, R. F., Manning, B. A., & Buntain, D. (1977). *The impact of teacher and student characteristics on student self-concept: A review of the research.* Austin, TX: University of Texas.

Pederson, P., & Carey, J. C. (Eds.). (1994). *Multicultural counseling in schools: A practical handbook.* Boston: Allyn & Bacon.

Peoy, D., & Suarez, V. (Eds.). (1992). *Iguana dreams.* New York: Harper Collins.

Pepper, F. C., & Henry, S. (1989). Social and cultural effects on Indian learning style: Classroom implications. In B. R. Shade (Ed.), *Culture, style, and the educative process* (pp. 33-42). Springfield, IL: Charles C. Thomas.

Perry, T., & Delpit, L. (1997). The real Ebonics debate: Power, language, and the education of African-American children. Special issue of *Rethinking Schools*, 12 (1).Milwaukee, WI: Rethinking Schools, Ltd.

Persell, C. H. (1977). *Education and inequality.* New York: The Free Press.

Peterson, P. L. (1993). Toward an understanding of what we know about school learning. *Review of Educational Research, 63*(3), 319-326

Pewewardy, C. D. (1994) Culturally responsible pedagogy in action: An American Indian magnet school. In E. R. Hollins, J. E. King, & W. C. Hayman (Eds.), *Teaching diverse populations: Formulating a knowledge base* (pp. 77-92). Albany, NY: State University of New York Press.

Philip, K., Estapa, A., & Dessetta, A. (Eds.). (1996). *Out with it: Gay and straight teens write about homosexuality.* New York: Youth Communications.

Phinney, J. S. (1993). A three-stage model of ethnic identity development in adolescence. In M. E. Bernal & G. P. Knight (Eds.), *Ethnic identity: Formation and transmission among Hispanics and other minorities* (pp. 61-79). Albany, NY: State University of New York Press.

Phinney, J. S., & Rotheram, M. J. (Eds.). (1987). *Children's ethnic socialization: Pluralism and development.* Newbury Park, CA: Sage.

Ponterotto, J. G., & Pederson, P. (1993). *Preventing prejudice: A guide for counselors and educators.* Newbury Park, CA: Sage.

Powell, A., & Frankenstein, M. (Eds.). (1997). *Ethnomathematics.* Albany, NY: State University of New York Press.

Powell, R. R., Zehm, S., & Garcia, J. (1996). *Field experience: Strategies for exploring diversity in schools.* Englewood Cliffs, NJ: Merrill.

Prager, J., Longshore, D., & Seeman, M. (Eds.). (1986). *School desegregation research: New directions in situational analysis.* New York: Plenum Press.

Presseisen, B. A., Sternberg, R. J., Fischer, K. W., Knight, C. C., & Feuerstein, R. (1990). *Learning and thinking styles: Classroom interaction.* Washington, DC: National Education Association.

Ramirez, G., & Ramirez, J. L. (1994). *Multiethnic children's literature.* Albany, NY: Delmar Publishers, Inc.

Ramirez, M. III., & Castenada, A. (1974). *Cultural democracy, bicognitive development and education.* New York: Academic Press.

Ramsey, P. G. (1987). *Teaching and learning in a diverse world: Multicultural education for young children.* New York: Teachers College Press.

Reck, U. M. (1982, March). Self-concept, school, and social setting: An in-depth view of rural Appalachian and Urban non-Appalachian sixth-graders. Paper presented at the Annual Meeting of the American Educational Research Association, New York, NY: (ERIC Document Reproduction Service No. ED 215 849)

Reck, U.M., Reck, G.G., & Keefe, S. (1987, April).Teachers' perceptions of Appalachian and non-Appalachian students. Paper presented at the Annual Meeting of the American Educational Research Association,Washington, DC.

Reed, D. F. (1993). Multicultural education for preservice teachers. *Action in Teacher Education, 15*(3), 27-34.

Reiff, J. C. (1992). *Learning styles.* Washington, DC: National Education Association.

Revicki., D. A. (1981). The relationship among socioeconomic status, home environment, parent involvement, child self-concept, and child achievement. (ERIC Document Reproduction Service No. ED 206 645)

Reyes, L. H., & Stanic, G. M. (1988, April). A review of the literature on Blacks and mathematics, Research/Technical Report 143. Paper presented at the Annual Meeting of the American Educational Research Association, Chicago.

Reyner, J. (1988). Bilingual education. In J. Reyner (Ed.), *Teaching American Indian students* (pp. 59-95). Norman, OK: University of Oklahoma Press.

Reyner, J. (Ed.). (1992). *Teaching American Indian students.* Norman, OK: University of Oklahoma Press.

Reynolds, M. C. (Ed.). (1989). *Knowledge base for the beginning teacher.* New York: Pergamon.

Reynolds, M. C. (1990). Educating teachers for special education students. In W. R. Houston, M. Haberman, & J. Sikula (Eds.), *Handbook of research on teacher education* (pp. 423-436). New York: Macmillan.

Rich schools, Poor schools (1989, December). *Teacher Magazine*, p. 15.

Richard-Amato, P. A., & Snow, M. A. (Eds.), (1992). *The multicultural classroom: Readings for content-area teachers.* White Plains, NY: Longman.

Richardson, E. H. (1981). Cultural and historical perspectives in counseling American Indians. In D. W. Sue (Ed.), *Counseling the culturally different: Theory and practice* (pp. 216-254). New York: John Wiley & Sons.

Riley, P. (Ed.). (1993). *Growing up Native American.* New York: William Morrow.

Rist, R. C. (1973). *The urban school: A factory for failure.* Cambridge, MA: MIT Press.

Rogers, T., & Soter, A. (Eds.). (1997). *Reading across cultures: Teaching literature in a diverse society.* New York: Teachers College Press.

Rodgers-Rose, L. F. (Ed.). (1980). *The Black woman.* Newbury Park, CA: Sage.

Rosenburg, M., & Simmons, R. (1971). *Black and White self-esteem: The urban school child,* Rose Monograph series. Washington, DC: American Sociological Association, 70-71.

Rossell, C. H. (1990). *The carrot or the stick for school desegregation policy.* Philadelphia: Temple University Press.

Rubovitz, P. C., & Maehr, M. (1973). Pygmallion black and white. *Journal of Personality and Social Psychology, 25*(2), 210-218.

Rutter, M. (1990). Psychosocial resilience and protective mechanisms. In J. Rolf, A. Masten, D. Cichetti, S. Nuechterlein, & S. Weintraub (Eds.), *Risk and protective factors in the development of psychopathology* (pp. 181-214). New York: Cambridge University Press.

Ryan, K., & Cooper, J. M. (1992). *Those who can, teach* (6th ed.). Boston: Houghton Mifflin Company.

Sadker, M., & Sadker, D. (1982). *Sex equity handbook for schools.* New York: Longman.

Sadker, M., & Sadker, D. (1986). Sexism in the classroom: From grade school to graduate school. *Phi Delta Kappan, 67*(7), 512-515.

Sadker, M., & Sadker, D. (1987). *The intellectual exchange—Excellence and equity in college teaching.* Kansas City, MO: The Mid-Continent Regional Educational Laboratory.

Sadker, M. & Sadker, D. (1995). *Failing at fairness: How our schools cheat girls.* New York: Touchstone.

Safilios-Rothschild, C. (1979). Sex-role socialization and sex discrimination: A synthesis of the literature. Washington, DC: National Institute of Education.

Sage, W. (1978). Loaded school bus. *Human Behavior, 7,* 20-21.

Sandowsky, G. R., & Johnson, P. (1994). World views: Culturally learned assumptions and values. In P. Pederson & J. C. Carey (Eds.), *Multicultural counseling in schools* (pp. 59-79). Boston: Allyn & Bacon.

Santos, R. A. (1983). The social emotional development of Filipino-American children. In G. J. Powell (Ed.), *The psychosocial development of minority group children* (pp. 131-146). New York: Brunner/Mazel.

Saracho, O. N. (1989). Cultural differences in the cognitive style of Mexican-American students. In B. J. Shade (Ed.), *Culture, style, and the educative process* (pp. 129-136). Springfield, IL: Charles C. Thomas.

Scagliotti, J. (Producer), & Spalding, R. (Director). (1993). School's out: Gay and lesbian youth [Film]. (Available from In This Life, Inc., 39 West 14th St., Suite 401, New York, NY 10011.

Schniedewind, N., & Davidson, E. (1983). *Open minds to equality: A source book of learning activities to promote race, sex, class, and age equity.* Englewood Cliffs, NH: Prentice Hall.

Schofield, J. W. (1982). *Black and White in school: Trust, tension, and tolerance.* New York: Praeger.

Schoem, D., Frankey, L., Zuniga, X., & Lewis, E. A. (Eds.). (1993). *Multicultural teaching in the university.* Westport, CT: Praeger.

Schweder, R., Mahapatra, M., & Miller, J. G. (1987). Culture and moral development. In J. Kagan & S. Lamb (Eds.). *The emergence of morality in young children.* Chicago, IL: University of Chicago Press.

Scollan, R., & Scollan, S. B. (1984). Cooking it up and boiling it down: Abstracts in Athabaskan children's story reading. In D. Tannen (Ed.), *Coherence in spoken and written discourse* (pp. 173-197). Norwood, N J: Ablex.

Scott, M. B., & Ntegeye, M. G. (1980). Acceptance of minority student personality characteristics by Black and White teachers. *Integrated Education, 18*(1-4), 110-112.

Scritchfield, S. A., & Picou, J. S. (1982). The structural significance of other influences for status attainment processes: Black-white variations. *Sociology of Education, 55,* 22-30.

Sears, J. (1987). Peering into the well of loneliness: The responsibility of educators to gay and lesbian youth. In A. Molnar (Ed.), *Social issues and education: Challenge and responsibility* (pp. 79-100). Alexandria, VA: Association for Supervision and Curriculum Development.

Sears, J. (1988a). Attitudes, experiences, and feelings of guidance counselors about working with homosexual students. Paper presented at the Annual Meeting of the American Educational Research Association, New Orleans. (ERIC Document Reproduction Service No. 296210)

Sears, J. (1988b). Growing up gay: Is anyone there to listen? *American School Counselors Association Newsletter, 26*, 8-9.

Sears, J. (1989a). Personal feelings and professional attitudes of prospective teachers toward homosexuality and homosexual students: Research findings and curriculum recommendations. Paper presented at the Annual Meeting of the American Educational Research Association, San Francisco. (ERIC No. 312222)

Sears, J. (1989b). The impact of gender and race on growing up lesbian and gay in the South. *NWSA Journal, 1*(3), 422-457.

Sears, J. (1990). Problems and possibilities in "Homophobia" education. *Empathy, 2*(2), 61.

Sears, J. (1991). *Growing up gay in the South: Race, gender, and journeys of the spirit.* New York: Haworth Press, Inc.

Sears, J. (1992). Educators, homosexuality, and homosexual students: Are personal feelings related to professional beliefs? In K. M. Harbeck (Ed.), *Coming out of the classroom closet: Gay and lesbian students, teachers, and curricula* (pp. 29-79). Binghamton, NY: Harrington Park Press.

Sears, J. (in press). The impact of culture and ideology on the construction of gender and sexual identities: Developing a critically-based sexuality curriculum. In J. Sears (Ed.), *Sexuality and the curriculum.* New York: Teachers College Press.

Secada, W. G. (1994). Equity and the teaching of mathematics. In M. M. Atwater, K. Radzick-Marsh, & M. Strutchens (Eds.), *Multicultural education: Inclusion of all* (pp. 19-38). Athens, GA: University of Georgia.

Shade, B. J. (1978). The social-psychological characteristics of achieving Black children. *Negro Educational Review, 29*(2), 80-86.

Shade, B. J. (1982). Afro-American cognitive style: A variable in school success? *Review of Educational Research, 52*(2), 219-244.

Shade, B. J. (1983). Cognitive strategies as determinants of school achievement. *Psychology in the Schools, 20*(4), 488-493.

Shade, B. J. (1986). Is there an Afro-American cognitive style? *Journal of Black Psychology, 13,* 13-16.

Shade, B. J. (Ed.). (1989a). *Culture, style, and the educative process.* Springfield, IL: Charles C. Thomas.

Shade, B. J. (1989a). The culture and style of Mexican American society. In B. J. Shade (Ed.), *Culture, style, and the educative process* (pp. 43-48). Springfield, IL: Charles C. Thomas.

Shade, B. J. (1994). Understanding the African American learner. In E. R. Hollins, J. E. King, & W. C. Hayman (Eds.), *Teaching diverse populations: Formulating a knowledge base* (pp. 61-76). Albany, NY: State University of New York Press.

Shade, B.J. (Ed.). (1997). *Culture, style, and the educative process: Making schools work for racially diverse students* (2nd ed.). Springfield, IL: Charles C. Thomas.

Shaw, C. C. (in press). Instructional pluralism: A means to realizing the dream of multicultural, social reconstructionist education. In C. A. Grant & M. L. Gomez (Eds.), *Campus and classroom: Making schooling multicultural.*

Shaw, C. C. (1993). Multicultural teacher education: A call for conceptual change. *Multicultural Education, 1* (3), 22-24.

Shortchanging education: How U.S. spending on grades K-12 lags behind other industrialized nations. Economic Policy Institute. Reprinted in "The President's Worst Subject," *U.S. News and World Report,* August 6, 1990, p. 46.

Shea, J. D. (1985).Studies of cognitive development in Papua New Guinea. *International Journal of Psychology,20,* 33-61.

Shulman, L. (1987a). Knowledge and teaching: Foundations of the new reform.*Harvard Educational Review, 57*(1),1-22.

Shulman, L. (1987b). Assessment for teaching: An initiative for the profession. *Phi Delta Kappan, 69*(1), 38-44.

Shultz, F. (Ed.) (1997). *Annual editions: Multicultural education 97/98.* Guilford, CT: The Dushkin Publishing Co.

Sikula, J. (Ed.). (1996). *Handbook of research on teacher education* (2nd ed.). New York: Macmillan.

Silverman, J. (1994). *Traditional Black music* (15 volumes). Broomall, PA: Chelsea House Publishers.

Simpson, A. W., & Erikson, M. T. (1983). Teachers' verbal and nonverbal communication patterns as a function of teacher race, student gender, and student race. *American Educational Research Journal, 20*(2), 183-198.

Singer, B. L. (Ed.). (1994). *Growing up gay, growing up lesbian: A literary anthology.* New York: New Press.

Singer, J. D. (1993). On faith and microscopes: Methodological lenses for learning about learning. *Review of Educational Research, 63*(3), 353-364.

Sizemore, B. A. (1979). The four M curriculum: A way to shape the future. *Journal of Negro Education, 48*(3), 341-356.

Slapin, B., & Seale, D. (Eds.). (1992). *Through Indian eyes: The native experience in books for children.* Philadelphia: New Society Publishers.

Slaughter, C. A. (1969). Cognitive style: Some implications for curriculum and instructional practices among Negro children. *Journal of Negro Education, 38*(2), 105-111.

Slaughter-Defoe, D. T., Nakagawa, K., Takanish, R., & Johnson, D. J. (1990). Towards cultural, ecological perspective on schooling and achievement in African and Asian American children. *Child Development, 61,* 363-383.

Slavin, R. E. (1980). Cooperative learning in teams: State of the art. *Educational Psychologist, 15,* 93-11.

Slavin, R. E. (1982). *Cooperative learning: Student teams.* Washington, DC: National Education Association.

Slavin. R. E. (1987a). Cooperative learning and the cooperative school. *Educational Leadership, 45*(3), 7-13.

Slavin, R. E. (1987b). Cooperative learning and the education of Black students. In D. S. Strickland & E. J. Cooper (Eds.), *Educating Black children: America's challenge* (pp. 63-68). Washington, DC: Howard University Press.

Slavin, R. E. (1990). Achievement effects of ability grouping in secondary schools: A best evidence synthesis. *Review of Educational Research, 60*(3), 471-499.

Slavin, R. E., & Madden, N. A. (1979). School practices that improve race relations. *American Educational Research Journal, 16*(2), 169-180.

Sleeter, C. E. (1985). A need for research on preservice teacher education for mainstreaming and multicultural education. *Journal of Education Equity and Leadership, 5*(3), 205-215.

Sleeter, C. E. (1992). *Keepers of the American dream: A study of staff development and multicultural education.* Washington, DC: Falmer Press.

Sleeter, C. E. (1994). White racism. *Multicultural Education, 1*(4), 5-9, 39.

Sleeter, C. E. (Ed.). (1991). *Empowerment through multicultural education.* Albany, NY: State University of New York Press.

Sleeter, C. E., & Grant, C. A. (1988a). *Making choices for multicultural education: Five approaches to race, class, and gender* (1st ed.). New York: Merrill.

Sleeter, C. E., & Grant, C. A. (1988b). *Turning on learning: Five approaches for multicultural teaching plans for race, class, gender, and disability.* Columbus, OH: Merrill.

Sleeter, C. E. (1992, Spring). Resisting racial awareness: How teachers understand the social order from their racial, gender, and social class locations. *Educational Foundation, 6*(2), 7-32.

Sleeter, C. E., & Grant, C. A. (1994). *Making choices for multicultural teacher education: Five approaches to race, class, and gender* (2nd ed.). New York: Merrill.

Smith, E. J. (1982). The Black female adolescent: A review of the educational, career and psychological literature. *Psychology of Women Quarterly, 6,* 261-288.

Smith, G. P. (1991). Toward defining a culturally responsible pedagogy for education: The knowledge base for educating teachers of minority and culturally diverse students. Paper presented at the Annual Meeting of the American Association of Colleges for Teacher Education, Atlanta, GA.

Smith, J. A. (1979). Ascribed and achieved student characteristics in teacher expectancy: Relationship of socioeconomic status to academic achievement, academic self-concept, and vocational aspirations. *Dissertation Abstracts International, 40,* 959-60B.

Smitherman, G. (1977). *Talkin' and testifying: The language of Black America.* Boston: Houghton Mifflin.

Smitherman, G. (1985). What go around come around: Keepin' perspective. In C. K. Brooks (Ed), *Tapping potential: English and language arts for the Black learner* (pp. 41-62). Urbana, IL: Black Caucus of the National Council of Teachers of English.

Smock, P. J., & Wilson, F. D. (1991, October). Desegregation and the stability of white school enrollments: A school level analysis, 1968-1984. *Sociology of Education, 64,* 278-292.

St. Clair, R., & Leap, W. L. (Eds.). (1982). *Language renewal among American Indian tribes.* Rosslyn, VA: National Clearinghouse for Bilingual Education.

St. John, N. (1971). Thirty-six teachers: Their characteristics and outcomes for Black and White pupils. *American Educational Research Journal, 8*(4), 635-648.

Stalvey, L. M. (1970). *The education of a WASP.* Madison, WI: University of Wisconsin Press.

Staples, R. (Ed.). (1971). *The Black family: Essays and studies.* Belmont, CA: Wadsworth.

Stewart, S. A. (1969, Spring). Urban Negro speech: Sociolinguistic factors affecting English teaching. *Florida FL Reporter, 7,* 50.

Stiffman, A. R., & Davis, L. E. (1990). *Ethnic issues in adolescent men 'al health.* Newbury Park, CA: Sage.

Strutchens, M. (1994). Mathematical empowerment and African American families. In M. M. Atwater, K. Radzick-Marsh, & M. Strutchens (Eds.), *Multicultural education: Inclusion of all* (pp. 257-269). Athens, GA: University of Georgia.

Sue, D. W. (1975). Asian Americans: Social-psychological forces affecting their life styles. In S. Picou & R. Campbell (Eds.), *Career behavior of special groups* (pp. 97-121). Columbus, OH: Charles E. Merrill.

Sue, D. W., & Sue, D.M. (1983). Psychological development of Chinese-American children. In G. J. Powell, (Ed.), *The psychosocial development of minority group children* (pp. 159-166). New York: Brunner/Mazel.

Sue, D. W., with chapter contributions by Richardson, E. H., Ruis, R. A., & Smith, E. J. (1981). *Counseling the culturally different: Theory and practice.* New York: John Wiley & Sons.

Swisher, F., & Doyle, D. (1992). Adapting instruction to culture. In J. Reyner (Ed.), *Teaching American Indian students* (pp. 81-95). Norman, OK: University of Oklahoma Press.

Swisher, K. G., & Paval, M. D. (1994). American Indian learning styles survey: An assessment of teacher knowledge. *Journal of Education Issues of Language Minority Students, 13,* 59-77.

Takaki, R. (1993). *A different mirror: A history of multicultural America.* New York: Little, Brown & Co.

Tatum, B. D. (1992). Talking about race, learning about racism: The application of racial identity development theory in the classroom. *Harvard Educational Review, 62* (1), 1-24.

Tavris, C. (1992). *The mismeasure of woman: Why women are not the better sex, the inferior sex, or the opposite sex.* New York: Simon & Schuster.

Tavris, C., & Offis, C. (1977). *The longest war: Sex differences in perspective.* New York: Harcourt Brace Jovanovich.

Taylor, M. C. (1979). Race, sex, and the expression of self-fulfilling prophecies in a laboratory teaching situation. *Journal of Personality and Social Psychology, 37*(6), 897-912.

Tellez,K. (1996). Authentic assessment. In J. Sikula (Ed.), *Handbook of research on teacher education* (2nd ed.), pp. 704-721). New York: Macmillan.

Thernstrom, S. (Ed.). (1980). *Harvard encyclopedia of American ethnic groups.* Cambridge, MA: Belknap/Harvard University Press.

Thompson, B. J. (1993). *Words can hurt you: Beginning a program of anti-bias education.* New York: Addison Wesley.

Tiedt, P. L., & Tiedt, I. M. (1995). *Multicultural teaching: A handbook of activities, information, and resources* (4th ed.). Boston: Allyn & Bacon.

Timar, R., & Shimanski, D. (1993). Categorical wars: Zero-sum politics and school finance. In C. Marshall (Ed.), *The new politics of race and gender* (pp. 19-35). Washington, DC: Falmer Press.

Tobias, S., Cole, C., Zibrin, M., & Bodlakova. (1982, February). Teacher-student ethnicity and recommendations for special education referrals. *Journal of Educational Psychology, 74,* 72-76.

Tobias, S., Zibrin, M., Menell, C. (1983, October). Special education referrals: Failure to replicate student-teacher ethnicity interaction. *Journal of Educational Psychology, 75,* 705-707.

Tomlinson, S. (1981). Multicultural teaching and the secondary school. In M. Craft (Ed.), *Teaching in a multicultural society: The task for teacher education* (pp. 133-140). Lewes, England: Falmer Press.

Tong, B. R. (1978). Warriors and victims: Chinese American sensibility and learning styles. In L. Morris, G. Sather, & S. Scull (Eds.), *Extracting learning styles from social/cultural diversity: A study of five American minorities* (pp. 70-93). Norman, OK: Southwest Teacher Corps. Network. (Grant No. G007-700-119, U.S. Office of Education, Department of Health, Education, and Welfare)

Torres-Guzman, M. E., Mercado, C. I., Quintero, A. H., & Viera, D. R. (1994). Teaching and learning in Puerto Rican/Latino collaboratives: Implications for teacher education. In E. R. Hollins, J. E. King, & W. C. Hayman (Eds.), *Teaching diverse populations: Formulating a knowledge base* (pp. 105-127). Albany, NY: State University of New York Press.

Tran, M., Young, R. L., & DiLella, J. D. (1994). Multicultural education courses and the student teacher: Eliminating stereotypical attitudes in our ethnically diverse classrooms. *Journal of Teacher Education, 45*(3), 183-189.

Trent, W. (1991). Desegregation analysis report. New York: The Legal Defense and Educational Fund.

Trueba, H. R., Guthrie, G. P., & Au, K. H. (Eds.). (1981). *Culture and the bilingual classroom: Studies in classroom ethnography.* Rowley, MA: Newbury House.

Turner, L. D. (1941). Linguistic research and African survivals. *American Council of Learned Societies, Bulletin No. 69,* 32, pp. 68-69.

Turner, L. D. (1949). *Africanisms in the Gullah dialect.* Chicago: University of Chicago Press.

Unks, G. (Ed.) (1995). *The gay teen: Educational practice and theory for lesbian, gay, and bisexual adolescents.* New York: Routledge, Inc.

U. S. Commission on Civil Rights. (1974). *Toward quality education for Mexican Americans.* (Report VI: Mexican-American Study). Washington, DC: U.S. Government Printing Office.

Valdez, G., & Figueroa, R. A. (in press). *Bilingualism and psychometrics: A special case of bias.* New York: Ablex.

Valdez, J. M. (Ed.). (1982). *Culture bound: Bridging the cultural gap in language teaching.* New York: Cambridge University Press.

Van Sertima, I. (Ed.). (1989). *Blacks in science: Ancient and modern.* London: Transaction Books.

Velie, A. R. (Ed.). (1991). *American Indian literature.* Norman, OK: University of Oklahoma Press.

Villegas, A. M. (1988). School failures and cultural mismatch: Another view. *Urban Review, 20,* 253-265.

Villegas, A. M. (1991). *Culturally responsive pedagogy for the 1990s and beyond.* Princeton, NJ: Educational Testing Service.

Villegas, A. M. (1992, February). The competence needed by beginning teachers in a multicultural society. Paper presented at the Annual Meeting of the Association of Teacher Educators, Orlando.

Vogt, L., Jordon, D., & Thorp, R. (1987). Explaining school failure, producing school success: Two cases. *Anthropology and Education Quarterly, 18*(4), 276-286.

Vold, E. B. (Ed.). (1992). *Multicultural education in early childhood classrooms.* Washington, DC: National Education Association.

Walberg, H. J. (1984). Families as partners in educational productivity. *Phi Delta Kappan, 65*(6), 397-400.

Walburg, H. J. (1984). Improving the productivity of America's schools. *Educational Leadership, 41*(8), 19-27.

Walsh, C. E. (1991). *Pedagogy and the struggle for voice: Issues of language, power, and schooling for Puerto Ricans.* New York: Bergan and Garvey.

Wang, M. C., Haertel, G. D., & Walberg, H. J. (1993). Toward a knowledge base for school learning. *Review of Educational Research, 63*(3), 249-294.

Ward, M. C. (1971). *Them children: A study in language learning.* Prospect Heights, IL: Waveland Press Inc.

Woreley, D., & Perry, J., Jr. (Eds.). (1993). *African American literature: An anthology of nonfiction, fiction, poetry, and drama.* Lincolnwood, IL: National Textbook Co.

Warren, K. (1989). Rewriting the future: The feminist challenges to the mainstream curriculum. *Feminist Teacher, 4,* 46-52.

Warren, R. L. (1982). Schooling, biculturalism, and ethnic identity: A case study. In G. Spindler (Ed.), *Doing the ethnography of schooling.* Prospect Heights, IL: Waveland.

Washington, V. (1980). Teachers in integrated classrooms: Profiles of attitudes, perceptions, and behavior. *The Elementary School Journal, 80*(4), 193-201.

Washington, V. (1982). Racial differences in teacher perceptions of first and fourth grade pupils on selected characteristics. *Journal of Negro Education, 51*(1), 60-72.

Wayson, W. (1988, April). Multicultural education among seniors in the College of Education at Ohio State University. Paper presented at the Annual Meeting of the American Educational Research Association, New Orleans.

Wells, A. S., & Crain, R. L. (1994). Perpetuation theory and the long-term effects of school desegregation. *Review of Educational Research, 64*(4), 531-555.

Wheelock, A. (1992). Crossing the tracks: How "untracking" can save America's schools. New York: The New Press.

Wiggens, G. (1988, March). Ten radical suggestions for school reform. *Education Week, 8,* p. 28.

Wilkerson, M. A. (1980). The effects of sex and ethnicity upon teachers' expectations of students. *Dissertation Abstracts International, 41,* 637A.

Williams, B. (1994). Restructuring to educate diverse learners: A decision making framework. Paper presented at the Multicultural Minority Education conference sponsored by FEA/United, Florida Department of Education, FTP-NEA, Orlando, FL.

Williams, D. L., & Chavkin, N. F. (1989). Essential elements of strong parental involvement programs. *Educational Leadership, 47*(2), 18-20.

Williams, F. (1970). Psychological correlation of speech characteristics: On sounding "disadvantaged." *Journal of Speech and Hearing Research, 13,* 472-488.

Williamson, J. V. (1975). A look at Black English. In R. L. Williams (Ed.), *Ebonics: The true language of Black folks* (pp. 11-23). St. Louis: Robert L. Williams and Associates.

Wilson, F. D. (1985, July). The impact of school desegregation programs on White public school enrollment, 1968-1976. *Sociology of Education, 58*(3), 137-153.

Wilson, P. S., & Padron, J. C. M. (1994). Moving toward culture-inclusive mathematics education. In M. M. Atwater, K. Radzick-March, & M. Strutchens (Eds.), *Multicultural education: Inclusion of all* (pp. 39-63). Athens, GA: University of Georgia.

Wilson, P. S., Padron, J. C. M., Strutchens, M. E., & Thomas, A. J. (1994). Annotated bibliography of multicultural issues in mathematics education. Athens, GA: The University of Georgia. Unpublished manuscript.

Wilson, W. J. (1984). *The declining significance of race: Black and changing American institutions.* New York: Cambridge University Press.

Winfield, L. (1991). Resilience, schooling, and development in African American youth. [Special Issue]. *Education and Urban Society, 24* (1), 5-14.

Wittrock, M. C. (1986). *Handbook of research on teaching* (3rd ed.). New York: Macmillan.

Woodward, W. D., & Salzer, R. T. (1971). Black children's speech and teachers' evaluation. *Urban Education, 6* (2/3), 167-173.

Woolridge, P., & Richman, C. L. (1985). Teachers' choice of punishment as a function of a students' gender, age, race, and I.Q. level. *Journal of School Psychology, 23*(1), 19-29.

Word, C., Zanna, M., & Cooper, J. (1974). The nonverbal mediation of self-fulfilling prophecies in interracial interaction. *Journal of Experimental Social Psychology, 10*(2), 109-120.

Wortman, P. M. (1983). *School desegregation and Black achievement: An integrative review.* Ann Arbor, MI: University of Michigan Press.

Yamamoto, J., & Iga, M. (1983). Emotional growth of Japanese American children. In G. J. Powell (Ed.), *The psychosocial development of minority group children* (pp. 167-178). New York: Brunner/Mazel.

Yu, K. H., & Kim, L. I. C. (1983). The growth and development of Korean American children. In G. J. Powell (Ed.), *The psychosocial development of minority group children* (pp. 147-158). New York: Bruner/Mazel.

Zaslavsky, C. (1979). *Africa counts: Number and patterns in African culture.* Brooklyn, NY: Lawrence Hill Books.

Zeichner, K. M. (1993, February). *Educating teachers for cultural diversity.* East Landing, MI: National Center for Research on Teacher Learning, Michigan State University.

Zeichner, K., Melnick, S., & Gomez, M. (Eds.). (1996). *Currents of reform in preservice teacher education.* New York: Teachers College Press.

Zimpher, N. (1989). The RATE Project: A profile of teacher education students. *Journal of Teacher Education, 40* (6), 27-30.

Zimpher, N. L., & Ashburn, E. A. (1992). Countering parochialism in teacher candidates. In M. E. Dilworth (Ed.). *Diversity in teacher education: New expectations* (pp. 40-62). San Francisco: Jossey-Bass.

APPENDIX 1
Knowledge Bases for Diversity in Teacher Education

1.0 Foundations of Multicultural Education

    1.1 Definitions of multicultural education

    1.2 Key terms that constitute the concepts and language of multicultural education such as diversity, cultural pluralism, assimilation, culture, enculturation, acculturation, xenophobia, ethnocentrism, Eurocentrism, racism, classism, sexism, homophobia, prejudice, discrimination, antiracism, antibias, inclusion, exclusion, etc.

    1.3 Principles and philosophical tenets of multicultural education (i.e., differences are not deficits; culture influences the way students learn, etc.)

    1.4 Models of multicultural curriculum infusion

    1.5 Models of personal stages of development from ethnocentrism to multiculturalism and globalism

    1.6 Literature of theory and research that undergirds Multicultural Education as a discipline

2.0 Sociocultural Contexts of Human Growth and Psychological Development in Marginalized Ethnic and Racial Cultures

    2.1 Ethnic patterns of social, physical, and cognitive development

    2.2 Patterns and stages of ethnic identity including self-concept and self-image development

    2.3 Influences of culturally determined and unique patterns of family organization, childrearing practices, and other processes of socialization and development

    2.4 Cultural influences on motivation

    2.5 Resilience among non-mainstream ethnic and racial cultures

    2.6 Critical theory perspectives regarding conventional norms and definitions of "developmentally appropriate practice"

3.0 Cultural and Cognitive Learning Style Theory and Research

    3.1 Descriptive profiles of cultural learning styles for African American, Hispanic American, Native American, Asian American, and other cultural groups

    3.2 Theory and research base that undergirds the cultural learning-style profiles for each group

    3.3 The skills to use cultural learning-style profiles wisely

4.0 Language, Communication and Interactional Styles of Marginalized Cultures

    4.1 The theory and research on language acquisition, particularly of native speakers of languages other than English and English dialects

4.2 Cultural communication and interaction styles (verbal and nonverbal)

4.3 Principles and strategies of teaching English as a second language to speakers of culturally unique English dialects and speakers of first languages other than English

- Black English

- Hispanic American Bilingualism

- Native American and low incidence minority languages

5.0 Essential Elements of Cultures

5.1 A schema for learning about any culture

- Patterns of knowledge and ways of knowing

- Patterns and relevance of values, belief systems, worldviews, customs, traditions, mores, and spirituality

- An ancient through modern history of a culture's people (heroines and heroes), artifacts, music, dance, science, technology, mathematics, philosophy, architecture, government, etc.

- Unique ways different voices of a culture express relationships to other cultures, particularly the dominant culture

- Patterns of unique skills and behaviors

- Patterns of perception and cognition (cognitive styles)

- Languages and communication styles including verbal and nonverbal nuances

5.2 A study of each of the above essential elements in the context of specific or regional cultures (i.e., African American, Mexican American, Navajo, Korean American, etc.)

6.0 Principles of Culturally Responsive Teaching and Culturally Responsive Curriculum Development

6.1 Principles of culturally responsive pedagogy

- definitions: culturally responsive pedagogy, cultural synchronization, cultural incongruity, etc.

- major premises

6.2 Principles of culturally responsive curriculum development

7.0 Effective Strategies for Teaching Minority Students

7.1 Effective teaching research

7.2 Effective schools research

7.3 Cooperative learning research

7.4 Craft wisdom research

7.5 Resilient child research

7.6 Parental involvement research

8.0   Foundations of Racism

    8.1   History of prejudice, discrimination, and racism in the United States

    8.2   Theory and research on how racist attitudes, stereotypes, and prejudices are learned and integrated into self image, personality structure, and ethnic identity

    8.3   Effects of racism on members of the dominant white culture and members of minority cultures

    8.4   The literature of theory and research on changing negative racial attitudes and negative attitudes toward diversity

    8.5   Scales and instruments that purport to measure racism and attitudes toward diversity

    8.6   A study of anti-bias, anti-racist curricula

9.0   Effects of Policy and Practice on Culture, Race, Class, Gender, and Other Categories of Diversity

    9.1   Effects of ability grouping and curriculum tracking

    9.2   Effects of segregated schools by race and class

    9.3   Effects of school choice, privatization and vouchers

    9.4   Effects of inequitable school funding

    9.5   Effects of discipline policy and practice on minority students

    9.6   Effects of teacher expectations and teacher-student interactions

    9.7   Effects of standardized testing

10.0   Culturally Responsive Diagnosis, Measurement, and Assessment

    10.1   Theory and research on skewed diagnosis

    10.2   The validity literature on specific intelligence tests, achievement tests, and aptitude tests, K-higher education

    10.3   The literature that questions the use of tests to allocate educational opportunity in a democratic society

    10.4   The literature on alternative and authentic assessment

11.0   Sociocultural Influences on Subject-Specific Learning

    11.1   Theory and research on the influence of cultural belief systems, values, and expectations that influence non-White ethnic children's learning and achievement in specific subject areas, i.e., mathematics, science, standard English, reading, art, etc.

    11.2   Theory and research on linguistic factors of non-native speaking and dialect speaking groups on mastery of skills in specific subjects

12.0   Gender and Sexual Orientation

12.1 Gender

- Definitions of key terms (nonsexist education, gender-free education, gender sensitive education, non-sexist and culturally inclusive education, feminism, androcentrism, sexism, sex discrimination

- History of sexism in the United States and a more inclusive history of women's lives and contributions in U.S. society

- Theory and research on principles of human growth and development, gender identity and moral development that challenge male-as-norm models

- Theory and research documenting sex discrimination against females in the education system (teacher-student interaction, testing, learning style and communication style preferences, and gender oppressive language, etc.)

- Principles of nonsexist-culturally inclusive curriculum development

- Knowledge of materials for gender and culture inclusive elementary, middle and secondary school curricula

12.2 Sexual Orientation

- Introductory level knowledge about human sexuality including gay, lesbian, and bisexual development and personal empowerment

- The unique psychological, emotional and educational needs of gay, lesbian, and bisexual students including research on internalized homophobia, alienation, and other psychosocial aspects of peer, family and societal rejection and acceptance

- Contemporary survey profiles and literature that present public attitudes regarding homosexuality

- A study of personal lives and voices of gay, lesbian, and bisexual teachers and students

- An examination of gay, lesbian, and bisexual orientation in a variety of cultural contexts, i.e., African American, Hispanic American, Asian American, Native American, and European American, etc., and in the context of other diversity variables such as social class, gender, and religion

- A history of case law on gay and lesbian teacher dismissal and credential revocation and on gay and lesbian students

- Survey knowledge of curriculum and school materials suitable for instruction about historical contributions to society of notable gay men and lesbian woken, instruction for self acceptance and peer acceptance, and instruction in HIV education

13.0   Experiential Knowledge

13.1 Personal and multicultural lifestyle experiences (informal and planned)

13.2 Supervised clinical experiences demonstrating culturally responsive teaching of culturally diverse student populations

Endnotes

[1] *The International Review of African American Art*, a quarterly academic journal, can be purchased by subscription from Hampton University Museum, Haughton, VA 23668 (tel: 804/727-5308). Subscriptions to *American Visions: The Magazine of African American Culture* can be purchased by writing American Visions, P.O. Box 614, Mt. Morris, IL 61054, tel: 1-800/998-0864.

[2] Educators for Social Responsibility publishes an annual catalog of antiracism and prejudice reduction classroom resources. Write Educators for Social Responsibility, 23 Garden Street, Cambridge, MA 02138, tel: 1-800/370-2515.

[3] *Multicultural Education*, the official magazine of the National Association for Multicultural Education, is free to members, or non-member subscriptions can be purchased from Caddo Cap Press, 3145 Gregory Blvd. Suite 275, San Francisco, CA 94118. *Multicultural Review* is a quarterly publication available from Greenwood Publishing Group, Inc., 88 Post Rd. W., P.O. Box 5007, Westport, CT 06881. *Teaching Tolerance* is a biannual magazine available from The Southern Poverty Law Center, 400 Washington Avenue, Montgomery, AL 36104.

[4] The National Women's History Project publishes an annual catalog of curriculum resources and videos that promote the study and appreciation of multicultural women's history for kindergarten through university-levels. Write the Women's History Project at 7738 Bell Road, Windsor, CA 95492-8518, tel: 707/838-0478. The Women's Educational Equity Act Publishing Center also disseminates curriculum materials and publications for educators and others committed to sex equity. Write Women's Educational Equity Act Publishing Center at 55 Chapel Street, Newton, MA 02160, tel: 1-800/225-3088.